THINGS OF
THE HIDDEN
GOD

THINGS OF THE HIDDEN GOD

JOURNEY TO THE HOLY MOUNTAIN

CHRISTOPHER
MERRILL

RANDOM HOUSE

NEW YORK

Grateful acknowledgment is made to the following for
permission to reprint previously published material:

Farrar, Straus & Giroux, LLC.: Excerpt from "The End of
March" from *The Complete Poems: 1927–1979* by Elizabeth
Bishop, copyright © 1979, 1983 by Alice Helen Methfessel;
excerpt from "Church Going" from *Collected Poems* by Philip
Larkin, copyright © 1988, 2003 by the Estate of Philip Larkin.
Reprinted by permission of Farrar, Straus & Giroux, LLC.
The Wylie Agency, Inc.: Excerpt from "Berryman" from *Flower
& Hand* by W. S. Merwin, copyright © 1997 by W. S. Merwin.
Reprinted by permission of The Wylie Agency, Inc.
Anvil Poetry Press Ltd.: "Chelandrion" is taken from *Vasko
Popa: Collected Poems,* translated by Anne Pennington, revised
and expanded by Francis R. Jones. Published by Anvil Press
Poetry in 1997.

LIBRARY OF CONGRESS CATALOGING-IN-PUBLICATION DATA

Merrill, Christopher.
   Things of the hidden God: journey to the Holy Mountain/
   Christopher Merrill.
      p.   cm.
   Includes bibliographical references.
   ISBN 0-679-46305-4
   1. Athos (Greece)—Description and travel.   2. Merrill,
   Christopher—Travel—Greece—Athos.   I. Title.

BX385.A8.M47 2004
271'.81949565—dc22   2004046814

Random House website address: www.atrandom.com

Printed in the United States of America on acid-free paper

9 8 7 6 5 4 3 2 1

FIRST EDITION

For Lisa, Hannah, and Abigail

Truly, thou art a God who hidest thyself.

ISAIAH 45:15

acknowledgments

I wish to thank the following individuals without whose help and inspiration this book could not have been written: Shirley Adams, Stephen Ainlay, William Albrecht, Robert Allison, Dick and Gabriele Anderson, Archbishop Chrysostomos of Etna, Krzysztof Czyzewski, Jennifer Baum, Lori Branch, Jeffrey Butler, Scott Cairns, Magda Carneci, Reverend David Carter, Robert Cording, Patrick Cox, William Decker, Natasa Durovicova, Hugh Ferrer, Thomas Flynn, Robert Fox, Reverend Andrew M. France, Jr., Mark Freeman, James Galvin, Tom Gavin, Susan Holahan, Paul Ingram, James Kee, Edmund and Mary Keeley, Elaine LaMattina, John and Maureen Leatham, Dennis Maloney, Thomas Martin, Richard Matlak, William and Paula Merwin, Charles Millard, Mary and Peter Nazareth, George R. Neumann, Patricia Porcaro, Scott Russell Sanders, David Skorton, Garrett Stewart, Frederick Turner, Russell Valentino, Frank Vellaccio, Benjamin Webb, Terry Tempest Williams, and Larry Wolff.

Special thanks to my literary agent at International Creative Management, Sloan Harris, who first understood my interest in the Holy Mountain and encouraged me at every step. I am very grateful to my editor at Random House, Webster Younce, for his inspired reading of the work in progress, and to my editor at HarperCollins in London, Michael Fishwick, for his sound advice at critical moments in the creative process. Michael Burke, Julia Cheiffetz, Mary Chamberlain, Catherine Heaney, Kate Hyde, Jonathan Jao, Jon Karp, and Vincent La Scala helped me in countless ways. In like manner Stephanos Bibas and Nicholas Samaras generously shared their knowledge of Mount Athos and of Orthodoxy, read the manuscript in its entirety, and saved me many errors. My wife, Lisa, and daughter, Hannah, endured long separations during my travels, which I hope will be redeemed by this portrait of a sacred world they cannot visit—a prohibition that extends to the newest member of our family, Abigail, whose birth blessed this work. Finally, I wish to express my gratitude to the monks, holy men all, who figure in this narrative, most of whom prefer to remain nameless. They taught me that "Those who trust in the Lord are like Mount Zion, which cannot be moved, but abides forever" (Ps. 125:1).

Ketchum, Idaho
Feast of St. Panteleimon

contents

STRYMONIC GULF

ESPHIGMENOU

CHILANDARI

ZOGRAPHOU

KASTAMONITOU

DOCHEIARIOU

• Chromitsa

Ouranoupolis

N. Thebais

0 1 2 miles

0 1 2 3 4 kilometres

Thessaloníki

CHALKIDIKI

THERMAIC GULF

STRYMONIC GULF

N. Thebais

Karyes

SINGITIC GULF

SITHONIA

GULF OF KASSANDRA

SINGITIC

THE PENINSULA
OF MOUNT ATHOS

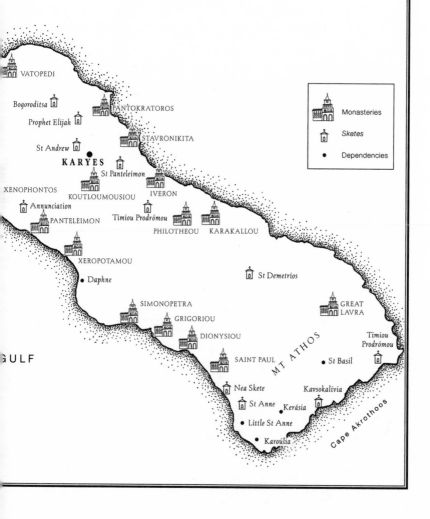

VATOPEDI

Bogoroditsa

Prophet Elijah

St Andrew

KARYES

PANTOKRATOROS

STAVRONIKITA

St Panteleimon

XENOPHONTOS

KOUTLOUMOUSIOU   IVERON

Annunciation

PANTELEIMON   Timiou Prodrómou

PHILOTHEOU   KARAKALLOU

XEROPOTAMOU

Daphne   St Demetrios

SIMONOPETRA   GREAT LAVRA

GRIGORIOU

DIONYSIOU   Timiou Prodrómou

GULF   SAINT PAUL   St Basil

Nea Skete   Kavsokalívia

St Anne   Kerásia

Little St Anne

Karoúlia

M T   A T H O S

Cape Akrothoos

Monasteries

Sketes

Dependencies

The ladder descends along the face of the cliff to a hermitage set on a rock high above the sea—a stone hut accessible to only the most daring spiritual athletes. Here in the desert of Mount Athos, a peninsula in northern Greece, Christian monks have climbed down these rickety steps for more than a millennium to devote their lives to prayer. They renounce everything, withdrawing from the world to praise God. For food they depend upon the generosity of passing fishermen to whom they lower baskets on pulleys, which is why this area of the monastic republic of Athos is called Karoúlia, the Place of Pulleys. And this image of asceticism guided my pilgrimages to the Holy Mountain, the first of which I made in March 1998.

I had reached a crossroads in my life—in my marriage, my work, and my health—which I attempted to navigate through the discipline of an ancient faith. *Things of the Hidden God*, the record of my journeys into the world of Orthodox monasticism, is thus an account both of a place little known in the West and of a spiritual reckoning. I walked the length and width of the peninsula, visiting all twenty monasteries and dozens of settlements, little expecting that my encounters with a tradition at once foreign and familiar would shake me to the core. But the liturgy and icons, the monks and pilgrims, the landscape and legends—these impressed upon me the need to forge a closer relationship to God. Mine became an excursion into what the theologian Paul Tillich called "the dynamics of faith," which reverberate now in every part of my being.

"Why have you come to Mount Athos?" was the question repeatedly asked of me. And the answers I gave — spiritual yearning; despair born of my reporting on the war in the Balkans; marital difficulties; the birth of my daughter; interest in Byzantium — took on new meaning in a land untouched by modernity, where my curiosity about monasticism led me to reexamine my own faith as a Protestant. Here is an unchanging order against which to measure the ceaseless changes of modernity, a thousand years of continuous religious practice to juxtapose with the ever shifting habits of contemporary belief. The vitality of the spiritual tradition carried on by Athonite monks is everywhere on display: in the mysterious beauty of the liturgy sanctified by fifteen centuries of daily performance; in the rigorous theology informing the monks' prayers; in the artistic heritage of architecture, iconography, statuary, metalwork, illuminated manuscripts, chanting, vestments, and ceremony. Yet even as I walked along the cliffs and paths, marveling at the strangeness of a place that creates its own time, its own singular history, I carried the burden of my life in the world. My spirits were low, and I was filled with existential dread: "Is there any meaning in my life that will not be annihilated by the inevitability of death which awaits me?" Tolstoy asks — a question I could not answer until I traveled to the Holy Mountain.

This change in my bearing was by no means easy to explain either to myself or to my secular friends. I had traded the physical dangers of covering the breakup of Yugoslavia for the psychic risks of opening my heart to the possibility of grace, war stories for Christ's parables. The stakes seemed higher on Mount Athos, where I was conscious of last things in a manner altogether distinct from the mortal threat I had faced on the streets of Sarajevo during the siege. Thomas Merton praised the purity of heart achieved by the desert fathers, the fourth-century anchorites who made a clean break from society in order to purge their false selves and permit "the emergence of the true, secret self in which the

Believer and Christ were 'one Spirit,' " inaugurating the Christian monastic tradition. This was the secret self that to my surprise began to emerge from my pilgrimages. From the depths of mental, physical, and spiritual exhaustion I discovered in the remotest circumstances new energy and meaning: direction.

Something started to vibrate in my soul when I first heard a monk calling his brethren to prayer. My pulse quickened, my heart soared, and I grew avid for the knowledge of spiritual things available in Scripture and patristic literature. The writings of the church fathers were a revelation to me like unto the pleasure and instruction I had always found in poetry. That for some time I had been unable to write my own poems reinforced the power of these divine words, which govern my thinking now and may one day inspire me to write a different kind of poem.

My first pilgrimage was undertaken in the shadow of the war in Bosnia, my last in the sunlit promise of the new millennium, before the war on terror darkened every sky. But what I learned on Mount Athos holds through the ages—through feast and famine, war and disease, love and loss. And if my course of travel on the peninsula and through the literature of faith resembled the meandering of a river that eventually empties into the sea, I understand it now in a new light. "The ladder that leads to the Kingdom is hidden within your soul," wrote St. Isaac of Syria. "Flee from sin, dive into yourself, and in your soul you will discover the stairs by which to ascend." This was the ladder I did not know I was seeking until I had already begun to climb it.

part one

PENITENCE

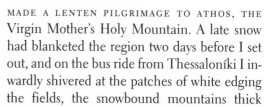

I MADE A LENTEN PILGRIMAGE TO ATHOS, THE Virgin Mother's Holy Mountain. A late snow had blanketed the region two days before I set out, and on the bus ride from Thessaloníki I inwardly shivered at the patches of white edging the fields, the snowbound mountains thick with clouds. In the grey dawn the bus wended its way through villages and towns, making brief stops to leave bundles of newspapers outside kiosks and cafés. The monk across the aisle from me dozed off in the stuffy air, his beard resting on his chest. At the sight of the Aegean, calm and lead-colored, a memory surfaced: I was lying on a hospital gurney, awaiting exploratory surgery, buoyant from the effects of a painkiller. I remembered watching the clock on the wall, cherishing its slow progress, wishing to put off for as long as possible the moment when the orderly came to wheel me into the operating room. The bus sped around a corner. The monk laid his head back against his seat. It occurred to me that my journey into faith might prove to be painful.

The sun was out by the time we arrived in the fishing village of Ouranoupolis, the jumping-off point for pilgrimages to Mount Athos. But the crowd at the administrative center inspired new fears: that I would be denied a permit for one of the ten places allotted each day to foreigners; that the ferry down the coast to Daphne—the only way, in winter, onto the easternmost of the three fingerlike peninsulas reaching into the sea—would leave without me. I was last in line, and I pictured myself having to return to Thessaloníki to secure another set of documents with which to enter the theocratic state. Ahead of me stood an old man in sandals, a crazed, rank-smelling German with a white beard and ponytail. He was muttering to himself when the policeman behind the counter asked him to declare his faith. Bewildered, he looked to his left and right before barking, "Lutheran." Then he shuffled off with his *diamonitirion*—a permit good for four days on the Holy Mountain. Soon I had one, too.

Monks, laborers, and pilgrims boarded the ferry, many choosing to stay outside, in a cold wind, for the duration of the two-hour journey. I climbed to the top level and stood near the forward railing. How often I had imagined this moment! Mount Athos had been a beacon for me during my travels through the war zones of the former Yugoslavia, a distant light I dreamed of following away from the sea of hatred I was charting. The suffering and carnage had darkened my outlook, and just before flying abroad I had sent my literary agent a new book about the war, the writing of which left me exhausted. I prayed that a walk around the peninsula that forms the spiritual heart of the Eastern Orthodox Church would restore me. In this monastic republic, which for more than a millennium has been a center for contemplative life, I hoped not only to witness ancient rituals and ways of living but also to experience, as the author of Ecclesiastes wrote, "a time to keep silence" (Eccles. 3:7). And what I saw as the ferry began to motor down the coast were burned-out buildings not unlike what I had seen in the war. Up a steep hillside around a promontory was a small monastic settlement of gutted houses, charred walls, and a roofless chapel: an abandoned *skete*, which resembled the razed villages common in Bosnia and Croatia.

The surrounding hills were thick with trees, in sharp contrast to the fields, pastures, and eroded slopes of the mainland. Spared the blight of clear-cutting, which has left Greece with Europe's lowest percentage of forested land, Athos is rich in chestnut and fir and holly oak—an ecological haven, 480 kilometers square, interspersed with monastic settlements ringed by terraced gardens, olive groves, and vineyards. A place apart, a poet said. And this is true not only in a physical sense—a stone wall topped with barbed wire runs along the northern border of the peninsula, harbor police in speedboats patrol the coastline—but also in terms of time: the Holy Mountain follows the Julian calendar, which is thirteen days behind the rest of the world, and in most of the monasteries time is reckoned according to the medieval Byzantine system—

sunset is midnight, which means the clocks must be reset each day.

A cellular phone rang. Under a canopy was an old monk surrounded by pilgrims eager for his counsel and businessmen working their phones—an incongruous sight that brought to mind the meeting of the Café Europa I had just attended in Kraków. Some Central European artists and writers had created a sort of traveling band to showcase their work, naming the group after the place where cultural life had long thrived, and one morning they gathered at the cultural ministry to debate the merits of various joint enterprises. The discussion drifted, though, until chocolates and vodka were served. A Lithuanian stage designer, who hoped the Café Europa would create what she called "a dramaturgy of their thinking," suggested they publish a literary almanac, with texts on a common theme. A Polish writer, declaring that European civilization was the problem, wondered if they possessed the right antennae to pick up the signals for whatever was going on in the world. He likened the Café to a troupe of wandering monks. Someone proposed writing on the subject of silence. A Slovenian poet caught fire at this idea, his voice rising in pitch as he declared the need for silence at the end of the millennium.

The Polish writer immediately agreed. "Our whole program must be a meditation on the subject of silence," he said with feeling. "Silence is more important for me than Central Europe or the *fin de millennium!*"

"Silence is a constant element in our meditations," the Slovenian poet said imperiously.

"We should be silent about silence," countered a Romanian art critic. "Some subjects are sacred."

But the Slovenian was on a roll. "Silence has a completely different meaning after Auschwitz and Sarajevo," he cried. And now whenever anyone tried to interrupt he spoke even louder. Soon he was shouting at the top of his lungs, "Silence! We need more silence!"

On an outcropping of rocks near the shore perched four cormorants. Gulls flew into the wind to stay even with the ferry, waiting for pilgrims to throw bread overboard. Fishermen spread nets from the boats in the distance, and occasionally the sun slipped out from behind the clouds around the peak of Mount Athos to reveal a snow-covered triangle rising more than two thousand meters from the sea. It is said that after forty days in the wilderness Jesus was led up this mountain by Satan, who tempted Him with "all the kingdoms of the world and their glory" (Matt. 4:9) if He would fall down and worship him. It is also said, with even less authority, that on a clear morning from the marble peak you can see the dome of Hagia Sophia in Constantinople—a legend underscoring the fact that the Holy Mountain is not only a staging ground for mystical visions and teachings but also a watchtower for Byzantium, the lost empire which in the modern imagination stands for a mysterious, sacramental world. Yeats wrote that Byzantium was the last place on earth in which "religious, aesthetic and practical life were one." But then the Irish poet never visited Athos, where everything is supposed to hold sacred value.

A boathouse and a two-story stucco building came into view, the *arsanas* or landing for the inland monastery of Zographou, which remained out of sight. The ferry put in, monks and laborers walked off in the direction of a waiting Land Rover, and within a minute we were under way again, sailing toward the monastery of Docheiariou, a walled city set on a wooded slope, with a crenellated tower looming in the background.

Docheiariou ranks tenth in the hierarchy of the twenty ruling monasteries, the ancient system of governance on the Holy Mountain, which houses the oldest unbroken monastic tradition in the West. The religious underpinnings of the peninsula go back further still. It was the first seat of the gods in Greek mythology, before they decamped to Olympus, and the story goes that during a family quarrel Poseidon's son, Athos, picked up a mountain in Thrace and hurled it at his father in the sea. To assuage Poseidon's feelings, the gods gave him the mountain, only to incur

Zeus's wrath; when Zeus claimed Mount Athos for himself the vengeful sea god retaliated, turning the waters off the headland into a graveyard for ships. Some see the prongs of Poseidon's trident in Chalkidiki's three peninsulas, and it is true that around Cape Akrothoos powerful storms rise without warning, one of which crippled the fleet of King Darius in 492 BCE, slowing the Persian invasion of the Greek city-states. Some years later, Darius's son, Xerxes, taking no chances with the weather, cut a canal through the isthmus of the Athonite peninsula, just north of the current border, to move his fleet overland. Of Xerxes' hubris against nature (he also ordered his slaves to lash the Hellespont for the crime of ruining a pair of bridges he had built between Asia and Europe) Herodotus wrote, "I cannot but conclude that it was mere ostentation that made Xerxes have the canal dug—he wanted to show his power and to leave something to be remembered by." And the Persian's landscaping ambitions were as nothing compared with those of Alexander the Great's court sculptor, Deinocrates, who proposed to carve his patron's likeness out of the mountain. Indeed a popular engraving by an eighteenth-century British artist features Alexander with one arm draped over a basin containing the waters flowing out of the peak and the other clutching the tallest structure in a city stretching from his lap to the ridge of the peninsula. But Alexander rejected the monument, not because he disliked the design but because he thought Athos had suffered enough at the hands of Xerxes.

With the advent of Christianity, though, came a different attitude toward the mountain. What was once the site of titanic battles between gods and giants, and man and nature, became the setting for what an Orthodox text calls "unseen warfare"—the war waged within the souls of those who have no wish to be remembered by the world. In this dispensation the Mother of God supplanted the Greek deities, in a dramatic fashion. Legend has it that in old age Mary accepted an invitation to visit Lazarus, who was then living in Cyprus, and set sail from Palestine with St. John the Evangelist. But a storm blew their ship off course, the winds carried them into a shallow bay off the east coast of Athos, and when she stepped ashore at the port of Clementos, near a temple of Apollo, all of the idols and pagan statues instantly crumbled—a miraculous story rooted perhaps in a historical event, a powerful earthquake that struck the region in 49 CE (although on Athos it is said that legend does not contradict reality—it is the very truth itself). In gratitude Mary blessed the mountain and converted its inhabitants. She prayed to her Son to give this special place to her, and His voice was heard proclaiming it to be her portion of paradise, "a haven of salvation for those seeking to be saved."

Tradition holds that in the Garden of the Virgin, as Athos came to be known, Constantine the Great built three churches, which were razed by Julian the Apostate. Archaeological evidence, however, suggests that it was not until about 800 that the deserted peninsula began to attract hermits from the region, as well as monks in flight from advancing Arab armies, which had leveled monasteries in Egypt, Syria, and Asia Minor, and from iconoclasts bent on destroying the religious imagery in Byzantium. The first historical mention of the Holy Mountain, in fact, records a delegation of Athonite monks attending the council in Constantinople, in 843, at which the veneration of holy images was vindicated. The defeat of iconoclasm, which became the Feast of Orthodoxy celebrated on the first Sunday in Lent, inspired the last flowering of Byzantine civilization—remnants of which I had glimpsed during my travels as a war correspondent.

What Yeats called "the artifice of eternity," the handiwork of nameless artisans laboring in the service of God, I found in the iconography of Orthodox churches in the former Yugoslavia; in a museum display of illuminated manuscripts in Sofia, Bulgaria; in the desecrated frescoes of a cell, in Thessaloníki, said to have been occupied by St. Paul. Here was the story behind the story I was writing, a ritualized narrative to counterpoint the tragedy unfolding all around me. A monk in Montenegro described Byzantine society as the embodiment of the spiritual imagination, and this was what I longed for in the chaos of war; his assertion that in Byzantium the price of bread had remained constant for six hundred years resonated in a land in which hyperinflation was forcing restaurant owners to raise their prices every fifteen minutes; his economic knowledge was murky, but his vision of a world outside time fascinated me. In the messiness of ordinary life I dreamed of a place in which ceremony and practice were united. And so in the late winter, with another war imminent in the Balkans, the stock market booming in New York, and the American president mired in a sex scandal, I traveled to Athos, arriving a week after the celebration of the Triumph of Orthodoxy, which ushered in the final glory of Byzantium.

Monasticism was at the heart of this renewal, which began with the redecoration of the churches and monasteries and ended long before the fall of Constantinople. Monks had the last word on religious practice—the liturgy, art, and music through which Byzantine men and women communicated with God; their spiritual advice was sought after by rich and poor alike; emperors ignored their views on political and ecclesiastical matters (often one and the same) only at their peril. But what peculiar figures they present to a modern sensibility. The first names associated with the Holy Mountain, two ninth-century saints named Peter the Athonite and Euthymios of Thessaloníki, endured unimaginable hardship in their quest for the divine, setting the pattern for later athletes of God, those who practice the strictest asceticism to partake "of the inheritance of the saints in the light" (Col. 1:12). Peter's circuitous route to Athos took him first to Syria to fight as a soldier, a more glamorous venture than the monastic vocation to which he had pledged himself; he blamed his capture and imprisonment by the Arabs on his decision to give up his vow. In atonement he prayed to St. Nicholas, promising to become a monk if he was freed, and upon his release he went to Rome to be ordained. From there he boarded a ship bound for the Levant. One night at sea he dreamed that St. Nicholas asked the Virgin Mary to lead the monk to a place where he might practice "what is lovable to God." She replied that in time the Holy Mountain would "fill from end to end with companies of monks, and the mercy of my Son and God, if they are steadfast in the saving commandments, shall never desert them."

The very next day the ship was approaching Athos, with a favoring wind, when it stopped dead in the water. Peter told the sailors they would not be able to continue unless they left him on the shore. Which they did, reluctantly. And for the next fifty years he lived in a cave, according to his hagiographer, with "more crawling animals than the sky has stars or the sea sand." Nourished by manna, fortified by prayer, he withstood the temptations of demons in every guise. In old age he met a hunter who promised to follow him in the ascetic life. But when the hunter returned with his brother and some monks they discovered that Peter had died. So they bundled his corpse into their boat and sailed along the east coast of the peninsula until they neared the monastery of Clementos, about which little is known beyond the legend that it was built where the Mother of God had come ashore. (The monastery of Iveron now stands there.) Suddenly their boat stood still, with its sails billowing. Intrigued, the monks from Clementos rowed out to them and, hearing their story, demanded Peter's relics. These they placed in a shrine to Mary. The hunter and his brother sailed home, forsaking their vows to become hermits, while the monks they had enlisted to join them on Athos stayed behind to steal the relics, which they took to Thrace only to have to surrender them to the bishop for a proper burial. Dream-visions, miraculous winds, divine interventions—these are the staples of Athonite legend, the underpinnings of a place apart.

The story of Euthymios, shorn of any traces of the fantastic, is no less strange. Not long after his marriage and the birth of a daughter, he renounced the world, first to live in a monastery, then in a *lavra* (a gathering of anchorites who assemble for weekly services), and then as a hermit on Athos; at his urging, his wife, mother, and sisters entered a convent; his daughter was instructed

to continue the family line. He and his companion in the eremitical life, one Joseph the Armenian, tested their resolve by imitat-
ing cattle, eating grass and crawling on their hands and knees for
forty days—"to realize the true degree of their spiritual depriva-
tion," writes Philip Sherrard, author of *Athos: The Mountain of Silence* (from which some of these details are taken). Then they
moved into a cave, planning to stay for three years—a trial that
Joseph could not endure. Word spread of Euthymios's spiritual
feats, though, and he emerged from his solitude to find several
monks waiting for him to guide them in a new *lavra*. From this it
was but a step to the creation of monasteries (the oldest Athonite
monastery still in existence is named Great Lavra), hundreds of
which were built over the centuries.

These competing visions of the ascetic life, the solitary and the
cenobitic or communal, shaped the character of the place, which
Emperor Basil I set aside for monks and hermits in 881. His
chrysobul (a document bearing his gold seal) was followed by
other edicts affirming Athonite autonomy, the most recent of
which, the Treaty of Lausanne in 1923, turned the peninsula into
a protectorate of Greece (which promptly confiscated monastic
properties on the mainland—their main source of revenue—for
use in resettling Greek refugees from Asia Minor). Seven *typika*
or charters, the first dating from the tenth century, spelled out
the Holy Mountain's organization: twenty ruling monasteries—
seventeen Greek, one each from the Bulgarian, Russian, and Serbian traditions—own the twelve *sketes* (smaller monastic communities) on Athos, as well as some 250 *kelliá* (dwellings, with their
own chapels, for three or more monks) and countless hermitages
and ruins. Each monastery is self-governing, under the rule of an
abbot elected for life; each sends a representative to serve in the
Holy Assembly in Karyes, the administrative capital of Athos,
which by the eleventh century held an unrivaled place in Orthodox monasticism.

The population of contemplatives rose steadily until Constantinople fell in 1453; as many as ten thousand monks may once

have lived here. But their numbers declined under Ottoman rule, a trend that continued into the modern age, for Athos's liberation from the Turkish yoke coincided with the liberation of mankind from God. By 1963, on the millennial anniversary of the Holy Mountain, fewer than 1,500 aging monks remained. Unable to maintain the monasteries, they were thought to be the last generation of monastics who would occupy Athos. The Greek government even proposed to herd them into Great Lavra and convert the peninsula into a tourist resort. The verdict of Byzantine historian John Julius Norwich seemed just: "Unless a miracle happens—a great nation-wide religious revival, nothing less—the Holy Mountain is doomed."

What happened next did border on the miraculous. Western societies did not undergo a religious revival, in the conventional sense of the term, yet the proliferation of eschatologies and New Age creeds, as well as interest in ancient religions imported from the Far East, testified to an enduring spiritual hunger. In the 1970s, young men found their way to Athos; within the decade the number of monks was on the rise. The political revolutions in the Eastern bloc in 1989, the end of the Cold War, the waning power of ideology, all provided fresh impetus for a spiritual reawakening. Orthodoxy was reestablishing itself in formerly Communist countries like Bulgaria, Romania, and Russia, even as it gained converts in the West—a renaissance rooted in the traditions of the Holy Mountain, where the average age of monks was declining and funding to renovate the monasteries was on the increase, especially from the European Union.

Thus when the ferry put in at Docheiariou, a pickup loaded with building supplies drove off behind the departing passengers, a scene repeated at the next two stops—the low-lying monastery of Xenophontos, once a favorite target of pirates, now a victim of neglect; and St. Panteleimon, the Russian monastery, a small city of churches with green onion-shaped domes and burned-out shells of buildings, all guarded by stone garrisons that had lain empty for decades. But now the Russikon, as it is known on Athos, was a hive of industry, with scaffolding draping the gutted buildings along the sea and the sound of jackhammers echoing off the walls. The ferry pulled away as an enormous bell tolled thirty-three times, one for each year of Christ's life.

We made landfall at Daphne (literally, "bay leaves"), the Athonite customs center, which looked like any fishing village— a string of stone buildings on the waterfront housing some shops, a taverna, a post office, a police station—except that the shops trafficked in icons, prayer ropes, and guides to the monasteries. Monks and pilgrims crowded onto an old yellow bus, which drove off to Karyes belching diesel fumes. I stayed behind, heeding the wisdom of those who say that Athos should be approached on foot, if not on your knees. One dictionary definition of *pilgrim* is "wanderer," and every pilgrim to the Holy Mountain is considered to be a sojourner in the scriptural meaning of the word: "Hear my prayer, O Lord, and give ear unto my cry; hold not thy peace at my tears: for I am a stranger with thee, and a sojourner, as all my fathers were" (Ps. 39:12). If I had learned anything during the war it was that our walk in the sun is brief, and so I resolved to wander from monastery to monastery, a sojourner in the world of last things. It was time for me to come to terms with the way my life had turned out: the love I had squandered, the misgivings I had about my vocation and my faith, the dread I felt at every turn.

PENITENCE, PURIFICATION, PRAYER—THESE ARE THE MEANS BY which mystics in the Eastern Church reach for the divine. For Orthodoxy is above all a mystical religion. "The eastern tradition has never made a sharp distinction between mysticism and theology," writes Vladimir Lossky, a scholar of the Russian Church, "between personal experience of the divine mysteries and the dogma affirmed by the Church." Nor is this call to the union of heart and spirit confined to ascetics. Everyone may partake of the divine mystery, if only they will redirect their passions toward God. Indeed *passion* has a special meaning for Orthodox theologians. An Athonite elder has defined it as a spiritual disease which arises from habitual sinning; you lose your way when it becomes second nature—a passion—to succumb to lust, hate, jealousy, and the like. To be healed of this disease—to recover your true nature— requires the transfiguration of your passions.

"You must change your life," Rainer Maria Rilke concluded after a visit to a museum in Paris to see an archaic torso of Apollo—a poetic insight integral to Orthodoxy. And while Rilke was shaken by the Greek god's gaze ("for here there is no place/ that does not see you"), the mystic, who likewise knows he cannot escape the will of God, focuses his attention on Him, seeking to arrive at the state of dispassion, an Orthodox term for a spiritual bearing described not as indifference but rather as the sanctification of the powers of both body and soul. No small task for those who devote their lives to praising the Lord, to say nothing of the rest of us.

I knew from my own experience how easily passion in the customary meaning of the word can turn on itself, dividing instead of uniting, for what had sustained my wife and me through a long marriage was now tearing us apart. Ours had been a kind of gypsy life: we moved from Santa Fe to New Orleans to the Northwest, pursuing artistic careers. Then Lisa took a break from her violin to give birth to our first child, a late gift which coincided with another move (I had accepted a teaching job at a Jesuit college); in our new home in New England, alone with our daughter, far from her friends, family, and music, Lisa fell into despair. I was too preoccupied with academic obligations, a book deadline, and the pressure to pay off the credit card debts we had accumulated as freelancers to give her the love and support she needed. We argued almost every day. Our passion for each other had turned into a destructive force.

But passion has a different meaning for Christians: the root of the Latin word derives from the suffering of Jesus on the cross. During the Lenten journey to Easter the penitent should dwell not on private pain but on the Passion of the Son of man, who died for our salvation. This is how to align your will with the will of God: what is required is a reordering of perspective.

I needed a map of Athos, which a pilgrim had said might be available in the capital, and so I adjusted my backpack and set out for Karyes along the dirt road that winds toward the ridge of the peninsula. The hills were tawny with heather, the air sweet with the scent of nectar. The twittering of finches brought me up short: when had I last heard birdsong? "Create silence," Kierkegaard advised. Just so I came upon an empty hermitage, where anchorites had once carved out lives alert to every sound in nature. The hut was perched on a rugged slope, beyond a stone wall studded with purple irises and prickly pears, and I was admiring its view of the sea—emerald water close to shore, fishing boats in the distance, the hilly peninsula of Sithonia across the Singitic Gulf—when a pickup barreled past. Dust hung in the air as I walked to the first switchback overlooking a hillside strewn with plastic garbage bags, five-gallon containers, scrap wood and metal—debris from the nearby monastery of Xeropotamou. It was unsettling to see that the monks had made no other provision for disposing of their trash.

The monastery—a walled town, really, on a plateau of gardens and orchards—was closed in preparation for the feast of the Forty Martyrs from Sebaste, a legion of Armenian soldiers from the Roman army who were condemned to a cruel death. One night in the fourth century, during a persecution of Christians, the soldiers were stripped naked and marshaled onto a frozen lake; a warm bath waited on shore for anyone who renounced Christianity. But the soldiers stayed in formation, praising God and singing hymns; when one broke from the ranks a pagan guard, seeing a bright light shine above them, took his place. Not all were dead by morning, when the guards broke their legs and threw them onto a pyre. The relics came into the possession of Xeropotamou (which also owns the largest piece of the True Cross on Athos— you can even see a nail hole in it), and in the seventeenth century an enterprising monk carted them around Europe, raising money to rebuild the monastery, which had been destroyed, repeatedly, by earthquakes, fires, and pirates. Cash trumps *chrysobuls*: the monk's tour was imitated by others, in defiance of an edict, in 1082, that sacred treasures should not be profaned by public outings. And the tour persists in a modern form: in conjunction with Thessaloníki's designation as an EU cultural capital, an exhibit at the new Byzantine Museum of icons, illuminated manuscripts, paintings, carvings, and embroidery from the Holy Mountain had just been extended by six months.

The sign at the monastery gate, in English, warned pilgrims away, so I returned to the road. Athos had survived natural catastrophes, imperial whims, the incursions of pirates and mercenaries, the machinations of occupying powers (Latin Crusaders, Ottoman Turks, Nazi Germans), and a dwindling monastic population to face a more insidious present-day threat: the rising volume of pilgrims and renovations undermined the solitude and silence necessary for the contemplative life. Thus the tinkling of bells at the approach of a pack of mules (until recently the only form of transportation on the mountain) was drowned out by the whine of a chain saw, which grew louder as I climbed through a chestnut forest above the monastery. Farther on, in a clearing off to the right, was a new *kellí* under construction. Bundles of cut aspens and brush were piled on one side of the road; from the other, a logging road led toward the peak.

Road building is the modern curse of Athos. The first road, linking Daphne and Karyes, was not built until the Holy Mountain's millennial celebration in 1963, but it was only a matter of time before roads connected most of the monasteries, supplanting footpaths used for centuries; only the distant reaches of Athos—principally in Eremos, the desert at the southern tip of the peninsula—are still served by mules; a monastic taxi service even runs to and from the capital. There is more: some phone lines put in by the Nazis to link their officers garrisoned in different monasteries have been hooked up to the World Wide Web; every monastery has a pay phone. In short, Athos has not avoided some of the trappings of modernity, though it remains largely immune to what Henry Adams diagnosed a century ago as the chief malady of the age: acceleration. The historian laid the blame for his inability to find inner peace on the force of the dynamo, the precursor to the Information Age technologies that have dramatically accelerated the pace of our lives. Fax machines, voice mail, e-mail: who can find peace today?

This was one reason why I had journeyed to Athos: my life was too complicated. But how to simplify? Never say no, Jean Cocteau advised artists, since there is no telling where any commission might lead—a maxim which had become second nature for me: a passion. During the war I chased stories, partly to write my way out of debt, partly for the thrill of recording history in the making. But even now I could not break the habit of accepting every assignment that came along. Mine was a visiting professorship, after all, and providing for a child was an expensive undertaking; our credit card bills continued to mount.

Near the ridge overlooking Karyes, six hundred meters above sea level, I stopped at an iron cross to rearrange my backpack. My shoulder throbbed, and I could not turn my head. The pain shooting through my neck seemed vaguely connected to a biopsy I had undergone, the week of my departure, on my thyroid gland, which had given out some years earlier, in Sarajevo. In the months before the problem was diagnosed a suicidal depression had come over me, which I attributed to the pressures of reporting on the war. My spirits improved with medication, although the melancholia returned long before a routine checkup revealed a suspicious nodule—which, my doctor explained, had nothing to do with my state of mind. And I did not learn the results of the biopsy until the night before my pilgrimage, in a phone call home.

Benign, said my wife. Isn't that good news?

What I felt was only emptiness.

WOMEN ARE BARRED FROM ATHOS. LEGEND HAS IT THAT IN BLES-
sing the mountain the Mother of God forbade other women from
setting foot in her garden. In fact it was the baleful influence of
Vlach shepherdesses that gave rise to the eleventh-century *avaton*,
still in effect, prohibiting women and even female livestock from
entering the peninsula. The Vlachs had migrated into the region
by the ninth century, and their strained relations with the hermits
led Leo VI the Wise to expel them from the Holy Mountain.
With the rise of the ruling monasteries, however, they returned to
tend the monastic flocks, deliver milk and cheese to the monks,
bake for their feasts—and sometimes more. The women, dressed
like men, "were very much liked by the monks to whom they were
as serfs," one observer remarked. "And the things that occurred
are shameful both to tell and to hear." The ecumenical patriarch
in Constantinople intervened to expel the Vlachs and excommu-
nicate the offending monks—an abuse of authority the Holy
Community regarded as more dangerous than the sins of the
weak-willed. Nevertheless the patriarch established the right to
interfere in the administration of Athos, a right which to the
monks' chagrin still exists.

The monks, though, welcome the Virgin's interference, especially when it comes to keeping women away. The monks say she
refuses to share their devotion with any woman; hence few have
set foot on the mountain, usually for very brief periods of time.
The experience of Sultana Maria, the daughter of a Serbian
prince, is telling. A devout Christian (even after her marriage to
Murad II in 1453), she sailed to Athos to present to the monastery
of St. Paul the gifts of the Magi, the gold, frankincense, and myrrh
brought to the Nativity of Christ. But no sooner had she stepped
ashore than she heard a voice: "Come no further, for here there is
another queen greater than you, the Queen of Heaven." The sultana, seeing no one, left her gifts with the monks and hastened
back to ship; a chapel stands where she heard the voice,
which through the ages has apparently spoken to other women

approaching Athos. A staple of Greek journalism, for example, features a female reporter attempting to sneak onto the peninsula only to be warned away by the Queen of Heaven. Unaccountably she did not deter an enterprising French journalist from having her breasts surgically removed so that she could pass herself off as a man, though perhaps it should be noted that the publication of the book the journalist wrote about her month with the monks coincided with the Great Depression.

Sir Steven Runciman, Byzantine scholar and patron of the Holy Mountain, tells a story about the exception made to the *avaton* for female cats. A century ago, when Athos was overrun by adders and the mainland merchants who supplied the monks with tomcats to hunt down snakes kept raising their prices, the Holy Assembly prayed to the Mother of God for help. Within a few days all of their tomcats had delivered litters, with as many female kittens as male. What to do? Some monks argued for drowning the tabbies. Wiser heads prevailed. Mary, they reasoned, had provided the kittens: if they got rid of them not only would the snakes return but she might be unwilling to perform a second miracle. And that is why there are so many cats on Athos.

The first ones I saw prowled the backyard of a *kellí* on the outskirts of Karyes, a town straggling southward under the eastern ridge, in a forest of chestnut and hazel trees. Wide cobblestones replaced the dirt road above the Russian *skete* of St. Andrew, which houses the largest church on Athos and a seminary with a dismal record of graduating monks. But there was no sign of life at the *skete*, which was once home to six hundred monks, or anywhere else as I strolled into town. A pilgrim had described Karyes to me as something out of Tarkovsky's *Andrei Rublev*, the masterly Soviet film about a medieval Russian iconographer who works in the face of religious cruelty, Tatar raids, and paganism, and the square did look like a deserted movie set. Four antique fire trucks parked by a stone terrace draped with ivy. Shuttered doors and windows in the facing buildings. All that remained of one balcony was the railing.

Tarkovsky's parable about the survival of the spirit, banned in his homeland during the Cold War, anticipated Orthodoxy's revival after decades of persecution. Nor was it an accident that Athos's changing fortunes over the last century corresponded to communism's rise and fall. Partisan guerrillas, including twenty-five women, briefly occupied Karyes during the Greek Civil War. (A firefight with the police, not the Virgin's voice, caused them to withdraw.) Bulgarian, Romanian, Russian, and Serbian monks died off without being replaced; pilgrimages from the Eastern bloc were rare until the Berlin Wall came down. But Slavs were flocking to Athos now, some to renew their spiritual ties, some to stay—although the Greek government, wary of losing control over immigration, was loath to uphold its treaty obligation of granting citizenship to Slavic monks; the delegation of bishops sent by the ecumenical patriarch in Constantinople to preside over the Holy Assembly's discussion of the issue was met with scorn. The fear was general among Athonites that the patriarch wished to silence them in a bid to reunite Eastern and Western Christendom. The stern monks of Esphigmenou, the poorest monastery, refused to remember him in their prayers, arguing that the spiritual war with communism was not won in order to surrender to the darker forces of the papacy and Protestantism. As a British writer dryly notes: "Athos has never been at the forefront of ecumenical dialogue."

The stillness in the square, the long shadows cast by the cypress trees on the hill beyond, the ravens wheeling overhead, all unnerved me. Sunlight hides as much as it reveals, a poet said, and the light striking the connected façades of Holy Spirit Street, a narrow rockway of stores, workshops, and residences leading from the square, seemed to seal off the possibility of contact with any living soul. There were no customers in the stores, which were crammed with dry goods, foodstuffs, postcards, and local handiwork—wood carvings, icons, prayer ropes. No maps. And the hotel was closed. Likewise the modern central administration building overlooking the Protaton, the oldest church on Athos. I had the name of a monk to look up and directions to his *konaki,* one of the houses maintained by each monastery for its representative to the Holy Assembly (except for the monastery of Koutloumousiou, which lies on the edge of town). But no one answered at his door. And when I went to the restaurant to eat a bowl of beans (the only available fare), the sole other customer, a monk smoking a cigarette, pointedly ignored me.

From the restaurant I wandered to the Protaton, the tenth-century church named for the Protos, or ruler of the world's last monastic state. Athenian democratic ideals may have vanished from the region under the Romans, yet Athos has always been governed democratically. The office of Protos evolved from a lifetime appointment, elected by an assembly of abbots, to a one-year position chosen by representatives of the first five monasteries in the Athonite hierarchy—Great Lavra, Vatopedi, Iveron, Chilandari, and Dionysiou. This pentarchy also controls the Holy Assembly, where the monasteries are divided into groups of four; every year a different group serves as the Holy Epistasia, the executive body responsible for the administration of Athos. The civil governor, who answers to the minister of foreign affairs in Athens, is in charge of security—i.e., the two police Land Rovers parked behind the Protaton, which sometimes needs protection even from its guardians. Tradition holds that after the Fourth Crusade and the Latin conquest of Byzantium (1204–61), which on Athos resulted in looted monasteries, razed churches, and murdered monks, the Byzantine emperor who reconquered Constantinople made an unusual conciliatory gesture to Rome: he destroyed the Protaton, with the support of the patriarch, who also acquiesced in the execution of several monks.

The rebuilt church, the only basilica on Athos, is dedicated to the Dormition of the Virgin Mary—that is, to her death, which in Orthodoxy is described as her falling asleep (from the Latin *dormire,* "to sleep"). And in the narthex, which leads to a cross-shaped nave, I felt the holy hush of death. Seepage had turned the walls into saltpeter; masons had chipped away at the white stone, careful to preserve the frescoes, dating from the fourteenth century, attributed to a painter from Thessaloníki named Manuel Panselinos, about whom nothing is known. These murals, the most beautiful on Athos, are arranged in four tiers around the church, with portraits of Christ's prophetic ancestors and saints — hermits, martyrs, warriors, patrons — enveloping a frieze of Gospel scenes from the Nativity to the Resurrection. This visual narrative (cartoons for the illiterate, said a pilgrim) has liturgical meaning, and I likened the feelings the murals conjured in me to the sense of awe I experienced at a retrospective exhibition of Mark Rothko's work, with this difference: Rothko's abstractions, which darkened year by year, chronicling his descent into despair (he committed suicide in 1970), enact the inescapable fact of our mortality, while Panselinos illustrates the path to redemption. St. John of Damascus (c. 675–749) called icons "windows into heaven": a fair description of these murals. The portraits of the Evangelists are painted on the pendentives in other Athonite churches, but in the domeless Protaton they are worked into the very stories they tell, à la postmodern fiction writers — all undergirded by pictures of saints like the founders of Athos, Peter and Euthymios, two gaunt, white-bearded figures who seem to look away from the viewer, as if afraid of encountering the devil.

A short, fat monk on a ladder was lighting candles in the corona, the large brass candelabra suspended in the nave. His heavy breathing I ascribed to exertion, not to irritation at my presence, until I strayed too close to the *Axion Esti* (literally, "worthy it is"), a miracle-working icon of the Virgin, the Holy Mountain's most precious treasure. The velvet curtain on the iconostasis (icon stand) was open, and in the sanctuary I could see a glass case containing the silver icon surrounded by gold and silver coins and pendants. The archangel Gabriel is said to have taught a monk praying before the icon in the tenth century to sing, "Worthy it is to magnify Thee, Mother of God." Then, with his fingernail, he carved the verses into stone — something to hide from the heathen, the monk lighting candles seemed to think. He climbed down the ladder, marched into the sanctuary, and yanked the curtain shut. Then he angrily shooed me out of the church.

This was my cue to leave town, and I had just gained the road down to the eastern seacoast when I heard what I thought was the sound of children shrieking in delight. "Pick up and read, pick up and read"—this was the chant from a children's game that St. Augustine thought he heard one evening in a garden in Milan. Opening his Bible to Paul's Epistles, he read the verses that changed his life: "Not in riots and drunken parties, not in eroticism and indecencies, not in strife and rivalry, but put on the Lord Jesus Christ and make no provision for the flesh in its lusts" (Rom. 13:13–14). The saint's anxieties about his conversion instantly dissolved. But when I looked back toward Karyes I saw only cawing ravens flapping their heavy wings above the Protaton. "Athos," writes John Julius Norwich, "has seen the deaths of many men, but the birth of none."

THE MONASTERY OF IVERON TAKES UP THE STRETCH OF COAST-line where the Mother of God (Theotokos, as she is known on Athos) was supposedly shipwrecked. A separate chapel dedicated to her lies at the southern edge of the cove, and in the fading sunlight the mountain rising above it in the distance was bathed in a creamy iridescence. Nearer to hand, waves pounded the seawall below the fortified tower. A green truck was parked by a shrine on the pier, ready for loading the long timbers milled at Iveron. The cobblestone path up to the monastery followed a stone wall, capped with red tiles, encircling a wide expanse of garden, tilled for the spring planting.

On a whim I had decided to spend my first night at Iveron. Third in the hierarchy of Athos, the monastery was founded by a courtier to David, ruler of Iberia—an ancient land, now known as Georgia, which was the second nation (after Armenia) to adopt Christianity, in the fourth century. Iveron remains a spiritual center for the faithful of the former Soviet republic, although its last

Georgian monk died in 1955—two years after the death of another seminarian from Tbilisi, Joseph Stalin, who deported hundreds of thousands of his fellow Georgians, including monks, nuns, and priests. Nor over the centuries has Iveron been spared the kinds of destruction that Stalin visited upon holy places in the Soviet Union. Crusaders and the Catalan mercenaries who drove the Latins from Byzantium, pirates and Turks, earthquakes and fire, all left their scars on the monastery, which by the fourteenth century had passed into Greek hands. That was when its Georgian character began to give way: henceforth services in the *katholikón*, the main church, were conducted in Greek; in 1913, in a fit of anger against the czar and things Russian, the monks burned their collection of Georgian manuscripts; what remains is the Georgian custom of telling time—sunrise is midnight, as it must often have seemed to Soviet Georgians.

Through a colonnaded porch I entered a stone courtyard. Tall cypresses stood at either end of the entrance to the *katholikón*, where vespers was under way. An Australian monk hailed me as I set my backpack down on a bench by the *phiale*, a marble fountain under a lead dome for the blessing of the waters. He was a straggly-bearded man whose first order of business was to tell me about Iveron's takeover in 1990: how he and several monks seeking more rigor had come from a neighboring monastery to reestablish Iveron along cenobitic lines. For centuries the monastery had followed the looser idiorrhythmic model, unique to Athos, in which monks devised their own schedules of work, prayer, and meals, assembling as a community only on feast days. St. Basil the Great (c. 330–79), Orthodoxy's first hierarch, warned against the dangers of solitude: "no single man is sufficient to receive all spiritual gifts, but according to the proportion of the faith that is in each man the supply of the Spirit is given; consequently, in the common life the private gift of each man becomes the common property of his fellows." Yet Athos has always accommodated eremitical and semi-eremitical forms of monastic life alongside its cenobitic monasteries. In the fourteenth century the Holy

Mountain gave rise to another type of solitary living. Idiorrhythmic monks acquired private property, servants, profane ideas; the office of the abbot was abolished in many monasteries; the rules about fasting were relaxed; and so on.

This decadence, mirrored in the West by the papal indulgences and clerical abuses that led to the Reformation, found no corrective in the Ottoman conquest of Byzantium. On the contrary. The Athonite authorities wisely submitted to Sultan Murad II before he captured Thessaloníki, sparing themselves the murder and mayhem that attended resistance in other quarters. But they paid a price for preserving their monasteries and autonomy: far from the patriarch (whose powers were now circumscribed), the monks could do as they pleased, and the canker of idiorrhythmia spread across the mountain. By the eighteenth century most of the ruling houses had adopted this freer system, which persisted through a rising in 1821 against the Turks, an abortive Russian attempt to occupy Athos, two Balkan Wars, two World Wars, and the Cold War. Only in the last decade had the remaining idiorrhythmic monasteries reverted to cenobitism—a dramatic and, according to the Holy Community, irreversible change.

It was part of a worldwide revolt, what Octavio Paz in a defense of poetry called "a return to the origin." The Mexican poet believed that in modernity's wake our search for meaning would lead either to regeneration or to original chaos. "The resurrection of buried realities," writes Paz, "the reappearance of what was forgotten and repressed"—these could inspire a renaissance or war. But the revival of religious, national, and tribal passions, and the resulting conflicts in Bosnia, Rwanda, Somalia, and elsewhere, suggested that chaos was a defining feature of the new world order, in which vast economic forces unleashed by information technologies were reshaping our lives in unimaginable ways. My province being the arts, I was interested in works that not only tested the boundaries of expression but also explored the origin, spiritual and artistic—the German artist Anselm Kiefer's paintings on Old Testament themes, the Estonian composer Arvo

Pärt's plainchant-inspired musical works. Some poets (and I was one) had rediscovered the usefulness of traditional forms: how meter and rhyme can distract the conscious mind, allowing mysterious currents of thought and feeling to surface. And these "buried realities" were for me increasingly religious in nature. But in the last few years I had stopped writing poetry altogether, imagining I could not continue until I addressed the questions inscribed by Paul Gauguin on a painting: Where do we come from? What are we? Where are we going?

The Australian monk led me up a creaking staircase to a room heated by a raised fireplace. On the table was a tray of empty water glasses and coffee cups. The custom is to serve pilgrims a glass of ouzo or raki (anise-flavored liqueurs), a rose-scented Turkish delight called *loukoumi*, a glass of water, and Greek coffee; during Great Lent, the liquor is dispensed with. Father Iakovos, the elderly guestmaster, greeted me like a lost son, although I had not taken the precaution of reserving a place for the night. He was a large monk with a long white beard and ponytail, a holy man (who might have passed for Jerry Garcia) blessed with the gift of discernment. A Vlach I knew from Thessaly, a sportswriter who called the guestmaster his spiritual father, had made three pilgrimages in the last year to talk to him about his engagement, which had broken over his fiancée's atheism and fear of his monastic leanings. Father Iakovos said he had no right to demand belief from her. Maybe this was God's way of testing her. In ten years she might feel differently. After all, once she wanted to put off having children, then she despaired of having waited too long to start a family. Father Iakovos did not think the journalist should become a monk.

"Don't worry, my son," he said. "You are like a budding rose."

The journalist burst into tears. The guestmaster told him to find another girl.

With me the monk wanted to discuss poetry. He felt a kinship with Robert Frost because, as he joked, they were both "a little strange in the head." But perhaps it was Frost's sober gaze into the abyss that stirred the monk's sympathies. For behind the genial mask of the farmer-poet lay a haunted soul I recognized: "Forgive, O Lord, my little jokes on Thee / And I'll forgive Thy great big one on me." Frost called poetry "a momentary stay against confusion." And Father Iakovos prayed for an eternal stay against the pain wrought by the theater of the world, which he advised pilgrims to view with skepticism. Even so he congratulated me on my long marriage.

"Do you have children?" he asked.

"A two-year-old daughter," I replied.

"Wonderful," he said, beaming. And my decision to make a pilgrimage on foot pleased him even more.

"The Holy Mother is counting your steps," he said.

"THERE ARE NO SHADOWS IN ORTHODOXY," THE SEMINARIAN EXplained. "Only lightness and darkness."

My roommate, a wine merchant from California studying in Thessaloníki, belonged to a new generation of Orthodox Americans raised outside the Church. Orthodoxy's tangled history in the New World, which begins with Russian missionaries crossing the Bering Strait in 1794 to set up churches in Alaska (there was even a seminary on the Aleutian Islands), is a study in migration and the myth of assimilation. Immigrants from Eastern Europe and the Middle East—Albanians, Bulgarians, Greeks, Romanians, Serbs, Ukrainians, Lebanese, Syrians—established churches in their own languages, while exiles from the Bolshevik Revolution founded another Russian church; several dioceses, each representing different ethnic groups, thus serve three million Orthodox Americans. The three largest jurisdictions—the Greek Archdiocese; the multiethnic Orthodox Church of America, which descends from the original Russian diocese; and the Antiochian Archdiocese, which oversees the Syrian and Lebanese Orthodox—are theoretically working toward unification. But deep divisions remain, not least because ethnic differences are hard to transcend, as my roommate revealed when our discussion turned to our fellow pilgrims at Iveron.

"The Greeks are so crude," he muttered. "They don't care about anyone else."

Our room was sparsely furnished: three beds, two chairs, a card table with an oil lamp, a wood-burning stove, one small window. On the white wall above my bed was an icon of John Chrysostom (c. 357–407), the "golden-tongued" saint who created the Divine Liturgy performed almost every day on Athos (except during Great Lent, when it is replaced by a more austere form of the rite). An English translation of the liturgy lay open on the table, and between pronouncements my roommate would read a page, frequently crossing himself. His convictions were unshakable, if sometimes contradictory. Thus he was torn between condemning the savage (his word) Serbian siege of Sarajevo and defending the Serbian clergy. "They can only bless and understand," he said. He called Orthodoxy the only uncorrupted apostolic creed; his disdain for Roman Catholic and Protestant innovations was profound. With a convert's fervor he argued that theology, a sophisticated art unavailable to heretics, demands constant attention and deepening of the spirit. Attracted to monasticism, he did not plan to take orders.

"I want to get married!" he cried. (Unlike his Roman Catholic counterpart, an Orthodox priest has the option of taking a wife.)

From the courtyard came the sound of the *sémantron*, a kind of double-bladed oar struck with a mallet to call the faithful to services, in a rhythm bearing an uncanny resemblance to the drumbeats of the Native American ceremonial dances I used to attend in the pueblos near Santa Fe. But in this cosmology the *sémantron* links the first and last books of the Bible, Genesis and Revelation: three times a monk circles the courtyard rapidly striking the *sémantron* on his shoulder, summoning the faithful into the ark of the church, just as Noah called the animals before the Flood—first the reptiles, then the four-footed creatures, then mankind. The *sémantron* also announces the hours set aside for private prayer, warning monks to attend to God's presence, like the last trumpet of the angel, according to St. Symeon of Thessaloníki. Up and down the board the mallet flies, now faster, now slower, pausing, then urgently resuming; sometimes the monk beats the *kopanos*, a wooden blade hung from a pair of chains or an omega-shaped piece of iron, and bells ring in the tower. With uncommon interest I watched the courtyard fill with monks and pilgrims, recalling a line from D. H. Lawrence's account of his last journey to New Mexico: "The moment I saw the brilliant, proud morning shine high up over the deserts of Santa Fe, something stood still in my soul, and I started to attend." Like the first Christian anchorites, the fourth-century desert fathers whose sayings endure as models of spiritual and literary compression, Lawrence went to the desert to heal himself (he was dying of tuberculosis), to become a new man. His "savage pilgrimage" to discover a better way to live than was on offer in modern industrial society had taken him to Sicily, Ceylon, and Australia. But "in the magnificent fierce morning of New Mexico one sprang awake," he wrote, "a new part of the soul woke up suddenly, and the old world gave way to the new."

We went into the ancient church, black with night and age. It took a few minutes for my eyes to adjust to the dark, and what I saw then was amazing. Sixteenth-century frescoes covered with soot. A wooden iconostasis carved with twisting tendrils. A silver lamp stand in the shape of a lemon tree, with thirty gilded lemons. The rose marble floor, a thousand years old, was inlaid with diamonds, in squares and circles; the corona, lit with candles and suspended like a halo from the ceiling, cast shadows on a circle of porphyry with an inscription—"I have set firm her columns, and for all ages she shall not be shaken. George the Monk, Iberian and Founder"—said to commemorate a foiled Persian raid. When fifteen ships appeared off the coast, the monks locked themselves up in the tower with their treasures and prayed to a miracle-working icon of Our Lady of the Gate. The raiders sacked the monastery, bound cables around the columns of the church,

29

and tried in vain to topple the dome. When the monks' prayers gave rise to a storm that swamped the fleet, sparing only the emir's ship, the emir repented. His reparations ensured that walls high enough to prevent another sacking were built.

Monks shuffled toward the tall wooden chairs—*stasidia*—lining the walls. Pilgrims bowed and crossed themselves and kissed the icons. A novice lit candles as the service commenced, an exquisitely choreographed affair of readings and plainchant. The solemnity of the ceremonial entrances and prayers was leavened by the sight of monks trading jokes and pilgrims wandering in and out of the narthex. I likened the effect to a strictly metered poem that incorporates looser rhythms; the tension between formality and freedom enhanced the complexity of the experience. What a departure from the rigid formalism of the Episcopal Church in which I was raised. St. Peter's Church in Morristown, New Jersey, I remembered for its sterility: a cavernous hall, a priest droning on to a few parishioners, a lame curate whose idea of discipline in confirmation class was to kick us with his steel boot. After my first Communion, I declined the invitation to become an acolyte. In high school and college I went to church only at Christmas and Easter.

Not until I was enrolled in a graduate creative writing program at Columbia University did I draw closer to God. Dissatisfied with my classes, I spent my free time at the Cloisters, a museum of medieval art designed to replicate a monastery and incorporating fragments of medieval architecture. I would take the subway from 116th Street and Broadway to the last stop—Fort Tryon Park, along the Hudson River—and stroll from the exhibits to the gardens, imagining a life apart from the literary world into which I was plunging, with uncertain results. The tapestries and altarpieces, the espaliered pear trees and quinces, the silence and solitude—soon I was contemplating a different course of study. Union Theological Seminary was just around the corner from the classes I had stopped attending (not long after a professor had introduced himself as the "legendary" author of a bestselling novel about a serial rapist and murderer); the course catalog for the divinity school I kept on my desk as a kind of map to a less indulgent future, spiritual and artistic.

One day I came upon Philip Larkin's poem "Church Going," which became a touchstone for me. This poem, from 1954, recounts Larkin's visit to a church — "A shape less recognisable each week, / A purpose more obscure" — in blank verse unsettled by so many metrical variations that its underlying pattern all but disappears, as if to say the orderly world of belief can barely be heard now. The poet wonders what will become of churches, which seem on the verge of obsolescence. Will some be turned into museums while the rest fall into ruin? Yet the impulse that gave rise to the construction of this church will never die, Larkin suggests, "Since someone will forever be surprising / A hunger in himself to be more serious" — a hunger I knew well.

But Union was not the place for me to become more serious. Instead I moved to Seattle to complete my graduate studies in creative writing. I found work in a nursery, shared a house with friends from college, and began to put together a thesis. An odd conjunction of events at Christmas altered the course of my life. First, in a used bookstore I came across an anthology of surrealist poetry, which inspired me to experiment with automatic writing — writing in the absence of conscious control to plumb the depths of the unconscious. Mad love, convulsive beauty, the marvelous — these were the names the surrealists gave to the ways in which dream and reality might meet. "Everything tends to make us believe that there exists a certain point of the mind at which life and death, the real and imagined, past and future, the communicable and the incommunicable, cease to be contradictions," wrote André Breton. And I was searching for that point when my housemates and I hosted a Christmas party. Just before our guests arrived, though, I discovered a lump in my neck, which I tried to ignore with the help of liberal quantities of hot cider-and-rum and passionate conversation with a visiting theology professor — a Union graduate, as it happened. By the time a glamorous violinist strolled in, dressed in black, I was flirting again with the idea of entering the seminary. My future wife, fresh from a performance of Handel's *Messiah*, thought I was destined for an ecclesiastical career.

Our courtship had a rocky start. Lisa moved to Portland to study. My doctor said I was suffering from either leukemia or Hodgkin's disease, confirming my premonition that I would not live past the age of twenty-five. Then came a flurry of encounters which I would jokingly describe as providential. The Sunday morning before I entered the hospital I hitchhiked to the nursery, and the first driver to pick me up, a Baptist minister who was listening to a tape of the Bible, pressed his card on me. The next ride I hailed was with a Jehovah's Witness, who gave me a copy of *The Watchtower*. And then in the hospital I shared a room with an Episcopal priest, who was dying of stomach cancer. He was in terrible pain, yet he never complained, not even when I woke from surgery and vomited on the floor between our beds.

My diagnosis was more fortunate—a benign tumor; and when I was released from the hospital I felt as if I had been granted a new life. Poems flooded over me. I was surrendering to the dictates of the language instead of attempting to control the process of discovery integral to creation, even as I learned that obeying formal imperatives could lead me into the uncharted waters of memory and desire. I wrote in the mornings, in the afternoons I walked to the park. Blossoming camellias, azaleas, apple trees— the world never seemed brighter to me than when my first collection of poems was taking shape. Lisa returned from Portland, and soon we were possessed with the sense of the miraculous dear to lovers: chance meetings led to walks along the bluff overlooking Puget Sound and picnics under madronas, nights of lovemaking, a cross-country train ride to Vermont: mad love. By the summer solstice we had decided to marry.

Yet now it all seemed for naught. My marriage was in tatters, war reporting had taken the place of poetry, and I was of an age to realize that the resolution of my latest health crisis was just a temporary reprieve—three reasons not only to make a pilgrimage to the Holy Mountain but to explain why in the last year I had returned to the Episcopal Church. On the first Sunday in Lent, a reading from Mark, in which Jesus prophesies His Second Coming, brought me to attention:

> Take heed, watch and pray; for you do not know when the time is. It is like a man going to a far country, who left his house and gave authority to his servants, and to each his work, and commanded the doorkeeper to watch. Watch therefore, for you do not know when the master of the house is coming—in the evening, at midnight, at the crowing of the rooster, or in the morning—lest, coming suddenly, he find you sleeping. And what I say to you, I say to all: Watch!
>
> [MARK 13:33–37]

The guestmaster had indeed encouraged me to stay awake for as much of the evening service as possible, neglecting to add that the vigil for St. Gregory Palamas was six hours long. Palamas, a fourteenth-century Greek theologian, is remembered for his defense of hesychasm (literally, "silence," "stillness," or "rest after warfare"), the tradition of contemplative prayer practiced on Athos. Inspired by Christ's parable of the publican and the Pharisee (Luke 18:9–14), hesychastic monks translate the publican's anguished cry for mercy into the Jesus Prayer: "Lord Jesus Christ, Son of God, have mercy on me, a sinner." Through constant recitation of the prayer and synchronized breathing, uniting the mind and heart, hesychasts claim to receive visions of God's uncreated light, the same light that surrounded Jesus at the Transfiguration, when He took His disciples Peter, James, and John up Mount Tabor and appeared to them beside Moses and Elijah. This light is how God reveals His presence to man, argued Palamas, the light through which God said, "This is my beloved Son, in whom I am well pleased. Hear him!" (Matt. 17:5). And the old monk leaning on the chair next to mine, running a black prayer rope through his fingers as if it were a fishing line, was practicing this prayer of the heart with such concentration that I could believe he had experienced the eternal light by which God is known.

Palamas wrote his *Triads for the Defense of the Holy Hesychasts* at a critical juncture in Byzantine history. The Ottoman threat he knew firsthand. From his birthplace in Asia Minor he had fled with his family to Constantinople, where his father served in the Senate. (There is a story of his father being too absorbed in prayer one day to hear the emperor question him on a political matter. The emperor, respecting his spirituality, did not demand an answer!) Palamas pursued a course of secular studies, chiefly Aristotelian metaphysics, until, at the age of twenty, he chose to leave the world, forgoing the emperor's offer of a career at court. He sailed to Athos and lived in a settlement near Vatopedi, then in Great Lavra, and lastly in a hermitage. When Turkish pirates made eremitical life too dangerous, he moved to Thessaloníki, bearing the gift of hesychasm. The prayer of silence is available to all, he said, carving out a private realm resistant not only to the imminent Muslim takeover but to any future regime inimical to Orthodoxy. St. Isaac the Syrian said prayer is "the conversation with God which takes place in secret." No authority can take that away (as Palamas himself demonstrated when, late in life, returning to Constantinople, his galley was captured by the Turks, and he spent a year imprisoned in Asia Minor).

In Macedonia, Palamas struck a balance between communal life and solitude, praying alone during the week before joining his brethren on the weekend to celebrate the Eucharist. By 1331 Serbian raids had sent him back to Athos, and it was from a hermitage above Great Lavra that he was spurred to his defense of hesychasm. Barlaam, a Greek theologian from Calabria, had made a name for himself in Constantinople by attacking the hesychasts, discounting their claims to see the uncreated light of God. Their presumption, he said, was of a piece with Scholasticism, the deductive theology by which Thomas Aquinas sought to prove

God's existence: man can no more see God's divine essence, Barlaam insisted, than he can discover Him by rational means.

In this Barlaam followed the thinking of Pseudo-Dionysios the Areopagite (c. 500), an enigmatic figure who until the nineteenth century was thought to be a disciple of St. Paul. God is unknowable, said Pseudo-Dionysios: we ascend to Him by a process of unknowing—the *via negativa* or apophatic theology. We can only say what God is not, not what He is, since He is by definition beyond all categories of thought. God points up the poverty of language; only by analogy, by poetry, can we speak of Him: "the ray of the divine shadow which is above everything that is," wrote Pseudo-Dionysios. And what distinguishes Eastern from Western Christendom is the East's emphasis on God's unknowability. Against Aquinas's elegant proofs of God's existence and the deductive reasoning sweeping over Western Europe (creating, among other things, the first modern university, in Paris), hesychast monks held that their knowledge of God was limited to their experience, in prayer, of His divine light.

The division between Constantinople and Rome, crudely summarized as the difference between Greek and Latin, patristic literature and jurisprudence, the embrace of mystery and the imperatives of logic, cannot be underestimated. It is a commonplace to say that Scholasticism rescued the West from the superstitious Dark Ages. And who can deny the benefits—scientific and medical, legal and political, artistic and economic—derived from the application of reason to the material universe? The glories of our civilization depend upon Occam's razor. But what if in our drive to master the world we lost sight of a vital spiritual tradition? Orthodox theologians, transformed by their encounters with the divine, offer an original vision of spiritual progress, rooted in monasticism. Pseudo-Dionysios said God could be experienced through purification, illumination, and union—the three ways of the mystical life (which may recall the Pauline triad of faith, hope, and love integral to salvation). This is an altogether different religious understanding from the systematic theology that, say, provided Dante with a map to the hereafter for his *Divine Comedy*—a map the Orthodox can read only in poetic terms.

Barlaam, an apophatic theologian imbued with the humanistic ideals of the Renaissance, might have built a bridge between Eastern and Western Christendom, if not for his unpleasant encounters with some hesychast monks in Constantinople and Thessaloníki. "I have been initiated by them," he wrote, "in monstrosities and in absurd doctrines that a man with any intelligence or even a little sense, cannot lower himself to describe"—and then went on to describe some of the products of their "rash imagination": marvelous separations and reunions of the mind and soul, the differences between red and white lights, shields around the navel. His chief objection, though, was to their certainty that they could see God's divine essence: how could He be inaccessible to the senses and still reveal Himself in prayer? What they imagined to be the uncreated light, he contended, was nothing more than a man-made vision.

Palamas was thus forced to distinguish between God's essence and His energies, a cardinal point of *Triads for the Defense of the Holy Hesychasts*, which has been described as the first theological synthesis of Eastern monastic spirituality. Barlaam's attack was useful, then, because it inspired Palamas to inventory the most vital features of the mystical life, the central province of Orthodoxy. God's essence is invisible, he argued, yet His energies are omnipresent in Creation: everyone and everything—rocks, trees, beasts, birds, sea, stars—contain His divine spark. "The world is charged with the grandeur of God," wrote the poet Gerard Manley Hopkins. *Inscape* was the word he coined to account for the ways in which the world's fundamental beauty reveals itself; the visions of eternity the Jesuit recorded in his journal and celebrated in his poetry, the elemental truths we glimpse from time to time, the saints see at every moment, according to Palamas. The Jesus Prayer is their route to the uncreated light.

"Pray without ceasing," Paul advised (1 Thess. 5:17), and monastics say the Jesus Prayer (or arrow prayer, which metaphorically shoots straight into the heart) unceasingly. On a practical level, the Jesus Prayer resembles the Buddhist discipline of chanting a mantra, except that it works by way of the name to build love between the believer and the Lord. As John Chrysostom wrote: "Abide constantly with the name of our Lord Jesus, so that the heart swallows the Lord and the Lord the heart and the two become one." The monk thus silently recites this prayer thousands of times a day—in church and in his cell, during work and at meals, even in conversation. With his eyes closed and head bowed to steer his words toward his heart, the monk takes a breath, saying, "Lord Jesus Christ, Son of God," then exhales to complete his prayer, "Have mercy on me, a sinner." This prayer of silence was what I now said. For what monks call *kenosis* or poverty, the emptying of the self to let God work through you in the same way that Christ emptied Himself into human form for our deliverance, is best achieved through prayer.

If poetry is a form of listening to the inner workings of the language, then prayer is how we listen to the divine, which we imagine to be always present, if rarely heard. The prayer rope used by the monk beside me, a tasseled chaplet made of black wool, was thus a kind of hearing aid: fingering the knots silences the endless chatter in the mind so that what lies in the deepest recesses may surface, in the same manner that a poet obeying the imperatives of meter can distract his or her logical thought processes enough to discover darker truths. Just as the poet engages in a dialogue with the language, taking soundings syllable by syllable, so the hesychast petitions God with every breath. For religious poets— St. John of the Cross and Sor Juana Inés de la Cruz, John Donne and George Herbert—inspiration is but another name for His divine inflowing.

No doubt the Jesus Prayer can be recited as mechanically as a poet with a tin ear composes blank verse. As the composer John Cage understood, music is continuous, listening intermittent. And certainly my listening was intermittent during the vigil, which consisted largely of Byzantine chant. The mystery of God's presence in the world: this is what the chant celebrates. "Be still, and know that I am God," says the Psalmist (Ps. 46:10). And this week the entire Psalter would be sung not once but twice in every monastic establishment on the Holy Mountain. For psalmody is another form of prayer. From the semicircular north and south ends of the nave two choirs trade antiphonal lines, so that it sounds as if one rich voice is echoing throughout the church. Under an oil lamp the leading chanter uses a series of liturgical books laid out on an octagonal book stand to tune the voices. Sometimes he walks back and forth between the choirs, reading lines before the chanters translate them into music. Monks and pilgrims hum and sing along. An old man with a cane, a traveling chanter I recognize from the ferry, has come to lend his voice to the vigil—one of about fifty annual celebrations at this monastery. He stands between the choirs, chanting to the congregation, his wizened features set in an expression of rapture.

Here is a chance to pay attention to the divine music, without and within your soul. Which I do, more or less, for the first hours of the vigil. But the longer the chanting goes on, the more I wonder what I am doing here. Like several pilgrims and monks, including the guestmaster, I doze off from time to time, and once I dream I understand every word of the service. "Your heart should be watchful even when your eyes are closed in prayer," wrote Cyprian, a third-century saint who was exiled and beheaded. But my imaginary vigil is all barracks ballads and dirty jokes, far removed from the Pentecostal gift of speaking in tongues by which people from everywhere suddenly understood the Holy Spirit. I wake with a start at the sound of the celebrant priest swinging a censer before the altar and icons, the pilgrims and monks. Following their example, I lean forward to inhale the sweet smoke, which is said to carry our prayers to God.

The Athonite fathers have a saying about a celebrant priest at Iveron who once passed by a high-ranking monk without censing him. After the liturgy, when the priest explained that he had not seen anyone in his place, the monk became contrite. "I was on my stand only in body," he said. "My mind was elsewhere." So was mine, for long stretches of the service. Yet when we filed out of the church, sometime after midnight, I felt a new—and curious— form of peacefulness flood over me. The moon was full, the wind off the sea had died, the monks and pilgrims left the courtyard in silence. Back in our cell my roommate lit a candle, placed an icon on his bedside table, and knelt to pray, reading aloud from the liturgy—a sight that made me uneasy. He had chanted ostentatiously during the service; his zeal left me at once wary and a little envious. This sophisticated devotee of fine wine and literature (he was as well read as many writers I knew) had translated his passion for the things of the world into a spiritual quest. Which was not without hazards. He was the first to say he was confused about his vocation.

"It's hard to answer a monk when he tells you to do what your spiritual father says when you don't have one," he sighed, and blew out the candle.

THE MEAL SERVED IN THE REFECTORY WAS ALMOST INEDIBLE: cold fish-and-potato soup, spinach, stale bread, olives, an apple, a tin cup of sour red wine—our reward for the short two-hour daybreak service following the vigil. The monks fast on Mondays, Wednesdays, and Fridays, avoiding dairy products and olive oil; during the Great Fast, which begins seven weeks before Easter, they take one meal a day; meat is never eaten; fish is served only at the feasts. The refectory was silent save for the monk at the lectern reading aloud from patristic literature. St. Basil, the Cappadocian father whose *Shorter* and *Longer Rules* codified Eastern monasticism, said monks should listen "with far greater pleasure than they eat or drink, in order that the mind may be shown not to be distracted by the pleasure of the body, but delighting rather in the words of the Lord."

No fear of that, I decided.

I recalled the time I treated a friend with a penchant for spicy food to Dungeness crab, which should be eaten with just a hint of butter. After one bite, though, my friend asked the waiter for hot sauce. Evidence of a ruined palate, I joked. But mine was little better. In the words of the Blessed Theodore, I could not "enjoy sensory things by the senses and intelligible things by the intellect"—the gift of those who have recovered their spiritual vitality. Indeed for some time I had been unable to concentrate on anything at all. I suffered from what Pascal identified as the cause of all evil: I could not sit still; at work and at home, my mind raced from image to idea, from memory to desire; even when I went for a run I could not refrain from mulling over past slights or from projecting myself into the future, all at the expense of living in the present. "In two years," I would tell myself, "such and so will happen." At night I would open a book and read no more than a paragraph or two before turning on the television to channel surf. An Orthodox theologian accurately diagnosed my condition two centuries ago: "the order of things has become inverted: instead of God within, the heart seeks for pleasures without and is content with them."

The Orthodox remedy is watchfulness, the practice of guarding the heart against fantasy, the source of sin—pride, envy, avarice, the pursuit of sensual pleasure. St. Hesychios the Priest (c. 800) called watchfulness a "spiritual art, which, with long and diligent practice and with the help of God, releases man completely from passionate words and from evil deeds." This art takes the form of attentiveness to the movement of the heart as it invokes the Divine Name of Jesus, refusing entry to "predatory and murderous thoughts." In His Sermon on the Mount Jesus said, "Blessed are the pure in heart: for they shall see God" (Matt. 5:8). And if watchfulness is a prerequisite to penetrating God's hidden mysteries, then fasting, which St. Basil called "a disengagement from the passions," is a necessary element of the spiritual journey: savoring each bite of food teaches you to pay attention to the holiness inherent in every moment of life. Prayer, vigil, and fasting: a sacred triad by which to return to the beginning.

But for this journey you need a teacher, someone to point the way to divine union—a path which begins in the fear of God and which, by His grace, ends in salvation. In *Directions to Hesychasts*, a manual on spiritual matters, Kallistos and Ignatios, two monks who lived on Athos at the same time as St. Gregory Palamas, ask:

> If a man is unlikely to take an unexplored path without a true guide; if no one will risk going to sea without a skillful navigator; if no man will undertake to learn a science or an art without an experienced teacher, who will dare to attempt a practical study of the art of arts and the science of sciences, to enter the mysterious path leading to God, and venture to sail the boundless mental sea, that is monastic life, akin to the life of the angels, and be sure of reaching his goal without a guide, a navigator and a true and experienced teacher?

My roommate was searching for such a guide. Meantime he ate Iveron's meager fare with gusto, squeezed lemon juice into his wine before gulping it down, and pocketed an extra apple when the abbot rang the bell to signal the end of the meal. A monk came to our table and crumbled into our paper napkins a sweet confection made of coconut and almonds. After the benediction, we walked out through two lines of bowing monks, blessed by the abbot, who held his right hand in the air, his thumb and first two fingers pressed together—the Orthodox sign of the cross. The pilgrims returned to their cells to retrieve their belongings. Hospitality at Athonite monasteries is generally extended for one night, but the guestmaster invited my roommate to stay until Easter, joking that he could help them to improve the wine they made. What the merchant hoped for was spiritual direction. Perhaps the guestmaster would become his spiritual father. Father Iakovos had different instructions for me. He gave me a photocopy of the only reliable map of Athos, drawn by an Austrian pilgrim, on which he had sketched out a route for me to follow to several monasteries north of Iveron. Then he kissed me on both cheeks.

"Be fruitful," he said, "and write many poems."

IT WAS A STRANGE FEELING. I KEPT THINKING I HAD STRAYED OFF the trail, but whenever I looked behind me the way was clear. Under overcast skies I was hiking north along a cliff, in heather and sage, cypresses and chestnut trees, relying on my instincts to navigate through the confusing terrain. The system of footpaths was overgrown in several spots, because most pilgrims preferred the taxi to walking from monastery to monastery. Descending from a cliff to a cove buffeted by a stiff wind, I came to a rocky beach where the path vanished under mounds of sea wrack, oil cans, and plastic containers. There was even the hull of a boat washed up on shore. The seaward rocks were covered with a mustard-colored lichen, and in the next cove a dog was barking in a stone tower overlooking the surf; the wooden bridge above the rocks swayed in the wind, and several steps were missing from the staircase to the third-story entrance. The shrine at the far end of the cove looked like a better destination, but when I reached the brick-and-stone hut I could not read the sign, in Greek, on its lintel. I turned around and saw that I was still on the trail.

This was the same sensation I experienced when I began to read patristic literature—the writings and doctrines of the church fathers, the most important of which for the Orthodox date from the New Testament to the works of John of Damascus (d. 749). It was as if I had stumbled onto a neglected path, a style of thought, at once metaphorical and penetrating, which seemed familiar; at every turn was a new vista beckoning further exploration. Mark Rothko said that in the writings of the early Christians everything "went toward ladders," and the first text to capture my attention was *The Ladder of the Divine Ascent*, the most popular guidebook to asceticism in the ancient Church. St. John Climacus (c. 579–649) composed it late in life, after reluctantly leaving his hermitage to become the abbot of the monastery of St. Catherine on Mount Sinai. When the abbot of a neighboring monastery asked him to write down what, like Moses, he had seen in divine vision on the mountain during his long years as a hermit, John Climacus said he was still learning. Nevertheless in obedience (a key feature of monasticism) he completed what he called an outline sketch, which on Athos is read in its entirety during Great Lent.

The thirty steps of *The Ladder of the Divine Ascent,* which correspond to Christ's years on earth before His baptism, reflect His hidden life, just as the steps of the ladder an Athonite hermit climbs to his remote perch symbolize the hidden power of faith — how prayers said in the most inhospitable circumstances hold the world together, according to John Climacus. But the ascent described by the saint is so arduous that, one monk told me, most people throw the book down in disgust. Still this monk believed we must imagine such efforts at faith, no matter how distant they may be from our own. The chapter on penitence, for example, reads like an improvisation on Dante's *Inferno.* John Climacus recalls his stay in a monastery known as "The Prison," a "place of true grief," where penitents stood outside all night; prayed with their hands tied behind their backs, like criminals; pounded their foreheads into the ground. They beat their breasts, imploring God to punish them. They ate crusts of bread, they drank only enough water to keep from dying of thirst, they thought constantly of death. And when one neared his end the others gathered around him, asking, " 'Has the door been opened to you, or are you still under sentence?' " Some even begged to have their corpses flung into a river or cast out to the wild beasts, in the hope of finding mercy in the next world. "Through repentance you have reached the fifth step," John Climacus concludes. "You have in this way, purified the five senses, and by choosing to accept punishment have thereby avoided the punishment that is involuntary."

My senses were far from pure, although this morning the salt air was invigorating and the sound of the waves clattering over the shells was as sharp as a drumroll. I climbed a narrow path to a cliff leading toward the monastery of Stavronikita. The sun came out, throwing into relief the sand and stiff clumps of dormant grass; at each switchback I could see the mountain behind me, laden with snow. *Bright sadness,* a phrase coined by John Climacus, is how Orthodox theologians describe Great Lent, and in the stark light of Athos a familiar sadness arose in my heart. Penitence is the theme of the Lenten journey to Easter or Pascha; the seven-week-long fast is not so much an exercise in abstinence as it is an occasion to meditate on the gulf between our actions and God's will. Our reflections on the inevitable disappointments of love and work should inspire a clearer sense of the import of Christ's summons to imitate His life—an effort doomed to failure, the church fathers remind us. Thus in Great Lent we are counseled to pay special attention to our sinfulness. "Sores, when revealed, do not get worse but are cured," wrote John Climacus. But as I mulled over my problems, wallowing in self-pity, my daughter's beautiful face rose up in my memory. "Daddy, come home," Hannah had cried over the phone on the eve of my pilgrimage. Her words struck with a particular force. A friend said that when his first child was born he felt as if the air was full of bullets. Nor could I protect my daughter from this distance. The tangle of circumstances that had led me away from her filled me with shame.

"Do not think I have come to bring peace on earth," Jesus tells His disciples in one of the New Testament's most troubling passages. "I have not come to bring peace, but a sword. For I have come to set a man against his father, and a daughter against her mother, and a daughter-in-law against her mother-in-law; and a man's foes will be those of his own household. He who loves father or mother more than me is not worthy of me; and he who loves son or daughter more than me is not worthy of me" (Matt. 10:34–37). The Gospels illustrate at every turn the sacrifices integral to discipleship, but who can bear up under such demands?

Everything in my being told me that my first obligation was to my family. Yet what I felt now was my unworthiness not only as a husband and father but also as a writer and pilgrim. How to reconcile my earthly love with my need to believe in something less transitory? I resolved to record for Lisa and Hannah the textures and dimensions of a sacred place forever hidden from their view.

CHRIST WAS THE FIRST MONK (FROM MONOS, "ALONE"). THE PRI-vations, temptations, and prayers He alternately endured, withstood, and offered during his forty days in the wilderness are crucial features of monastic life. And monastics obey His injunction—"If anyone would come after me, let him deny himself and take up his cross and follow me" (Matt. 16:24)—with varying degrees of the fervor displayed by the first Christians, who followed Him into martyrdom, including most if not all of His disciples. Indeed the threat of execution—the practice of Christianity was a capital offense in the Roman Empire—fueled the fires of belief once it became apparent that the Second Coming had been postponed. If the Day of Judgment was not at hand, then Christian eschatology needed to be reconfigured along a different axis, conveniently provided by the Roman authorities. The practice of crucifying, beheading, and stoning Christians to death only solidified the faith of the survivors. As Tertullian remarked, "the blood of the martyrs is the seed of the church," which in time grew large enough to end the persecution—and inspire monasticism.

The Christian monastic movement dates from the fourth century, when Egyptian ascetics fled the city and settled in desert caves to create an alternative city of God. This coincided with Constantine's conversion to Christianity in 312, the decisive moment in Western history. The story is well known: how Constantine, needing to secure his position against Maxentius, marched on Rome; how on the eve of the battle of the Milvian Bridge he saw in a dream a cross bearing the sign: *In hoc signo vinces* ("In this sign you will conquer"); how he celebrated his victory by granting favored status to Christianity. The political expediency of the emperor's dream is not often remarked upon, although it was instrumental in his unification of the Roman Empire. This may explain why he did not reveal its contents until the Council of Nicaea in 325—the first ecumenical council, which secured the unity of the Church in the East and produced the first draft of the Nicene Creed, the Christian statement of faith. By then the emperor had established a new Rome in Constantinople, and Byzantium—"the image of the heavenly Jerusalem," in one theologian's words—became a Christian theocracy, which endured for nearly twelve centuries.

To absolve his sins, Constantine waited until he was on his deathbed to be baptized. But what the writer James Carroll, in a historical study of the fraught relationship between Christians and Jews, calls "the old Constantinean cloud—how Christians behave when they come fully into power," was apparent from the moment the cross became a sword, when Christ's radical idea of love was transformed into political power. Any consideration of Byzantine and Roman glory must be balanced, then, by a reckoning of the iniquity committed in the Church's name. As Carroll explains, "Christian faith can be seen to triumph over every evil except Christian triumphalism." The Crusades, the Inquisition, the Final Solution—the seeds of the darkest events in Western history, Carroll argues, were planted in Constantine's dream. Nor should the centuries of persecution the Eastern Church suffered at the hands of the Crusaders, Ottomans, and Communists obscure its own propensity for evil: from Russian pogroms to Serbian massacres of Bosnian Muslims, Orthodox Christians have not spared the Other; the discrimination against Albanians in Greece, Turks in Bulgaria, and Gypsies throughout the Orthodox world, tacitly condoned by state and religious authorities alike, attests to a continuing refusal to obey Christ's second commandment: "you shall love your neighbor as yourself" (Matt. 22:39).

The Orthodox Church has a complicated relationship to political power. Unlike the Latin Church, which retained a universal outlook even after the Reformation, Orthodoxy divided into national or autocephalous churches, each of which must work out its relationship to the state. "Render therefore to Caesar the things that are Caesar's, and to God the things that are God's" (Matt. 22:21), said Christ, instructions that Orthodox clergy interpret in a stricter fashion than their Western counterparts, preferring to minister to the spiritual needs of the faithful than to enter into the political realm. Not that every Orthodox prelate remains distant from politics. Until the Bolshevik Revolution in 1917 the Russian Church played a vital role in state matters. And in the Soviet bloc the clergy who were not imprisoned or executed had little choice but to collaborate with the godless authorities—one reason why they have yet to reclaim every vestige of their spiritual authority. Nor has the Greek Church fully recovered from accepting the military dictatorship of 1967–74. (The Colonels' futile attempt to stamp out demotic Greek, which in the end discredited formal Greek, helps to explain the declining church attendance: many cannot understand the liturgy.) And the warmongering clergy of the Serbian Church, restored to positions of spiritual authority, still must answer for their support of Slobodan Milošević's project to carve a Greater Serbia out of Yugoslavia, the zeal with which they exhorted their flocks to turn on their neighbors, the blessings they offered to the paramilitaries whose crimes against humanity included killing sprees and rape campaigns in Croatia and Bosnia.

"There is a way in which success disagrees with Christianity," John Updike remarks, "and its proper venue is embattlement— a furtive hanging on in the catacombs, or at ill-attended services in dying rural and inner-city parishes. Its perilous, marginal, mocked existence serves as an image of our own, beneath whatever appearance of success is momentarily mustered." When Christianity enters the political arena, that is, the true religious light out for the desert. For just "as in the pagan Empire the Church herself was a kind of 'Resistance Movement,' " writes the Russian theologian Georges Florovsky, "*Monasticism was a per-*

47

manent 'Resistance Movement' in the Christian Society." And while some Egyptian anchorites retreated to the desert because of economic pressures or to escape justice, the majority embraced their white martyrdom, continuing the conciliar or democratic tradition of discussing, imagining, and then deciding on a course of action, pleasing to God, by which they might work out their fates according to His will.

The most famous desert father was St. Antony, traditionally regarded as the founder of Christian monasticism. His biographer, Athanasios, reports that Antony inherited a large estate in Egypt. One day he was reflecting on the apostles' renunciation of their worldly goods to follow the Savior when he entered a church and heard the Gospel reading of Christ's imperative: "If thou wilt be perfect, go and sell that thou hast, and give to the poor, and thou shalt have treasure in heaven" (Matt. 19:21). Antony immediately gave his lands to his tenants, made provisions for his sister, and went to the desert to become a hermit. He lived in solitude for more than thirty years, until he attained the wisdom to discern God's will in those who came to him in search of a healing word. (Indeed he was known as the physician to all Egypt.) This is a common pattern among holy men: withdrawal and return—for example, Christ's sojourn in the wilderness before His public ministry, or the way in which St. Gregory Palamas's writings on hesychasm drew him out of his hermitage and into the public fray. (He spent his last years as archbishop of Thessaloníki.) But St. Antony said, "Just as fish die if they remain on dry land so monks, remaining away from their cells, or dwelling with men of the world, lose their determination to persevere in solitary prayer." And St. Basil thought total separation from the world was necessary for the monk's progress:

> One becomes stateless and homeless. One gives up possessions, friends, ownership of property, livelihood, business connections, social life and scholarship. The heart is made ready to receive the imprint of sacred teaching, and this mak-

ing ready involves the unlearning of knowledge deriving from evil habits. To write on wax, one has to erase the letters previously written there, and to bring sacred teaching to the soul one must begin by wiping out preoccupations rooted in ordinary habits.

To return to the beginning, then, you must unlearn everything you know, untelling the story of your life in order to write a new one based on Scripture and patristic literature. Monastics thus retreat to the desert, literally or figuratively, to purify their souls in a landscape burned clean of association, practicing the virtues of renunciation, obedience, chastity, fasting, vigils, and manual labor, as described in the writings of St. Basil. The father of Eastern monasticism chose the middle path between self-indulgence and austerity, proposing what one commentator calls "a rhythmed schedule" of prayer, work, and reading of the Bible. The Psalter provided the communal prayer; a night office was chanted until dawn; and, in a departure from Antony's anchoritical ideal, Basil proposed a communal approach, arguing that "in the common life the private gift of each man becomes the common property of his fellows." All must be saved, or none.

Basil's reading of Holy Writ informed his thinking to such a degree that he was reluctant to use any word not found in it. Here is the rub: his *Rules* exist only in Latin translation, the Greek copies of the original having vanished—one more instance of the Latin filter through which we view our origins. St. Benedict, who codified Western monasticism, is much better known for his *Rule,* which owes a debt to Basil. The difference between Benedict's *Rule* and Basil's *Rules*? Benedict writes a brief, Basil replies to questions—the difference, that is, between the traditions of Hebraic lawmaking and Hellenic dialogue, Jerusalem and Athens. Roman Catholicism produced several monastic orders—Benedictine, Cistercian, and so on—but in Orthodoxy there is only one, the governing rules of which vary slightly from monastery to monastery depending on its *typikon.* At Great Lavra, for example,

Athanasios amended Basil's rule to accommodate eremitic and semi-eremitic monks, a practice that spread across the Holy Mountain.

An Athonite monk's day is divided into equal parts of prayer (public and private), work, and sleep. Vespers, compline, matins, the liturgy—these are the main services in what Basil calls "the sevenfold daily praise of God," the larger part of which occupies the monk from shortly after midnight, Byzantine time, until daybreak. A verse from the psalm known as the Law of the Lord—"At midnight I will rise to give thanks to You, because of Your righteous judgments" (Ps. 119:62)—prompts monks to gather in the dark to praise God; in their private worship they say the Jesus Prayer; the rest of their waking hours are given over to labor because, as the desert fathers teach, "the monk who works is tempted by one devil only; the lazy monk is tempted by a thousand devils." Each monastery is self-sufficient, each task performed, ideally, in a sacramental manner; laborers are hired from the mainland to supplement the workforce. Every January the elders assign the monks to work for that year in the gardens, kitchen, storerooms, choir, library, or the infirmary; to paint icons, carve crucifixes, weave prayer ropes, or bind books; to provide food and lodging for pilgrims, or strike the *sémantron* and ring the bells. A man who was a banker in the world read lessons in the refectory; an engineer may care for the aging and infirm. Monks rarely sleep for more than two hours at a stretch, yet they are generally long-lived.

Why does a man become a monk? John Cassian (c. 360–435), a Scythian monk and theologian, discerned three sources of inspiration for the monastic vocation—God, man, and circumstance. God may call someone to the monastery; or he may follow the example set by another monk; or something in his life—grievous loss, dissatisfaction with life, economic pressure, the threat of criminal prosecution—may lead him to abandon the world. In the monastery he serves as a novice for three years, receiving instruction in what Abba Philemon calls "the way of silence," a course of study designed to cleanse his mind of images, fantasies, and passions. And at his tonsuring, barefooted and bareheaded in the narthex of the church, penitent as the prodigal son returning to his father, he is baptized again and receives a new name, signifying the death of his old life. St. Isaac of Syria says the monk who takes up the cross has a double service: "first, patience in the face of bodily afflictions, which is called 'practice'; and, second, the subtle service of the mind, in intercourse with God, constant prayer, and so on, which is called contemplation. The first purifies through zeal the passionate part of the soul, the second the intellectual part": a lifelong project. Once he puts on the habit, "the garment of gladness," he will always be a monk, even if he is expelled from the monastery.

My reasons for making a pilgrimage to the Holy Mountain — to gain perspective on my life, my writing, the war; to untell the story of my walk in the sun; to draw closer to God—were not so distant from those of any anchorite. H. L. Mencken once remarked that in the modern age religion "is used as a club and a cloak by both politicians and moralists, all of them lusting for power and most of them palpable frauds." And in my discomfort with the trappings of Christianity everywhere on display in America—televangelists begging for money, politicians invoking God's blessing—I went in search of the authentic, obeying the impulse that in the fourth century sent Egyptians into the desert. In my imagination Athos came closest to inhabiting the spirit of those early Christian communities, where the faithful met to sing hymns of praise to Christ our Lord, to share their resources, to await His Second Coming. "Waiting in patience" was how Simone Weil described her journey to God. I had come to Athos to learn to wait.

THE RENOVATIONS ON STAVRONIKITA HAD STARTED NOT A MO-ment too soon. The long vertical crack in its foundation was tilting the last of the ruling monasteries into the sea. From a distance,

though, everything seemed in order—the stone walls and crenellated tower, the aqueduct and gardens, the bare arbor above the
gate; the narrow flagstone alleys revealed nothing of Stavronikita's
history of fire and neglect. The smallest Athonite monastery, with
few resources and fewer monks, had often gone up in flames or
been deserted, notably during the Latin occupation and the
Greek War of Independence. In fact it was on the verge of disin-
tegration in the 1960s, when a group of zealots settled here; their
decision to adopt the cenobitic way of life, which set an example
for the rest of the Holy Mountain, had dramatically improved the
living conditions. Now the monastery of the Conquering Cross
(*stavros* means cross) was rising again. The scaffolding draped
across its foundation was visible evidence of Stavronikita's renewed vigor.

In the guesthouse an old monk was arguing with five young
Greek pilgrims, who were distressed to learn he would not serve
them raki during Great Lent. Nor would he open the library at
this hour. But he did unlock the church to show us a fourteenth-
century mosaic of St. Nicholas, Stavronikita's patron saint. He
said the crack in the saint's forehead dated from the iconoclastic
controversy (c. 725–843), when Byzantine emperors ordered the
destruction of religious images and the persecution of monks who
persisted in venerating icons. A heretic struck the mosaic and
tossed it into the sea; five hundred years later, when a fisherman
brought it up in his net, an oyster had lodged in the crack—a sign
of the icon's miracle-working powers; the oyster shell was preserved as a holy relic. Miracles are integral to the Athonite imagination, and I was thinking of all the icons miraculously plucked
from the sea, when the monk took us to examine the progress of
the stonemasons on the foundation. The legend of an icon at
Iveron came to mind as I peered from the balcony at the scaffolding and the whitecapped water. When agents of an iconoclastic
emperor confronted a widow and her son over an icon of the
Blessed Virgin hidden in their house they set it in the sea, where
it sailed, upright, for seventy years. One day the monks at Iveron

noticed a pillar of fire rising from the sea into the sky; taking to their boats, they discovered the floating icon, which was too heavy to lift. A voice from the icon said it would not come to shore unless a hermit named Gabriel walked across the water to retrieve it. This he did. Three times the icon was placed in the *katholikón*, three times it moved in the night to the old gate of the monastery. Then the Blessed Virgin appeared to Gabriel with instructions to build a new chapel for her icon at the main gate, "for I have not come here for you to guard me, but for me to guard you." Which is why the icon is called Our Lady of the Gate.

The guestmaster stared for some time at the crack in the foundation before taking his leave. I went outside with the pilgrims, who rolled cigarettes and smoked. The previous night they had spent at Pantokratoros, the next monastery up the coast, which they advised me to avoid: the monks were too strict. So I could not fathom why they wanted to spend the week at Stavronikita, which was well known for its austerity. And they were surprised, when they asked about my religion and line of work, to hear of a Protestant teaching at a Jesuit college. This provoked a heated discussion among them about the differences between Orthodoxy and Roman Catholicism; when they switched to Greek, their voices rising, I departed for Pantokratoros, following a path along a low stone wall northward into the woods.

The schism between Rome and Constantinople traditionally dates from the anathemas exchanged between a delegation of papal legates and the ecumenical patriarch in 1054. The immediate cause of the break was Patriarch Michael Keroularios's refusal to support the papal military campaign against Norman incursions in southern Italy. These were Byzantine lands. Pope Leo IX's dream of exercising power over them was viewed with alarm in Constantinople. But he was taken prisoner by the Normans, and we may infer the patriarch's reaction to this news from the hostile reception he accorded the delegation sent to persuade him to come to the pope's defense. And when the legates placed a bull of excommunication on the altar of Hagia Sophia, saying,

"Let God look and judge," the patriarch replied in kind, issuing his own anathemas against the pope, who had since died. The Eastern and Western Churches severed relations, according to the standard interpretation of what were personal, not institutional, excommunications.

The two sides of the empire had in fact been growing apart for centuries, owing to the physical distance between Rome and Constantinople, linguistic and cultural differences, and the separate economic and political challenges facing them. Theological disagreements masked the main dispute: papal claims. Eastern and Western prelates divided over the Latin practice of using unleavened bread in the Eucharist and Rome's decision to introduce into the Nicene Creed the so-called *filioque*, the doctrine that the Holy Spirit proceeds not from a single fount of divinity but from the Father *and* the Son. But the real issue was power. Jesus anointed Peter as the rock upon which to build His church (Matt. 16:18); after His Crucifixion, when the apostles regrouped to create an institutional framework in which to await His Second Coming, Peter emerged as the leader of the Jerusalem Church; and while he was never the bishop of Rome his martyrdom in the imperial capital fueled the legend upon which the papacy was founded. It is true that in the five sees established in the early Church, in Alexandria, Antioch, Constantinople, Jerusalem, and Rome, the patriarchs regarded the bishop of Rome as first among equals. Nonetheless papal claims to speak for the entire Church, notably under Pope Nicholas I in the ninth century, offended theologians schooled in the conciliar tradition. The Orthodox Church is in fact known as the Church of the Councils, following the example, recounted in Acts 15, of the apostles meeting to settle the dispute over whether Gentile converts should be circumcised. "But we believe that through the grace of the Lord Jesus Christ we shall be saved in the same manner as they," said Peter (Acts 15:11). No doubt the Church's subsequent growth was fostered by the apostles' prudent decision to leave their converts' genitalia intact.

We cannot underestimate the importance that Orthodoxy attaches to the seven ecumenical councils held between 325 and 787. Hundreds of bishops and clergy met in Nicaea and Ephesus, in Chalcedon and Constantinople, to settle issues of church organization and to define doctrine, chiefly concerning the Trinity and the Incarnation: that God is three persons in one essence—God, Christ, and the Holy Spirit; that the Virgin Mary is Theotokos, the Mother of God; that Christ had both a divine and a human nature, as well as a divine and a human will; that He suffered in the flesh; that because God took human form it is appropriate to venerate Him through icons of Christ, the Virgin Mary, and the saints. These are the basic tenets of Orthodox theology; any innovation unsanctioned by tradition or ecumenical council is thus viewed with suspicion, from the *filioque* to the doctrine of papal infallibility promulgated at Vatican I. Indeed the Eastern Church does not recognize the decisions taken in the fourteen ecumenical councils convened by Rome since the schism; the councils at Lyons and Florence, in the thirteenth and fifteenth centuries, respectively, which attempted to reunite the Churches, are remembered with particular disdain in the East. The papacy, Orthodox divines argued, was evolving in a hierarchical fashion, centralizing power at the expense of the conciliar tradition. Heresy was the result.

The unilateral addition to the Creed of the *filioque* (literally, "and the Son"), a sixth-century Spanish innovation, was by Orthodox lights heretical in two ways: 1) the Creed can only be changed in an ecumenical council, and 2) the dual procession of the Spirit blurs the definition of the Godhead spelled out at Nicaea and Constantinople, subordinating the Holy Spirit to the Father and the Son. The controversy may be a semantic matter for Western theologians—what difference is there between saying the Holy Spirit proceeds from the Father or from the Father *and* the Son?—but Orthodox prelates say the distinction cuts to the heart of the Divine Mystery: three persons, one essence. The delegates to the first and second ecumenical councils spoke with a common mind about the Godhead, emulating the apostles in Jerusalem who justified their decree about circumcision by invoking the presence of divine authority: "It seemed right to the Holy Spirit and to us" (Acts 15:28). Why should one man imagine he knows better than a council guided by the Holy Spirit? A pope acting alone can make mistakes. And as the poet William Matthews wrote, "Who is by himself except in error?"

But this clash over vertical and horizontal models of authority, between a feudal idea and democratic stirrings, did not lead to formal schism and enduring Eastern antipathy toward the papal office until the Fourth Crusade culminated in the sack of Constantinople. Indeed the first Crusaders put on their scarlet crosses to come to Byzantium's aid against advancing Ottoman forces. But this holy war to save the Eastern Empire and liberate the Tomb of Jesus in Muslim Jerusalem degenerated into a campaign against infidels of any stripe—Jews, Turks, heretics. In 1204, when the Crusaders stormed Constantinople, they slaughtered men, women, and children, looted and desecrated churches and monasteries (much of Constantinople's art now resides in Venice), and set fire to the city. Byzantium never recovered, even after the paleologue Michael VIII reclaimed the capital in 1261. And the Orthodox have forgotten neither the Latin occupation, when the Franks repeatedly raided Byzantium, nor Michael's subsequent efforts to consolidate his power by reuniting the Churches. The price of healing the breach was steep. At the Second Council of Lyons, in 1274, the emperor accepted the *filioque* and papal primacy, which led to widespread resistance and counterresistance. On Athos, for example, when more than two dozen monks locked themselves in the tower of the Bulgarian monastery and censured the imperial envoys sent to convince them to support reunification, the Latinizers burned the tower down; the saints' martyrdom is commemorated every year in a special service—one reason why Athonites, and the Orthodox in general, are said to have long memories.

This was a constant refrain during the Balkan Wars, when all sides appealed to histories of injustice to explain the unfolding tragedy. And if arguments over the *filioque* seemed remote to me in the woods beyond Stavronikita, where leaves littered the trail under a canopy of vines and branches, my mind was filled with images from the war—razed villages, gutted churches, lines of refugees—testifying to the schism's legacy. Some Balkan observers invoked Freud's theory of "the narcissism of minor differences" to account for the hatred displayed by the "ethnic cleansers" in Bosnia and Croatia—the idea that it is the little things that most upset people who are otherwise alike. But this was not an ethnic conflict—there are no ethnic differences among Croats, Serbs, and Bosnians. It was a religious civil war waged, ironically, in a predominately secular country. In Yugoslavia the Communist policy of brotherhood and unity papered over the religious identities of Roman Catholic Croats, Orthodox Serbs, and Bosnian Muslims; what emerged after the Cold War was fractious tribal myths rooted in religion; hence the phenomenon of people sharing a language, food, and customs while inhabiting vastly different spiritual landscapes. If recognition of papal authority had oriented Croats to the West, Serbs looked eastward, remembering the cruelties their ancestors had suffered at the hands of the Vatican and the Ottomans. Thus many Serbs welcomed the destruction of their neighbors' churches and mosques in Croatia and Bosnia, a sentiment echoed throughout the Orthodox world. This was their revenge for the Latin Conquest and the fall of Constantinople, the Battle of Kosovo in 1389 (when Turkish forces conquered Old Serbia), and atrocities committed in World War II by the Croatian Ustaša—the Nazi quislings who tried to convert, expel, or annihilate the Serbs on their lands.

I passed a stone shrine covered with ivy, a *kellí* with a tin roof, and several sets of ruins, rounding three more coves before emerging from the woods near Pantokratoros, a monastery on another promontory by the sea. Beyond fields readied for planting was a cobblestone path to the gate, bright with red camellias; orange trees in white cement planters lined the sloping courtyard. In the guest quarters a fat monk in an apron served me water and *loukoumi*. He looked put out when I asked for coffee, then whisked me through the small red church of the Transfiguration. I was left with an impression of soot-stained frescoes, including a portrait of Christ the Pantokrator (or Almighty) staring down from the central cupola—a common feature of Byzantine churches, usually bearing a verse from St. John: " 'I am the Alpha and Omega, the Beginning and the End,' says the Lord, 'who is and who was and who is to come, the Almighty' " (Rev. 1:8). With the monk all but asking me to find other accommodations I recited the Athonite formula of leave-taking: *Evloyite*—your blessing. And he replied, *Tou Kyriou*—the Lord's.

Twelve levels of scaffold encircled the tower, which from the road above the monastery looked like an office building. I marched uphill to the Russian-Ukrainian *skete* of the prophet Elijah, a dependency of Pantokratoros set among acres of terraces carved out of the woods. Green onion-shaped domes, red tile roofs, white walls: a settlement larger than many monasteries. From its founding in 1759 there were problems with its size. One hundred and fifty Russian monks moved in, and while disputes with Pantokratoros soon led them to abandon the *skete* their spiritual progeny returned a century later to rebuild it, with generous help from Russia's last czar. The *skete's* rapid growth before the Bolshevik Revolution, resulting in the construction of a refectory, a hospital, a mill, a bell tower, and many chapels, is a political story disguised as a religious awakening, as so much Church history is.

Consider the *skete's* founder, a monk named Paisios, whose Ukrainian heritage bespoke a complicated spiritual inheritance. It is said that Vladimir the Great (980–1015), the pagan prince of Kiev, then the center of Russia, sent envoys everywhere to discover the true religion. They visited Muslim Bulgars on the Volga

River, churches in Germany and Rome, and the Hagia Sofia in Constantinople. The Byzantine rite dazzled them. "We knew not whether we were on heaven or earth," they told the prince, "for surely there is no such splendor or beauty anywhere upon earth." Like Keats's nightingale, Vladimir proclaimed beauty to be truth and Christianized the Eastern Slavic lands. But when Kiev was destroyed by the Mongol Golden Horde in 1240 and the metropolitan moved to Moscow, Ukraine (literally, "on the edge") became another fault line: on one side were Polish and Lithuanian princes allied with Rome, on the other, the Third Rome, as Moscow came to be known after the fall of Constantinople. Ukraine's partition between Poland and Russia, formalized in 1667, enforced a spiritual division that continues to this day.

Many Orthodox, caught in the middle, were converted by Jesuit missionaries, often reluctantly. Thus at the Council of Brest-Litovsk, in 1596, negotiators seeking a path between East and West created a new category of Christians: Greek or Eastern Catholics—members of an Eastern rite in full communion with Rome. These churches and communities, which the Orthodox lump together under the derisive title of Uniate, include Romanians, Ruthenians, Slovaks, and Ukrainians, as well as Copts, Maronites, and Syrians, all heeding the principle for reunion enunciated at the Council of Florence: "a diversity of traditions in unity of faith." In return for fealty to the pope they were allowed to conduct services in their own languages (no small matter in the wake of the Inquisition, when the first question put to heretics was whether they knew any Scripture in their mother tongue: those answering yes were led straight to the stake to be burned), and they retained their customs and canon law—married clergy, for example. But the Orthodox fear of a papal ploy, borne out by Vatican efforts to Latinize the Greek Catholics, made them rather an obstacle to reunion. And while the Communists forced the Greek Catholics underground or into union with the Orthodox, in the post-Soviet era the divisions between these communities had reemerged. Confusion reigned as Greek Catholics tried to reclaim their spiritual identity and church property. Thus Ukraine had two patriarchs (representing Kiev and Moscow), three Orthodox Churches, and the Greek Catholic Church, each following essentially the same rite. Nor had the *skete* of the Prophet Elijah been spared political machinations in the new world order: in 1992, the Slavic brotherhood was expelled for refusing to commemorate the ecumenical patriarch. The Greek monks living there now had little incentive to accept new monks from Ukraine.

I was circling the *skete* in search of the gate when three pilgrims and a monk appeared. No one inside was awake, said a pilgrim, who offered to show me the trail to the monastery of Vatopedi. So we went down the path into the woods, where the monk, a plump young man with a wisp of a beard and a walking stick, carried on a lively conversation with the pilgrims. I assumed he had no English until we reached a crossroads. Then he turned to me.

"Follow this road until you come to your first left," he said, waving his walking stick. "You will be there in two and a half hours."

He was right. Wood was stacked at regular intervals along the winding mule track to Vatopedi. The wind had picked up, the sun rarely came out from behind the clouds, my shoulder ached. A British traveler compared Vatopedi, the largest Athonite monastery, to Windsor Castle, and from the cliffs above the Bay of Vatopedi it resembles a medieval fortress. It has the usual history of miracles and misfortune, of creativity and calamities; its decline in the twentieth century was precipitous. Only in the last decade had a group of monks, led by a cave-dwelling elder, come from another *skete* to transform Vatopedi, second in the hierarchy, from spiritual and physical dilapidation into the most powerful monastery of all. This was a familiar story: energetic monks adopting the cenobitic way of living, with dramatic results. Vatopedi was so popular now that reservations were required, as I learned upon my arrival at dusk. The guestmaster allowed me to stay, though, cautioning me not to let my valuables out of my sight.

"The Holy Mountain has no influence on thieves?" I said.

"They bring the devil with them," he replied.

He directed me toward the *katholikón*, where vespers had just ended. More than sixty pilgrims, including the wandering cantor who had sung with the choir at Iveron, were filing into the refectory. A paralytic from Cyprus bellowed at me from a balcony, shaking his staff as if to steer me toward or away from the church, I could not tell which. And he was still there when I returned from a meal that was only marginally better than what had been served at Iveron. An American monk, taking me to the *katholikón* for compline, described the Cypriot as a practitioner of black magic struck down while casting a spell—a victim of the Prince of Darkness, said the monk. The Cypriot made regular pilgrimages to Vatopedi to atone for his sins.

The monk himself, a soft-spoken man with a long grey beard, had lived here for five years, having left a Roman Catholic monastery in the Midwest to get closer to the source of Christianity. When I pressed him about his own origins he looked uncomfortable.

"Come," he said, ushering me into the outer narthex, where non-Orthodox pilgrims may attend services. Then he went into the nave.

"What did you expect?" a pilgrim later asked when I recounted the monk's reaction to my line of questioning. "His past is dead to him."

THE VIRGIN MARY'S BELT, A RED SASH EMBROIDERED WITH GOLD thread and ornamented with pearls, is the only relic of her life on earth. She supposedly wove it out of camel's hair and gave it to Thomas at her Assumption into Heaven—proof for the doubting apostle that she was the Mother of God. From the sanctuary of the *katholikón* a monk had brought forth the belt and other relics to spread on the holy table, and now he told their stories, which the American monk translated for me. This belt gave new meaning to

the notion of wonder-working. It came to Vatopedi in the fourteenth century as a gift from Lazar, the Serbian prince remembered in medieval epics for choosing the heavenly kingdom at the
Battle of Kosovo over earthly dominion; under Ottoman rule the
monks carried it around the Mediterranean to end plagues of
cholera and locusts—even a sultan reverenced it. If once the sight
of the belt was enough to bolster the spirits of enslaved Greeks,
now it is thought to cure infertility. Pieces of a cord tied around it
are snipped off and blessed for pilgrims to take home to their wives.

"If they have faith," said the monk, "they become pregnant."

I was not prepared to dismiss such talk. After all, many things
about my daughter's birth had seemed miraculous. Ours was a
late pregnancy (a miracle in itself), and my wife was nearly full
term when a stranger providentially entered our lives. We were
stuck in traffic one autumn evening, on Storrow Drive in Boston,
when our car overheated. I parked on the side of the road and
opened the hood. Lisa stood beside me, the contours of her pregnant belly visible to the drivers of the expensive cars and sport util-
ity vehicles inching by. No one stopped or even rolled down a
window to offer to call for help. A half hour passed—night was
falling—before an old Toyota pulled over. Out stepped a large
Hispanic woman and a smaller man who spoke no English. The
woman peered at the engine, and within minutes she had fashioned a makeshift solution for a faulty switch. Then she retrieved
a bottle of distilled water from her car, refilled our radiator, and assured us that we would be able to drive home safely.

She was the quintessential Good Samaritan. You recall Jesus'
parable of a Jew fallen among thieves whose cries for help go un-
heeded by a priest and a Levite from the temple (Luke 10:30–37);
only a Samaritan shows compassion, binding his wounds, then
taking him to an inn, where he promises to pay for his expenses.
The Samaritan is his enemy—think of him in contemporary
terms as a Palestinian coming to the aid of an injured Israeli—but
basic human fellowship leads him to act more generously than
the members of the religious establishment. And the revolution-

ary import of Christ's injunction to love your enemy has hardly diminished over the millennia. The Hispanic woman, from one of Boston's poorest neighborhoods, who helped us in the face of all the passing motorists, embodied that marvelous biblical phrase: loving-kindness.

That was not all. She traced her finger down Lisa's belly and announced that our daughter (we had not told her we were expecting a girl) would be born on a Saturday, between sunrise and sunset. Do you have some kind of knowledge about these things? I asked. We'll meet again, she replied enigmatically, and drove away. As it happened, Lisa entered the hospital on a Friday night, experiencing what were later diagnosed as false labor pains; not until daybreak did her true labor begin. And Bach's *St. Matthew Passion* was playing on a portable tape deck when Hannah was born, minutes before the sun went down. That Hispanic woman had foreseen our future. I lived in dread of our next encounter with her, imagining it would portend tragedy.

"Don't you feel as if you've joined a club you didn't even know existed?" a friend said after Hannah's birth. The cost of membership was constant anxiety. Unable to guard against every contingency, I understood the desperate measures that parents take to protect their children. How could I scorn the use of charms and amulets when every night I prayed for my daughter with a fervor I had never known before? I was reluctant to scoff at the American monk's claim that a miracle-working icon of the Madonna and Child had cured hundreds of Russian children suffering from cancer. The story goes that its powers were discovered when an adept of black magic kissed the icon, and the Virgin's face lit up; a mysterious force knocked the sorcerer unconscious. When he awoke he renounced his former life and became devout.

I asked the monk if it would help a Protestant to venerate the icon.

"God's mercy is great," he said, but admitted that Orthodoxy declares there is a right way to receive these blessings. For Orthodoxy means right thinking, right worship, right praise.

The words of St. John Chrysostom are instrumental in this praise, and here was his skull on display, in gilt casing, with his incorruptible ear sticking out like a sponge. It is said that as he composed his commentaries on Paul's Epistles the saint was seen at his side, whispering into his ear, guiding him in his interpretations: a literary critic's dream. Imagine writing with such purity of intention. But my ambition to listen to the language with the same openness that characterizes the great works of the spirit was undercut by doubts about the worth of my endeavors. I was not so different from the sacristan responsible for the icon of Our Lady Esphagmeni housed in a nearby chapel who, in a fit of madness after years of toiling in her service, stabbed the icon. Blood ran down her face—the last thing he saw before she blinded him and took away his wits. For three years he sat in the stall opposite the icon, praying for forgiveness, until she restored his health—and then condemned for all eternity the hand that had wielded the knife. Here for our inspection now was what remained of the incorruptible hand, bits of which used to be given to Russian pilgrims. Ear and hand: vital elements of the poet's trade, the one attuned to the music of the spheres, the other consigned to the earthly labor of making verses.

The monk in charge of the sanctuary, the *vematoris*, opened a box containing a piece of the True Cross, another gift of Lazar. Constantine's mother, Helena, discovered the cross, in 326, on a pilgrimage to the Holy Land, and returned with an imperial emblem for her son's earlier vision on the eve of battle: *In hoc signo.* Did Jesus die on the cross dug up at Calvary? There is no way of knowing, but much of the promise and tragedy of the West resides in the sacred wood, which was divided into nineteen pieces (to preserve it from the Persians and Turks) and distributed to the centers of Christendom. If the Church of the Holy Sepulcher in Jerusalem holds the largest piece of the cross, Athonite monasteries have the most slivers. The *vematoris* kissed the relics and invited the pilgrims to do the same. I could not bring myself to put my lips to the cross, to the Virgin Mary's belt, or indeed to any of the relics. And at the sight of the Cypriot sorcerer leaning over the Holy Table I remembered how Serbian monks had paraded Lazar's bones around Yugoslavia to whip up support for Slobodan Milošević's project to create a Greater Serbia. "Everything begins in faith and ends in politics," said the French poet Charles Péguy, a maxim borne out by the route the Serbian monks took when they removed Lazar's relics from their burial place in the patriarchate in Belgrade and displayed them in monasteries in Bosnia, Croatia, and Kosovo. These were to be the boundaries of a new Serbian state: Serbs would rule where Serbian bones were buried, even if they were in the minority. This macabre journey culminated in a celebration, at a monastery in Kosovo on June 28, 1989, of the six-hundredth anniversary of Lazar's defeat. A million Serbs, waving pictures of their fallen hero, marched to the nearby battlefield, where Milošević urged them to remember their former military glory. It was but a step from veneration of the dead to the creation of more killing fields.

After the relics were put away, the monks circled the outer narthex, bowing and crossing themselves, their feet shuffling across the floor with the sound of beating wings. "Come," said the American monk, directing my attention to a fresco of the Apocalypse: a woman stands behind two long fish holding a man dressed only in a loincloth as he pitches into the water; in each corner are the heads of the Evangelists and of various beasts—to remind us, said the monk, that we will be judged eternally for our every action. Then he took me to the guest quarters, promising more conversation in the morning. A monk who was learning to compose Byzantine hymns showed me to a room heated by a smoky wood-burning stove. Cats screeched in the courtyard. The wind howled off the sea. I fell into a deep dreamless sleep. In the morning, after the liturgy, I looked in vain for the American monk, then joined the pilgrims for a breakfast of bread, olives, and coffee. The monk-composer gave me oranges and a bag of sweet wafers for my hike. Under the reproachful gaze of the Cypriot sorcerer, I shouldered my backpack and set out for the north, intending to spend the night at the Serbian monastery of Chilandari.

THE SCENE WOULD RETURN UNBIDDEN: THE TIME I HUDDLED behind a tree with two friends in Sarajevo, under Serbian sniper fire. Dusk in autumn. A Bosnian curator, a French humanitarian, and I were on our way to a film festival titled *Beyond the End of the World*, part of an international effort to open a cultural corridor into the besieged city. The emptiness of the street connecting the Olympic ice arena and downtown Sarajevo was unnerving. "Something is not right," said the Bosnian—and then a bullet flew by, not with a whine but an explosion as loud as a grenade. We ducked into a nearby courtyard to line up behind a tree, where for close to an hour the sniper fired at us, round after percussive round. To calm the Frenchwoman and me (the bullets were passing within a foot of our heads), the Bosnian described the latest exhibition at his gallery, *Witnesses of Existence*, a series of conceptual works culminating in a terra-cotta sculpture, in the shape of a mass grave, from which the glassed-in faces of victims of the siege stared out. At the opening of the exhibition the artist covered the faces with dirt; just outside the gallery, a man was wounded by a sniper.

In the end we escaped under the cover of darkness, but the sound of the gunshots haunted me long after I left Sarajevo. Indeed the memory would rise up before me almost every day—the damp leaves on the ground, the acrid yellow trails of the bullets. Out for a walk, I would stop in my tracks, shaken; driving my car, sometimes I had to pull over to the side of the road to collect my wits. And I wrote as if possessed, hoping to exorcise the sights and sounds and smells of war—the smoke and fire from mortar shells, the gutted houses and cars, the stench of death. D. H. Lawrence said we write in order to shed our sicknesses. Yet the writing of my book had brought me no peace. So I turned to the Psalms: "I have become a stranger to my brothers, and an alien to my mother's children" (Ps. 69:8). The war had estranged me from my loved ones: the chill in my relations with Lisa surely owed something to my experiences in Sarajevo—the eerily beautiful spectacle of tracer rounds lighting the night sky; the firefights that sent pedestrians scurrying into doorways; the dingy rooms in which refugees tallied their losses (husbands, houses, sons). Nor was the bloodletting over in the Balkans. Milošević had taken advantage of a distracted American president—Bill Clinton's sex scandal was headline news around the world—to attack rebel Albanians in Kosovo; the recent massacre of forty-five Albanian villagers was the prelude to more of the death and destruction already visited upon Bosnia and Croatia.

If the fighting in Slovenia and Croatia ultimately derived from the Church's schism, the origins of the war in Bosnia and the looming conflict in Kosovo lay in the fall of Constantinople, which marked the end of the Byzantine Empire and the beginning of the saddest chapter of Orthodox history. The legacy of Turkish rule lives deep in Orthodox memory. From the rise of the Ottomans in the fourteenth century to the fall of the last despot in 1922, Christians were treated as second-class citizens—heavily taxed, forced to wear distinctive dress, forbidden to ride horses or to serve in the military. The sees of Alexandria, Antioch, and Jerusalem fell under the sway of the ecumenical patriarch, who assumed a civic function under the sultans. "For the Muslims drew no distinction between religion and politics," writes Bishop Kallistos Ware; "from their point of view, if Christianity was to be recognized as an independent religious faith, it was necessary for Christians to be organized as an independent political unit, an Empire within an Empire." The Orthodox Church—the *Rum Millet* or Roman nation, in Turkish usage—evolved into a national institution, ensuring the survival of a Greek national consciousness and the confusion in the Orthodox mind between church and nation, which continues to this day.

The remarkable thing is that the Church survived at all. Proselytizing was outlawed—it was a capital offense for a Muslim to convert to Christianity—and since only Muslims were allowed to pursue serious careers the pressure to embrace Islam was high, especially in places like Bosnia, where there was relatively little religious organization. (This is why many Bosnian Croats and Serbs—that is, Roman Catholics and Orthodox—dismissively call their Muslim neighbors Turks, although they are of the same ethnicity as themselves.) In fact Muslims regarded Christians and Jews as fellow people of the Book: as long as they accepted Ottoman rule they could practice their religion without interference. Indeed Turkish forces spared those cities and religious centers that surrendered to them, including the Holy Mountain, which made overtures to the advancing infidels and then submitted to the new civil authorities when Thessaloníki fell in 1430.

On Athos, among the hesychasts, Orthodoxy preserved its mystical character, against all odds. The sultans recognized the sacred power of the Holy Mountain—which did not stop them from exacting tribute from the monasteries and occasionally seizing monastic properties on the mainland. This compounded the fiscal crisis set off by the loss of their patron, the emperor. The monks turned elsewhere for support—to the princes of the Danubian principalities of Moldavia and Wallachia, the Orthodox nobility in Georgia and Serbia, Russian czars, Jewish moneylenders in Thessaloníki—and still the debts of the monasteries spiraled, forcing the monks to pawn sacred vessels; the libraries fell into ruin as manuscripts were sold off or rotted. The center was gone, the Great Church was under the Turkish yoke, monastic discipline broke down. Before long the idiorrhythmic system had replaced cenobitic rule on Athos.

This looser model dates from the last days of Byzantium, when the empire was in disarray and the rise of humanism fostered a new intellectual climate in the monasteries, which had grown wealthy from their land holdings. The office of the abbot was weakened—a lifetime appointment devolved to a one-year position staffed by a committee of elders—and monks abandoned their vows of obedience and poverty to live in separate dwellings, retaining their worldly possessions and sometimes even their servants. Free to serve God as they saw fit, they cooked for themselves, earned money, and worshipped together only on Sundays. Meanwhile pirates kept raiding the peninsula, and in the early fifteenth century, with Turkish forces on the advance, Emperor Manual II Palaiologos confiscated half of the monastic estates to defray the costs of defending his dwindling empire—a move that impoverished the Holy Community and infuriated the monks; his edict reminding them of their vows fell on deaf ears. By the time Constantinople fell, the idiorrhythmic system was firmly in place; its spread under the Ottomans was as much a reaction to economic straits—the monks now had to support themselves—as to the spirit of individualism. But all was not lost. Far from the center of political power, with little supervision, the hesychasts chanted and prayed, saving the light of the world.

I found a modern analogy in Octavio Paz's report that at the end of his life André Breton urged his fellow surrealists to return to the catacombs, just as Christians had once said mass in the burial vaults of the Appian Way, hidden from the Roman authorities. Surrealism, in Paz's words, was the great negation of the West, all roads of which had led to World War I; the artistic and spiritual vitality displayed in its initial phase—the manifestos, pranks, and exhibitions; experiments in automatic writing; discovery of dream imagery; invention of collage—offered an escape route from the trap of Enlightenment rationality. But the surrealist exploration of the *via negativa*—an artistic version of apophatic theology, if you will—had run its course, with poets entering academe instead of going underground; and if the mysterious currents charted by Breton and his friends still held poetic promise, as I sometimes thought, the mystery of the Incarnation, steadfastly celebrated on the Holy Mountain, seemed even more promising. Who could not admire how the hesychasts had kept the flame of Orthodoxy burning through four centuries of foreign rule?

For the sultans closed or converted churches to mosques; shut down centers of higher learning (the decline of the clergy was

pronounced); corrupted the patriarchate with their fiscal demands, offering the office to the highest bidder, and with the civic
power they bestowed upon it. In effect the patriarchate reunified
the Byzantine lands, under Greek auspices; what was once a religious institution became a tool of political administration—
subject, of course, to the dictates of the Antichrist. Which is to
say: an organization with little moral authority.

Thus when the spirit of nationalism swept across the Balkans
the Orthodox leader did not possess the influence to restrain his
flocks. The Serbs were the first to revolt, in 1804; the Greeks followed suit in 1821, winning independence over much of the mainland (though not on Athos, from which five thousand monks who
joined in the rising against the Turks fled for their lives); separate
national churches were established in Bulgaria, Greece, Romania, and Serbia. When the Holy Mountain was finally liberated,
in 1912, the Turkish civil governor confided in a French traveler.
"Look round you," he said,

> "look at these thousands of monks; visit their monasteries,
> question them yourself. Of what, in reality, can they com-
> plain? Have we touched their rules? Have we violated their
> property? Have we forbidden their pilgrimages? Have we al-
> tered a single item of their secular organization? . . . Always
> the West is talking of Turkish fanaticism. But what race, I
> ask you, what conqueror could have treated these people
> with greater humanity, greater moderation, greater religious
> tolerance? Under our law they have remained as free, even
> freer, than under the Byzantine Emperors. And they have
> not had to endure under our domination a hundredth part
> of the vexations that you have imposed on your monks in
> France . . . *Allez, monsieur.* They will regret us, monsieur.
> Greeks, Russians, Serbs, Roumanians, Bulgars, all those
> monks hate each other like poison. They are bound to-
> gether only by their common loathing of Islam. When we
> are no longer here, they will tear each other to pieces."

His prediction did not come true. The Holy Community's decline under Greek protection left the monks with no incentive to turn on their neighbors: they were too busy trying to survive. Now the war in Bosnia had united them again (and the entire Orthodox world) in a "common loathing of Islam." I recalled a tour of a monastery in Montenegro. An unpleasant monk (a recent convert, as it turned out) assured me that a Bosnian Muslim new to his faith (five hundred years after his ancestors had converted to Islam!) would happily kill his family, since he was living a lie. The monk's lecture was salted with slurs against Muslims and Roman Catholics, which I duly recorded in my notebook until he grabbed my pen and insisted that I let his words enter my heart, not my intellect. But too many people were listening to propagandists in Athens, Belgrade, and Moscow with their hearts, not their minds. Orthodox prelates often led the charge.

Debris lined the shore curling around the gulf of Vatopedi. The waves gleamed in the sunlight, which gave off little warmth. But the high winds diminished once the trail veered inland. I was hiking among violets when the figures of two prominent Bosnian Serbs floated into my mind—poet-psychiatrist Radovan Karadžić and General Ratko Mladić, the indicted war criminals responsible for the siege of Sarajevo, the massacre of Muslims at Srebrenica, and other crimes against humanity. There were rumors of them hiding out at Chilandari, to which they had sent emissaries to arrange for their asylum; they were thought to have fled here when peacekeeping forces in Bosnia appeared, briefly, to be serious about apprehending them. Outlaws have always found refuge on Athos because, as a canon of the sixth ecumenical council states, "Any Christian man is permitted to make choice of the monastic life, and to wear the *schema* [habit] of monks, even though he may have committed any sin whatsoever when he was living in the world; and no one may prevent his doing so." I detected a perverse symmetry at work in the Holy Community's sympathy for Serbian war criminals, which recalled the Roman Catholic monastic practice of helping Nazis to escape justice.

Serbs who dismissed or approved of the horror committed in their name—the rape camps and massacres, the razing of villages and shelling of cities, the sniper attacks against children—found plenty of support on Athos.

Theodicy is the branch of natural theology concerned with understanding the place of evil in Creation, which Orthodox Christians believe is intrinsically good. How, then, can God sanction evil? Why did Karadžić and Mladić, believers both, order their troops to commit genocide? The Orthodox answer is that God has endowed us with free will, with which we twist the good to fit our myopic designs. Still I could not fathom the reverence with which Karadžić and Mladić were held in Orthodox quarters. The argument that the Church is made up of fallible individuals comforted me only insofar as I worried about my own cowardice in the war zone—another moral failing which, I feared, would be held against me on the Last Day.

A loud crash, as of artillery fire, shook the earth. I ducked behind a tree, imagining the tectonic plates had shifted— earthquakes have flattened several monasteries over the centuries. In the sky was a Greek fighter jet's vapor trail; the sonic boom was the pilot's greeting to the monks. My shoulder was throbbing when I continued on my way.

THE HIKE TO THE MONASTERY OF ESPHIGMENOU—MY INTERME-diate stop this day—took two and a half hours, along a narrow wooded path that in places was inches deep in snowmelt. Around a hill I came to the sea and the sight of monks hoeing up rocks in a field by the monastery. Above the high walls flew the flags of Byzantium and Greece, as well as a black banner reading ORTHO-DOXY OR DEATH. Esphigmenou means "Tight-belted," not because it is the poorest monastery but because its founder may have worn a tight cord around his waist: a symbol of the lengths to which its monks have always gone to protect their notion of the True Light. They receive scant government subsidy, because they refuse to mention the ecumenical patriarch in the liturgy—a decision taken after an inter-Orthodox conference, convened in 1923 by the patriarch, voted to adopt a modified version of the Gregorian calendar for ecclesiastical use, a vote that caused a split within Orthodoxy. The churches of Jerusalem, Russia, and Serbia did not accept the new calendar, the Bulgarian and Romanian churches enacted it reluctantly, and in Greece a movement arose of Old Calendarists who objected not so much to the change of dates as to what they viewed as the patriarchate's drift toward papism and the "heresy" of ecumenism.

The patriarchate's 1920 encyclical, *Unto the Churches of Christ Everywhere,* called for rapprochement among the denominations, despite doctrinal differences. But some Orthodox accused the patriarch, "first among equals," of a neo-papal attempt to harness the national churches and dilute tradition to accommodate Western Christendom. Old Calendarists, fiercely opposed to any commerce with the West, broke communion with Constantinople, asserting that truth resides not in the authority of faith and dogma but in Christ and a commonality of vision. And their fears of the marriage of church and state were realized when the government refused to recognize weddings and baptisms performed in their parishes, imprisoned priests, and razed churches. Persecution bolstered their resolve, though, and the Old Calendarist movement spread to Bulgaria and Romania to counter another unholy marriage of church and state—the one that Orthodoxy made with the Communist authorities, which will long haunt the Church. For communism posed a greater immediate threat to the faithful than ecumenism. Those who created the True Orthodox Church of Russia, breaking communion with the Moscow patriarchate in 1927, took their lives into their hands—as did all Orthodox clergy in the Stalin era. Their bishops either were murdered or went into hiding; their successors were consecrated in secret, which is why the True Orthodox were also known as Catacomb Christians. Coincidentally they began to emerge from hiding around the time that Breton advised the surrealists to go underground. With the end of the Cold War they had again become "a magnet," in one scholar's words, "for the many Orthodox unhappy with the ecumenical movement."

The reaction to ecumenism on Athos took a different form. Some monks became Zealots, following the example of Simon the Zealot, who is thought to have been the bridegroom at the wedding in Cana of Galilee, where Jesus changed the water into wine—the first of His seven signs in the Gospel of John. Tradition holds that Simon the Zealot left his bride to become a disciple of Jesus. And some Zealots on Athos left their monasteries to become wandering monks, illustrating the wisdom of Symeon the New Theologian (949–1022): "He who is a monk keeps himself apart from the world, and walks forever with God alone." While the first generation of wandering monks had probably died off, rumors abounded of their spiritual descendants—a hidden band of disciples, scattered around the mountain, known as the Twelve Invisibles. Monks spoke of them in reverential terms. Pilgrims left rusks of bread for them in plastic bags hung from trees and traded stories of encounters with wild men dressed in rags. In the woods I sometimes had the sense that someone, perhaps one of the Twelve Invisibles, was watching me.

Zealots are plentiful on Athos, particularly in the *asceteria* at the southern end of the peninsula, the desert home of the most rigorous spiritual seekers. But Esphigmenou was the only monastery to adopt the Zealot position, severing relations with both the patriarchate and the Holy Community. It declined to send a representative to meetings of the *Epistasia*, the governing body; its black banner dated from 1972, when its protest of the patriarchate's efforts to bridge its differences with Rome prompted the military junta to intervene. For four months police and coast guard laid siege to the monastery from the land and sea, in a futile effort to bring the recalcitrant monks to heel. *Orthodoxy or death*, they said. The siege was lifted, but the Holy Community refused to recognize the abbot or to accept the List of Monks, the *Monachologion* sent to register the brethren; hence more than a hundred monks were considered to be illegal occupants. There was talk of evicting them and moving new monks into the monastery. But some Athonites admired Esphigmenou's purity and formidable isolation. A request for information about the status of the monastery from the Friends of Mount Athos, a British charitable organization dedicated to the Holy Mountain's preservation, elicited a memorable rebuke from the abbot: "The History of my Nation teaches me that I should not trust any more such 'friends.' "

The elderly guestmaster treated me with similar wariness. He was a picture of severity, a thin contemptuous man with a long grey beard. Without a word he served me a guest tray (minus the raki), grudgingly obeying the biblical injunction to provide hospitality to all. No one knows when the Messiah will return; to guard against the danger of His appearing at a monastery without being recognized, monks are obliged to treat every pilgrim as if he were the Son of man. Jesus says God will judge us on the Last Day by virtue of the ways in which we treat everyone, because every man, woman, and child partakes of divinity: "for I was hungry and you gave Me food; I was thirsty and you gave Me drink; I was a stranger and you took Me in" (Matt. 25:35). The guestmaster must have deemed it unlikely that I had come to judge him for eternity. I made a show of examining the icons for sale in a glass display case before purchasing a magnet emblazoned with a picture of St. George, then went out to the courtyard. The *katholikón* was locked, but a workshop was open, where monks in goggles were soldering strips of silver, their faces dark with dust. They plainly did not wish to be disturbed.

To get to Chilandari, a half hour inland, I walked up a wide dirt road past a wheat field, an olive grove, and a beekeeper's *kellí*. A laborer was building a wooden shrine at a crossroads; coils of electrical wire and telephone line lay under the ancient cypresses, the trees of mourning, leading to the Serbian monastery, which was preparing to celebrate its eight-hundredth anniversary. There is some uncertainty about the etymology of the word Chilandari, which may refer to the thousand mists that periodically descend over the thick woods around the monastery or to the tradition that a thousand pirates intent on pillage killed one another when the mists made it impossible for them to distinguish friend from foe. This day the sky was clear, and the laborers smoking outside the gate had different designs on the monastery. They were refurbishing the guest quarters; wood ripped from the walls was stacked in the courtyard to be hauled away by an old monk on a tractor.

I went to the refectory, where seven monks and a dozen laborers were standing around a table. A fresco caught my eye. An angel in monastic garb was instructing a monk: "In this Habit shall flesh be saved." I was given to understand that a new novice, a Bosnian Serb, might have a dubious war record. The habit could save him, according to tradition, even if he had committed crimes against humanity. The abbot rang the bell. We sat down to a lunch of soy-and-potato soup, pickled vegetables, plump olives, and fresh bread—my best meal yet on Athos.

"Food, wine, and politics are the three things Serbs are weak for," said the laborer seated to my right. "That's why the food here is so good."

THE GUESTMASTER WAS TRANSLATING *THE LIFE OF MOSES* BY Gregory of Nyssa (c. 332–95). Aleksander was a layman from Novi Sad, a soft-spoken accountant in his thirties who feared he had waited too long either to marry or to become a monk; now, while waiting to discern if he had a religious vocation, he was rendering into Serbian the central work of the Cappadocian father regarded as the founder of mystical theology. In a sunny niche above the courtyard, facing a wall decorated with photographs of monasteries in Kosovo and engravings of Serbian heroes, Aleksander served me lemonade, coffee, and *loukoumi* arranged in the shape of a cross. Then he sat down and described how Gregory had discovered in Moses's life a symbol for the spiritual journey adequate to his brother Basil's efforts to organize monasticism. If Basil outlined the rudiments of cenobitic living, Gregory focused on what he called the "greater philosophy" of withdrawal from the world, arguing that the discipline of the desert was central to the prophet's revelations; asceticism was the means by which Moses prepared himself for the revelation of God's word, just as Jesus went into the wilderness to purify Himself before launching His ministry.

Gregory's exegesis of the Old Testament worthy relied on typology: Moses was a type of the Messiah, anticipating Him in a number of ways. The burning bush, the rod changed into a serpent, the manna from Heaven—these were figures for the Incarnation. And the tabernacle shown to Moses on the mountain, which furnished the archetype for the portable sanctuary the Hebrew people carried with them in the wilderness, was nothing less than *"Christ who is the power and the wisdom of God,"* a divine image destined to take human form. At every turn in the prophet's story the Cappadocian found links to the Gospels, bridging Greek philosophy and Jewish Scripture, Mosaic law and the new covenant of Jesus. "But the word is very near you; it is in your mouth and in your heart," Moses told the Israelites (Deut. 30:14). And it was Gregory's genius to connect the prophet's word to the revelation of how "the Word became flesh and dwelt among us" (John 1:14). Christian doctrine thus took shape in this marriage of the Old and New Testaments, in the fulfillment of the prophesies, the embodiment of types.

God spoke to Moses, then, because he embodied virtue, which lies in constant striving toward perfection. Virtue is not static but dynamic, Gregory writes: just as there is no boundary to God, so there is no limit to virtue, which takes the form of eternal progress. If you reach for God, He will offer you a ladder on which to transcend the evil part of your nature. And just as Moses "continually climbed to the step above and never ceased to rise higher, because he always found a step higher than the one he had attained," so the pilgrim cannot rest in the assurance that he has attained the good. The prophet kept discovering new prospects, which the guestmaster interpreted to mean that anyone could make spiritual progress, if only they would try.

"If you're Orthodox and don't go to church," he said, "it's like living in a city with the best dentists and having rotten teeth."

As it happened, Aleksander spent little time in church, claiming to be overworked. Yet he was content to while away an afternoon with me. He served more lemonade, coffee, and *loukoumi* and talked about his journey to Chilandari: how he had come here on a whim the previous summer, when friends asked him to share driving expenses.

"But it was not accidental," he insisted. "It was God's will."

It was not long before he returned for a week's stay, and then he took a year's leave from his job. Now he was examining his conscience and personal habits. He said he was afflicted by his past. But when I asked him to explain he began to fidget. He mentioned something about dabbling in Eastern religions and a lot of partying. Did you fight in Bosnia? I asked. He did not answer.

Just then two laborers approached to beg the guestmaster for raki. Grateful for the distraction, Aleksander said the abbot let them drink during Great Lent to keep them happy. The laborers, thirty in all, some of whom had lived here for a decade, were crucial to Chilandari's survival. The monastery needed two hundred monks to be self-sufficient; it had eighteen, many of them elderly. One monk in his nineties worked all day in the garden; another was celebrating the sixtieth anniversary of his tonsuring. Aleksander attributed their longevity to inner peace, acquired through prayer, work, fasting, and faith. He remembered a story about a Serbian bishop, driving from monastery to monastery in Kosovo, who stopped to offer an old woman a ride.

She shook her head. "I have no money to give the church," she said. "I can only give my labor of walking."

The bishop slapped his forehead: now *that* was faith!

I steered the conversation back to the war. Aleksander waxed philosophical, tracing Serbian aspirations to Chilandari's founding in the twelfth century, when King Stefan Nemanja gave up his throne and followed his son, Sava, to Athos. It was the triumph of Serbianism: Sava returned to Serbia to be consecrated archbishop, while his father built a monastery, fourth in the hierarchy, that formed the spiritual heart of a growing empire. The monks translated, printed, and distributed Church Slavonic texts; trained bishops, archbishops, and patriarchs; produced a good red wine. With donations from Serbian rulers, Russian czars, and Danubian princes, Chilandari became one of the richest monasteries before it fell into decline—inevitably, the guestmaster seemed to think, just as it was inevitable that at the point of its greatest expansion the Serbian Empire had been destroyed. Had the Battle of Kosovo doomed the Serbs? In the epics Lazar is portrayed as a Christ-like figure whose nation will not be resurrected until its lands are cleansed of the Christ killers. And if the Turks were gone, Bosnian Muslims and Kosovar Albanians remained. Indeed Christian mythology applied to the entire Serbian nation, which had been betrayed and crucified, repeatedly, by its friends . . . Aleksander was lost in history.

"Empires rise and fall," he said wearily.

By way of contrast, three Greeks on a pilgrimage to venerate the icons at every monastery came to pay their respects to the abbot. On their quickstep march they had no time for coffee or conversation. And it grieved me that I was not allowed to accompany them into the *katholikón* to see the icon of the Three-Handed Virgin. Legend has it the third hand was placed there by St. John of Damascus, after his own hand was cut off by a caliph and then restored by the Mother of God—although the icon dates from the fourteenth century. Still another tradition holds that it arrived from Serbia in 1371, on the back of a donkey, divinely guided, which dropped dead in sight of the monastery. I knew about the icon from reading the contemporary Serbian poet Vasko Popa, who celebrated "the black Three-Handed Mother," pleading for her intercession:

Reach out your third hand to me
Let me sleep in a nest of verses

I've come in from the road
Dusty and famished
Longing for a different world

Popa's poetic exploration of Serbian legends, which began
with a pilgrimage to Chilandari (a daring literary quest to undertake in a Communist country, in 1950), was my introduction to
Balkan history; wedding surrealist imagery to Serbian folklore, his
work inspired me to imagine my own nest of verses. I, too, longed
for a different world, which was, alas, closed off to me at Chilandari. "I will not speak of thy mystery to thine enemies," the Orthodox promise God before communion. But what harm could
come from my contemplation of an icon?

I recalled the front-page article in a Belgrade newspaper,
in the first winter of the war, that had sparked my interest in
Athos. A Serb's glowing account of his pilgrimage to Chilandari,
unthinkable in the Communist era, made no mention of any
limitations on Christian fellowship. "Reach out three small ten-
dernesses / Before a thousand mists fall on my eyes / And I lose my
head," Popa beseeched the icon of the Three-Handed Virgin,
which I could not see through the man-made mists of Orthodox
prohibitions. I wondered, had I already lost my head?

"SCIENTISTS ARE SHOWING THAT WE'RE NOT DESCENDED FROM
monks," said Lefteris, a toothless, wild-eyed man who had joined
us on the bench above the courtyard.

"Monkeys," I corrected him.

"Oh my God!" he exclaimed in horror, as if in misspeaking he
had committed a mortal sin.

The Greek entomologist had traveled the world for twenty
years in search of a new insect; after discovering a butterfly in

Madagascar he retired to Chilandari—refusing, however, to be tonsured. For the profession of the monastic life not only requires the novice to have his hair clipped but also to take a new name, usually that of a saint with the same first initial: symbols of his new life in Christ. Just as Saul became Paul after his conversion on the road to Damascus, so the novice signals his turning toward God by taking a new name. Jesus promises hidden manna, the bread of Heaven, to anyone who repents. "And I will give him a white stone, and on the stone a new name written, which no one knows except him who receives it" (Rev. 2:17). But Lefteris was unwilling to give up his name, which means liberty. And he was a free spirit—he claimed, among other things, to have sailed up the Amazon, worked in a leper colony, and lived on an estate in Connecticut. He would never be able to honor a vow of obedience. Instead he was opening a health clinic to dispense herbal remedies—because, he explained, the monks were leery of Western medicine. Through his sniffles (he suffered from a chronic sinus condition) he described the microscopes and equipment he had ordered for performing blood and urine tests.

"This will be a drug-free monastery," he joked.

His humor had a dark edge. The misogyny girding his discourse on evolution made the Byzantine *avaton* against women seem tame by comparison. "Women are abortions," he said, lighting a cigarette in defiance of the no-smoking rule that obtains in every monastery. Then he launched a diatribe against his ex-wife, which was preempted by another drama, when the cook followed a novice into the courtyard and screamed at him for several minutes.

"What was that about?" I asked when the cook returned to the kitchen.

Aleksander shrugged. "He's been doing that all day, but I don't understand Greek."

I turned to Lefteris. He was gazing at the peak rising behind the monastery. "I don't hear him," he said. "The words come to my ear, and then I block them out."

AT VESPERS, THROUGH THE IVORY-INLAID DOOR TO THE NAVE OF the *katholikón*, I could barely hear the chanting, so I walked down to the sea, past a wheat field lined with garbage—a landfill extending for nearly a kilometer. The sight left me in despair. The Holy Community lacked the manpower to clear the trash that washed up on the beaches, but in my mind the landfill pointed to something more insidious. Right worship entails right relations to nature: how can you praise God and defile His Creation? If other monasteries burned or recycled their waste, why did the Serbian monks let theirs pile up? They were understaffed, but in their resumption of cenobitic living did they also retain some of their idiorrhythmic ways? Or were they afflicted with *acedia*, spiritual indifference, what Evagrius of Pontus identified as "the noonday demon"—a sin I was well acquainted with. The remedy for depression, according to the desert fathers, is prayer and psalmody. I decided the monks were unable to strike a balance between heavenly concerns and earthly matters.

The conflict between attending to the things of the world and eternal truth is spelled out in the Gospel story of Martha and Mary. When the Lord visits the sisters, Martha prepares food and drink for Him while Mary sits at His feet; when Martha complains about Mary not helping, Jesus says, "Martha, Martha, you are worried and distracted by many things; there is need of only one thing. Mary has chosen the better part, which will not be taken away from her" (Luke 10:41–42). The Savior's words generally raise more questions than answers, and this is a story especially suited to monastic life, for *acedia* fells monks and laymen alike. It occurred to me that in preparing for their anniversary celebration the Serbian monks had lost sight of the better part. Orthodoxy teaches that right worship leads to right action, an insight reinforced at every turn in the monastic tradition. But the *evergetinos* or sayings of the desert fathers underline the difficulty of maintaining that vigilance. In one of my favorite stories, when a sinful monk is ordered to leave the community, another monk accompanies him, saying he is also a sinner. The fear of God should inspire such humility—which is of course not always the case, even on the Holy Mountain. But the ideal of Athos must never be confused with the image, a monk warned me. It is one thing to be a conduit through which spiritual light flows, quite another to reflect static electricity. Athos was once a conduit—its energy can still be tapped—but much of what shines today takes its energy from thin air. The brightness is observable, said the monk. It still speaks of the source.

The discrepancy between Christian ideals and practice on the Holy Mountain, though, was only part of the problem. Out of sight, out of mind: this was how I explained the average Serb's indifference to the siege of Sarajevo (or the average American's, for that matter), but it was also a working definition of my relationship to certain personal matters. I had lived for too long in my imagination, measuring the real against the ideal, with unhappy results. The dream of transcendence—in marriage and literary work, in travel and faith—is conditioned by gravity. And the anguish I experienced in my daily life extended into my pilgrimage, which I had undertaken in part to escape the pull of the earth. My journey into faith was collapsing on account of an aching shoulder and exasperation over Orthodox prohibitions.

A vineyard lay beyond a six-story tower, with a gutted interior, and beyond that was the sea. The poet A. R. Ammons discovered a metaphor for the mutability of our earthly pursuits in the refuse we generate, dedicating a book-length work "to the bacteria, tumblebugs, scavengers, wordsmiths—the transfigurers, restorers." And for all its scientific lore, *Garbage* shimmers with religious meaning, because it seeks to redeem—well, everything. My task now was to transform what I had wasted—love and luck—in the light of the eternal life promised to Martha and Mary when Jesus raised their brother, Lazarus, from the dead (John 11:1–45). But my shoulder spasm had spread to my neck, and I could no longer turn my head. I belonged to the tribe of stiff-necked sinners, the stubborn ones saved by Moses's intercession with God—and damned by St. Stephen, the first Christian martyr. My faith was as hollow as the tower overlooking the trash.

MY INVOLVEMENT IN THE WAR BROUGHT MORE TROUBLE, AS IF I carried a pestilence in my backpack. My *diamonitirion* listed my profession as writer, and when the monks learned (via the Internet) that I had published a book about Balkan refugees they voted to send me packing—after dark, in below freezing temperatures, with jackals howling outside the walls and the gates of the nearest monastery, Esphigmenou, locked at sunset. This I was told by their "spokesman," a newly minted graduate of the public relations program at Boston College. Nenad was trying to decide whether to become a monk or to look for work in Belgrade. Fortunately for me, he used his powers of persuasion to convince the monks to let him discover my views, though when we retired to his cell he was more interested in setting me straight about the perfidy of the Bosnian Muslims and Kosovar Albanians. He said the Holy Community had sent Greek mercenaries to Sarajevo to protect the local Orthodox church, dismissing my objection that if the mercenaries had attempted to take up arms in the center of the besieged capital, where the church was located, they would have met with considerable resistance from Bosnian government forces.

"They went there to defend Christianity," he insisted in his Boston accent.

He shared his tiny cell with two laborers and an American college dropout the monks had nicknamed Clinton. This was no term of endearment, the American said when Nemad stepped out for a moment. He told me the monks believed that Milošević and Clinton were Freemasons in league to destroy the Serbian people; that Coca-Cola and McDonald's were owned by Jews bent on forging a world government and culture; that democracy, like communism, was an ideology of the devil—the monks called it "demonocracy." And if it was true, as a pilgrim said, that Serbia creates great saints and terrible sinners, precisely the conditions for a religious revival, then this "Clinton" believed he had come to the right place to witness the stirrings of new spiritual life, which might give rise to a saint. Chilandari was well acquainted with sin.

Which was why the monks had lately turned to music, Nenad said when he returned. Into a portable tape deck he inserted a cassette of folk songs written by the monks and recorded by a Montenegrin singer; on the cover was a photograph of a helicopter hovering over the monastery garden. *Invasion of Chilandari* was the monks' answer to Milošević's recent visit. All but two of the monks had fled to caves in the hills before he arrived; those who stayed were greeted as comrades, not fathers. Milošević had just two questions about the monastery: 1) What is it worth? and 2) How much does it cost in upkeep? This confirmed for the monks his diabolical nature, in contrast to the true defenders of Christianity—the Bosnian leaders the world condemned as war criminals. "If the pope came to the Holy Mountain he would convert to Orthodoxy," sang the Montenegrin. Likewise the sultan and every visitor, except Milošević.

"It is unfair to persecute Mladić and Karadžić while Milošević goes free," said Nenad, fingering a medallion containing a sliver of the True Cross—a gift from the monks.

"Will Mladić and Karadžić be offered asylum here?" I said.

"Anyone may find asylum at Mount Athos," he replied. "Even you."

A CONVERSATION THROUGH A DOOR IN WHICH THE WORDS ARE cut off: this was how Robert Frost described the sound of sense, the quality he prized in poetry. What I heard of the liturgy through the door to the nave was a muffled petition: *Lord, have mercy.* Better to speak softly on Athos, is the proverb, but I was frustrated not to see the church interior. At sunrise, as I strolled around the grassy courtyard, songbirds trilled in the cypresses, a laborer watered boxwoods and potted geraniums, Lefteris and "Clinton" scraped moss from the wall of a stone tower. I sipped cool water drawn from St. Sava's well, by a grapevine supposedly grown from his father's marrow. A tall monk set down his wheelbarrow and beckoned "Clinton" and me to follow him up the steps into the tower to see the vestments, portable icons, and illuminated manuscripts.

A tour of the treasury was the last thing I expected. Nor did it last long enough for me to gather more than an impression of beauty—centuries of praise for God figured in the handiwork of nameless men. Still I was grateful for the monk's gesture. And when we emerged from the tower Nenad was waiting to show me more. Beyond the gate, where a laborer was examining a truckload of broken windows delivered the day before, we went to a cemetery the size of a kitchen garden. There were three new graves, which would be dug up in three years. The bones would be stored in the cellar of the stone chapel next door, the skulls marked with the monks' names and added to the shelves lining the ossuary, a dank place lit by a lantern. Nenad handed me an ochre-colored skull, which had a sweet earthen fragrance.

"A good monk," he said.

Monks believe that for your relics to acquire this fragrance not only must you live a holy life but the Holy Spirit must live inside you to set the vibrations going by which Divine Light will keep filling your bones even after you die. I recalled a conversation with an American poet, who envisioned a dramatic memorial service for herself, complete with arias from her favorite operas; she wanted young poets to make love on her grave. What a different approach from the monastic tradition. Nor would the monks approve of my Protestant wish to be cremated—anathema to the Orthodox, who believe the body must be kept intact in order to be resurrected after death.

And judged.

Here, for example, was a black skull. A corrupt monk, Nenad explained, whose sinfulness was not revealed until after his death.

The ossuary was thus a kind of forensic laboratory in which monks learned about the secret lives of their departed brethren, examining their bones in the spirit of a war crimes investigator at a mass grave. Nenad opened a trap door to show me hundreds of femurs and ribs, spines and kneecaps, shinbones and shoulder blades. My head began to spin.

"Write something good about the Serbs," he said.

AT NENAD'S INSISTENCE I CAUGHT A RIDE WITH A LABORER driving to the port to meet the ferry. The pickup followed a twisting mountain road through thick forests, past woodcutters loading logs onto a flatbed, and descended along a ravine toward the sea. The sky was a shade of magenta, the sunlight blinding. On the radio Don McLean was singing "American Pie," and when Elvis Presley launched into "Suspicious Minds" the laborer switched to a Bulgarian station broadcasting folk songs from Sofia. The ferry put into the harbor not long after we arrived.

Sailing down the coast, I saw the passing landscape in a new light—the red earth, the thick woods, the mountain—and got out at the Russian monastery full of hope, ignoring a pilgrim's warning not to expect to find any peace there during its renovations. From the walkway below the courtyard rose a wall of sound: two monks with chain saws were cutting up olive trees, another jackhammered cement, the bell tolled in the tower. In a stone building that once housed a hospital I met a short, red-faced monk, who interpreted my request for a guest tray in an unusual manner, hurrying me through the nearby Church of the Holy Shelter—a paean to gold, with a huge gilded iconostasis. He screamed at the top of his lungs, waving first at a portable icon, then at a gold box containing the relics of a saint whose name escaped me. I had no idea what he was saying.

From its beginning Athos was a pan-Orthodox center, with Slavs living alongside Greeks more or less harmoniously. In the nineteenth century, however, when large groups of Russian monks began to settle at St. Panteleimon, a Greek house with a Russian pedigree, the national dynamics changed. This influx of Russian monks owed more to Great Power politics than to religion. Corruption, waning military strength, the Serbian and Greek rebellions—these left the Ottoman Empire "the Sick Man of Europe." Russia seized the chance to gain access to the Mediterranean through Athos. Spies mixed in with monks; the czar's men bought up twenty *kelliá* and the *sketes* of the Prophet Elijah and St. Andrew in Karyes, which swelled in size; at St. Panteleimon a Russian was elected abbot and the last Greek monks were expelled. A British traveler wrote: "It cannot be disguised that Russico has more concern with politics than religion." The Russian machinations were indeed part of Nicholas II's plan to oust Turkey from Europe, break the Greek stranglehold on the patriarchate, and assume the emperor's throne in Constantinople—which, he believed, was his birthright, Russia having succeeded Byzantium after the fall of Constantinople. The czar was Orthodoxy's protector, Moscow the third, and last, Rome.

By the turn of the century, when Russians outnumbered Greeks on Athos by nearly two to one, the very character of the peninsula was under assault. The Russians introduced a garish element—five-story barracks, green onion-shaped domes, monumental icons; they even erected a chapel near the summit, with monks lugging stones up the mountain daily for six months. And they were on the verge of usurping control of the Holy Community when the first Balkan War broke out in 1912. But after Greek forces seized Thessaloníki, delivering Macedonia from Islam, the Great Powers refused Russian entreaties to increase its influence on Athos. Then the Russian monks divided over a vision granted to a former hussar that even God's name was divine. In 1913 troops from a Russian warship stormed St. Panteleimon and deported six hundred monks to Siberia. The prospect of Athos becoming a Russian principality vanished with the Bolshevik Revolution. But Greek fears of Communist infiltration, which prevented Russian monks from settling here until the end of the Cold War, had given way to xenophobia. The authorities were still reluctant to allow Russian monks to move to the Holy Mountain.

St. Panteleimon's renovations thus proceeded by fits and starts. The deserted barracks by the sea, the charred walls of buildings gutted in a devastating fire in 1968, the weeds growing up through the ruins—the monastery looked like a blighted city. It was said that a Russian who had made a fortune in the privatization of state industries was providing money for the restoration of the collapsing buildings and chapels, though the red-faced monk whisking me out of the church would neither confirm this rumor nor invite me to spend the night.

My mind was taken up with human things—politics, housing, my stiff neck—and when the monk departed it occurred to me that, impatient as he was to return to his work, something else had fed his anger, his righteous indignation: a scriptural element, a lesson to impart, perhaps, from the Gospel story of Peter taking issue with Jesus prophesying His death and Resurrection, read at the service on Sunday. "And Peter took him aside and began to rebuke him. But turning and looking at his disciples, he rebuked Peter and said, 'Get behind me, Satan! For you are setting your mind not on divine things but on human things' " (Mark 8:32–33). This is not the last time the Son of man will single Peter out for instruction or condemnation; in his all-too-human foibles Christ's vicar on earth is an apt symbol of our failure to heed the saving word that God offers at every moment—the Word that governs the Lenten prayers and readings.

I took an overgrown path to the cliff, wading through thorn bushes and mountain tea, and crossed two footbridges to reach the road from Daphne. Hoping to extend my *diamonitirion*, which expired this day, I headed for Karyes with some foreboding. There was an autumnal feeling in the air. A cold front was moving in, the sunlight gave way to clouds, the wind kicked up leaves under the bare trees. Below the ridge a laborer gathered firewood. Ravens cawed overhead. From the edge of town I followed a monk on a bulldozer to the administrative office, which was closed. Likewise the hotel and restaurant. So I set out for the monastery of Koutloumousiou, which lies in a valley just south of town, passing through a vineyard and orchards, where monks sprayed insecticide and an elder, straddling a ditch, was teaching a novice to pick greens. The guestmaster at Koutloumousiou did not examine my *diamonitirion*. Then again, neither did he offer me anything to eat or drink. But I was grateful to have a place to stay.

These were not monks to trifle with. In the nineteenth century they had cast a curse on the village of Moudros, on the Aegean island of Limnos, for provoking a massacre of monks from the monastery of St. Marina, a dependency of Koutloumousiou. The villagers had killed some Turks and dropped them in the well at St. Marina, prompting the Ottoman authorities to take revenge. Two monks escaped to Koutloumousiou, which decreed that no one in Moudros should ever sleep again, as penance for the massacre—a curse the monks chanted for more than a hundred years before the penance was lifted. I was too tired to take any chances with them.

AN ITINERANT ARTIST WAS IN THE GUEST QUARTERS, UNLOADING his duffel bag of wares, which he hauled around the mountain on a mule. On his bed he laid out icons, carvings, and wine bottles in which black wooden crosses were propped, like ships—Byzantine crosses, each with a pair of bars, the lower of which was slanted upward on the left, symbolically pointing to the thief, on Christ's right side, who said, "Lord, remember me when You come into Your kingdom" (Luke 23:42). The Orthodox pray these words to remember that a repentant criminal was the first to gain paradise with Christ: salvation is available to all. It is sometimes thought the slanted bar represents Christ's agony on the cross. Not so. In Orthodoxy His Resurrection is more important than His Passion, the crowning moment of the Roman Church. "Union with Christ, for western saints, has tended to mean participation in His sufferings," observes an Orthodox theologian, "a participation made visible in the stigmata of St. Francis; whereas the eastern saint is invested rather with the glory of the risen Christ, and shines with divine light."

In this interpretation of the Scripture invisible things outweigh what we can see with the naked eye. The difference between stigmata and light is not unlike the difference between fact and metaphor, prose and poetry. Insight trumps logic in Orthodoxy: a direct encounter with God means more than rational proof of His existence. Better to pray for grace to reveal the spiritual truth dwelling in your soul than to study the *Summa Theologica*. But in the West we are trained to be skeptical, wary of the very language of the conversion experience central to a life in Christ. The gushing testimonies of born-again Christians grated on my nerves, even as I understood, intellectually, that a radical overturning of everything I knew lay at the heart of Christianity. For it was a divine light that appeared to Saul on the road to Damascus, converting him from a zealous persecutor of Christians into Paul, the new covenant's first theologian.

But my education in irony had blinded me to the revolutionary nature of his writings. I had even missed their poetic elements: the yoking together of disparate realms of experience—law and grace, the Old and New Testaments, the sacred and the profane; the flights of imagination: "we do not look at the things which are seen, but at the things which are not seen" (2 Cor. 4:18); the topsy-turvy reasoning. Consider the cross, which in the Epistles is transformed from a sign of dread into a symbol of hope uniting the various peoples of the Roman Empire: "For the message of the cross is foolishness to those who are perishing, but to us who are being saved it is the power of God" (1 Cor. 1:18). Indeed Paul's rhetoric helped to upend the old order: "For Jews request a sign, and Greeks seek after wisdom; but we preach Christ crucified, to the Jews a stumbling block and to the Greeks foolishness, but to those who are called, both Jews and Greeks, Christ the power of God and the wisdom of God. Because the foolishness of God is

wiser than men, and the weakness of God is stronger than men"
(1 Cor. 1:22–25). In a ship of Paul's devising the cross set sail
around the world—a message my roommate embedded in bottles
and sold in the shops and monasteries on Athos.

At dusk the artist took me to the kitchen, where a thin, toothless Albanian served bean soup, bread, and canned peaches. The
Albanian was a shifty character who demanded payment as soon
as I had finished eating, then followed me to the guest room to ask
for more money for my accommodations. I did not think it wise to
refuse him. And once he had enough drachmas from me he
cadged cigarettes and cognac from my roommate.

The room was quite smoky by the time an elderly hermit arrived, with a cassette to play on the Albanian's portable tape deck.
Above the din of a thunderstorm we listened to a Cypriot monk
tell miracle stories, which the hermit translated for me. It was Paul
who defined the place of miracles in the spiritual life: "God has
appointed these in the Church: first apostles, second prophets,
third teachers, after that miracles, then gifts of healings, helps, ad-
ministrations, varieties of tongues" (1 Cor. 12:28). Athonites trade
miracle stories like gossip (which on the Holy Mountain is said to
travel faster than the speed of light), and so I heard about a priest
who lived in a village without electricity. He stayed in church the
night his parishioners went to the next village to watch the first
moon walk on television; when they returned, he accurately described for them what they had seen. For after his prayers he had
lain down on his bed for only a moment before being transported
to the moon, with a strip of cloth knotted around his mouth; when
he removed the cloth and tried to breathe he found himself back
in bed.

"And you know," intoned the hermit, "the astronauts saw someone else there."

Lightning blazed across the sky. The rain turned to snow. We
huddled around the tape deck, as if listening to breaking news.
But these were timeless stories—of a monk, granted a vision of the

Lord and angels, who prayed so hard for the evil abbot under whom he had suffered for forty years that God let the abbot go to Heaven; of a Russian saint who saw water underground; of a Greek saint who set fire to a man's hands for refusing to let his son enter a monastery. The miracles blended together, but the hermit's English was improving with each story—of a wounded soldier healed by oil; of a man chopped apart by Jews who was then made whole. I was convinced he was mad until he described, in the most lucid terms, the long hike I was planning the next day to Great Lavra. I did not know what to think of him when he left toward midnight.

"This is the age of miracles," the hermit said with a smile. "God sends many miracles to help men fight the devil."

WHEN I WOKE AT DAYBREAK MY ROOMMATE WAS WRAPPING HIS bottled crosses in newspaper. From the doorway he tossed me a parting gift, a small black cross made of twisted wool, held fast by a silver bead—something to rub between my fingers to keep Christ in my thoughts. I shouldered my backpack, gingerly, and headed for the gate. The courtyard was deep in snow, which weighed down the branches of the blossoming camellias and fruit-laden orange trees. The Albanian left off sweeping the walkway to the *katholikón* to demand more money. I told him to get lost.

The hotel in Karyes was still closed, the shops shuttered against the cold. In the Protaton I heard the end of the liturgy, a cascade of voices arcing up to the ceiling before the deacon chanted the service to a close. Then I crossed the plaza and climbed the staircase to the headquarters of the Holy Community. A night of miracle stories had not prepared me for the humming efficiencies of a modern administrative building, with photocopiers and facsimile machines. A monk served me a glass of coconut juice and took my *diamonitirion*, returning it within minutes. In black ink, below a stamped likeness of the Virgin Mary and the Orthodox insignia of a double-headed eagle, was a handwritten five-day extension.

I stepped buoyantly into the brilliant sunlight, determined to make the most of this second chance on Athos. "He gives snow like wool," the Psalmist sings of God; "he scatters hoarfrost like ashes" (Ps. 147:16). And this morning the snow glittered with a cold fire. *Kyrie, eleison. Kyrie, eleison.* Lord, have mercy—this was what the songbirds trilling in the cypresses south of town sounded like. But there was no other sign of life until I came to a chapel under renovation, in the *skete* of St. Panteleimon, halfway between Karyes and Iveron, where a boy hauling sand in a wheelbarrow gave me a sullen look. The water trickling down the path below the chapel turned into a stream, so I followed a narrower trail into the woods. The sky clouded over, and soon I wandered into snow up to my hips. I stumbled and fell; my jeans soaked through; a freezing rain started, with sleet mixed in. The tree boughs as I brushed past dumped snow on me. I nearly slipped off a stone bridge, then lost the trail. How had I gotten into so much trouble so quickly?

Jackals howled near the stream I forded to an empty *kellí.* Shaking with cold, I wandered for an hour before emerging at a landfill, with gulls circling overhead. What joy I felt at the sight of a hillside covered with garbage. "It is risky to swim in one's clothes," John Climacus wrote in *The Ladder of the Divine Ascent.* "A slave of passion should not dabble in theology." Undaunted, I changed into dry jeans and found the road to Great Lavra, six hours away by foot. I had not gone far before a blizzard started, which stopped just as I was debating whether to abandon my hike.

This was to be a day of such extremes. The sun came out; the dirt road along the cliff was thick with mud; with each step my boots grew heavier. Yet the sea was shimmering, and rising before me was the snow-crowned peak of Athos. The road wound in and out of ravines and canyons, under waterfalls and into shadows where the snow had not melted. There were three sets of footprints in the road, and I took comfort in the knowledge that the Virgin Mary was guiding others to Great Lavra, even as the spasm in my shoulder slowed my progress. I recited the Jesus Prayer to take my mind off the pain. I dwelt on the bitter turn my marriage had taken—the way that every conversation now seemed to contain the seeds of an argument. Anything could set Lisa off—a word, a look—and I was wondering if her irritability could be traced to a physical problem when I came upon a flatbed truck parked at an angle, on a cliff above the sea; the two monks peering into the engine did not return my greeting. Miffed, I continued on my way. The road cut back into the mountain, following the contours of a gorge, at the bottom of which lay a settlement in ruins; in the shade on the other side, where the snow had iced over, I kept slipping and falling, I lost heart again. Then the air brightened, the road turned to mud, and the orange peels scattered among the footprints of the pilgrims ahead of me curiously bolstered my resolve. From time to time the splendor of the Holy Mountain—the sunlight and sea, rocks and pines, stone towers and *kelliá*—transported me out of myself. And it was at such a moment of exhilaration, three hours into my hike, when I had sweated through two shirts and put my hat and gloves away, that a monk in a Land Rover stopped to offer me a ride, which I cheerfully declined.

Within minutes I was regretting my decision. Another snow squall, a pain shooting down my arm, a succession of unhappy memories: I fell into an abyss of despair from which I could not extricate myself, not even when the clouds lifted and the mountain gleamed with an unearthly light. I trudged along the cliff, registering little of my surroundings. Black hours passed until a monk sped by in a pickup, splattering me with mud. I burst into tears.

Orthodox theologians praise the gift of tears, which comes with the surrender of the self. Only by letting go of our determination to solve every problem on our own can we open ourselves to God's grace. St. Peter, Keeper of the Keys of Heaven, provides the type for this gift, when he weeps at the realization that he has betrayed Jesus, denying Him three times on the eve of the Crucifixion (Luke 23:62). And St. Isaac the Syrian suggests that "The fruits of the inner man begin only with the shedding of tears. When you reach the place of tears, then know that your spirit has come out from the prison of this world and has set its foot upon the path which leads towards the new Age." My tears, though, were the fruit of physical pain and self-pity, not spiritual tears. Still I remembered the apostle's words: "Even though our outward man is perishing, yet the inward man is being renewed day by day" (2 Cor. 4:16).

It was then I rounded a corner and saw Great Lavra, less than a kilometer away.

MY FATHER'S SILENCE IS SEVERE, EVEN BY THE STANDARDS OF his generation. He has been a mysterious presence in my life, observing, judging, condemning, perhaps taking pleasure in my achievements. I say perhaps because, aside from displays of his titanic temper, which in my childhood terrified me, I can only speculate about his feelings. I recall just one substantive conversation with him. (The subject, of all things, was capitalism: he was a banker, I was a student reading Marx.) He worked long hours, commuting from our home in rural New Jersey to Manhattan; his civic responsibilities—he served on the board of education, on the planning and zoning commission, as mayor of our village— kept him out several nights a week. Then, just as I was preparing to leave for college, he moved our family to North Carolina to embark on a new career of rescuing failing banks. I spent vacations at my grandmother's house, hoping to preserve some connection to my hometown. Under her spell I began to appreciate my father's silence.

She was an amateur artist whose last years were given over to intractable suffering. Afflicted with neuralgia, she would fasten clothespins to her fingers to distract her from the blazing pain in her cheek. She painted winter landscapes dominated by an empty barn, listening to taped sermons by a minister who preached the power of positive thinking. At dusk she poured herself a Scotch and served cheese and crackers to her Welsh terrier and a blind German shepherd she had adopted from the Seeing Eye. Once she told me that after my grandfather's death my father would sit at her kitchen table of a Saturday morning, without speaking. His silence comforted her.

It was not that he had nothing to say but that he valued words too much to spend them on small talk. What mattered was that he came to see her—just as he showed up at my baseball games and soccer matches, though he stayed in the background, refusing to emulate the men who helped coach in order to promote their sons. He insisted on me making my own way, instilling in me a haughty independence. "Trust thyself: every heart vibrates to that iron string," Emerson wrote. In the face of insoluble problems it was but a step from the transcendentalist's skepticism about the tenets of faith to the confusion of an unchurched poet like me.

Schooled in silence, I was obsessed with what was left unsaid, the hidden life of things, the gaps that govern our understanding of the world. Writing was my way to initiate a conversation, first with myself, then with my loved ones. And if in my apprenticeship I lived in fear of the blank page, I had hardly learned to view fallow periods in the same way as the white space between the stanzas of a poem or the quiet moment at the end of the day, which is celebrated at vespers. From silence to silence: this is how poets translate their encounters with language. But how could I translate what I could no longer hear—the music of silence?

In my hiatus from poetry I studied the work of Paul Celan, who plumbed the depths of silence. He called poetry a message in a bottle; his poems are at once emblems of the bloodiest century and explorations of the distant reaches of consciousness. "There's nothing in the world for which a poet will give up writing," he said, "not even when he is a Jew and the language of his poems is German." Celan was determined to redeem the language of his people's executioners—a language which he famously said had to "pass through the thousand darknesses of deathbringing speech." Yet for all his efforts to find words capable of confronting history's greatest crime he could not escape the memory of those darknesses. In 1970, on Hitler's birthday, Celan threw himself into the Seine and drowned. He was forty-nine years old.

Born in Czernowitz, the polyglot city in Bukovina, Celan grew up hearing German, Romanian, Ukrainian, Yiddish, and many dialects: fuel for this linguistically gifted poet. By the age of six he could recite Schiller's "Song of the Bell"; as a schoolboy he translated Shakespeare and Yeats, Apollinaire and Esenin. But the German invasion interrupted his university studies in philology. Herded into the Jewish ghetto, then interned in labor camps, Celan continued to write and translate, discovering that "language doesn't only build bridges into the world, but also into loneliness." His parents' murders at the hands of the Nazis, the central tragedy of his life, only confirmed his notion about the limitations of language.

He remained a solitary, first in Bucharest, where he settled after the war, and then in Paris, where he fled, in 1948, from the new Communist regime. He married, fathered a son, worked as a translator and teacher. Yet he is remembered as a brooding, silent man. The Polish poet Zbigniew Herbert never forgot the night that he and Celan walked through the streets of Paris without saying a word until they parted at daybreak. Celan's poetic interrogation of silence, the most compelling figure for God in the aftermath of the Shoah, is equally unsettling.

He said he wrote to orient himself, a task that grew more difficult with each year. Poems in his view were "gifts to the attentive," and from his readers he demands more than ordinary powers of attention. His work brims with allusions, coinages, puns, and associative leaps:

The hourglass buried
in peony-shadow:

when my thoughts finally come down
Pentecost Lane
they will inherit the Reich
where
trapped in sand, you still
get whiffs of air.

In the opening couplet Celan distills the story of the Fall—in six words: the mortal consequences of Adam and Eve eating fruit from the Tree of Knowledge are compressed into an image of the sands of time, the Garden of Eden into the shadow cast by the flower of the gods. Then the poet boldly promises that his words will appear at a new Pentecostal harvest—of grains? ideas? souls? What they will inherit, and perhaps purify, is the distorted language used to create the Third Reich's millennial nightmare. For poetry offers "whiffs of air" to those trapped in the sand, just as the Psalms comforted many of those condemned to die in the Nazi gas chambers.

I recalled my visit, with the Café Europa, to Kraków's Jewish ghetto, lately restyled as a tourist destination devoted to Holocaust sites, complete with advertisements for *Schindler's List* tours of Auschwitz. But very few Jews remained—the synagogue could barely fill the minyan of ten adult men for a public service, the Noah's Ark Café featured live Jewish music played by Polish Catholics, et cetera—and as we walked from one empty street to another, in the cold, blustery gloaming, I was haunted by their absence. "We have Jewish restaurants, Jewish hotels, Jewish bookstores, and no Jews," said a Polish writer, ushering us into a Singer sewing machine factory which had been converted into a café. On each table was a sewing machine; in the corner a couple was locked in a kiss. It was darker inside than out. The Polish writer wondered whether his countrymen should be viewed as fellow victims of the Nazis or as collaborators—a question complicated by the collapse of communism. And nowhere were the ambiguous relations between Jews and Roman Catholics more on display

than at Auschwitz, where a cross had just been raised to commemorate Christian victims of the Nazis, angering Jews around
the world. From the café we went to a synagogue under restoration. Two crosses cut into the floor and filled with white pebbles
marked the destroyed altars; life-size cardboard cutouts of men
who had once prayed here were propped in the aisle. A silent
black-and-white film from the Nazi archives, documenting the
emptying of Kraków of its Jewish population, played continuously. Over and over we saw old men, women, and children carrying their belongings to the ghetto.

The critic Theodor Adorno thought it barbaric to write poetry
after Auschwitz. Celan replied with a body of work predicated on
the very silence that Adorno deemed the appropriate response to
evil. And if the Shoah seemed to confirm Nietzsche's prediction
that mankind had killed off God, the current worldwide resurgence of religious feeling suggested the contrary. Indeed the
killing fields and concentration camps, from the Turkish deportation of Armenians to the Nazi destruction of European Jewry,
from Cambodia to Rwanda to Srebrenica, confirm the notion that
God is silence—a silence that for Christians is embodied in the
figure of Jesus on the cross, who recited the first verse of Psalm 22
before dying: "My God, my God, why hast thou forsaken me?"
(Matt. 27:46). His despair was spoken in the name of humanity to
end our separation from God, but we may imagine Him inwardly
praying the entire psalm, which promises salvation, even as His
disciples silently filled in the other verses.

Psalm 22 enacts the central crisis of the human condition—
the distance between man and God, best illustrated in the conclusion of the first verse, in what remains unspoken by Jesus: "why
art thou so far from helping me, and from the words of my roaring?" The psalm's power in the Gospel depends on silence, on
what Jesus does not say. Israel's trust in the Lord; David's faith despite his humiliation; his plea for salvation; his revelation that
God is with him: "for thou hast heard me from the horns of the
unicorns" (a richer translation than the New King James Version:

"You have answered me"); his promise to praise Him "in the great congregation"—Jesus gives voice to none of this, trusting His listeners at the foot of the cross, and down through the ages, to pray the rest of the psalm in His name: "All the ends of the world shall remember and turn unto the Lord: and all the kindreds of the nations shall worship before thee" (Ps. 22:27). And His silence, which extends through Holy Saturday, makes His first word, on Easter Sunday, the most powerful of all: "Rejoice!" This was what He said to Mary Magdalene and the other Mary, outside His empty tomb (Matt. 28:9). They heeded His command to tell the apostles to go to Galilee, where He charged them with spreading the good news of His return. Thus the Church was born: Christ has died, Christ has risen, Christ will come again.

From silence to silence: this is the message of the hush that settled over Calvary. And it is what animates the last verse of the Gospel according to John: "But there are also many other things which Jesus did; were every one of them to be written, I suppose that the world itself could not contain the books that would be written" (John 21:25). Christianity is predicated on mystery, on what we do not know about the Son of man—any public records containing references to Jesus were destroyed in the Roman razing of Jerusalem in 70 CE. In fact the Jesus Seminar, a group of modern biblical scholars searching for what they call the authentic Jesus, has concluded that less than 20 percent of the acts and sayings attributed to Him in the New Testament may be rooted in historical truth; the rest, they argue, from the Virgin Birth to the Resurrection, belong to myth and legend—in short, Christianity's very premise. How, then, can anyone believe in Christ?

"You ask me how to pray to someone who is not," Czeslaw Milosz writes in a poem, and then explains that prayer builds a bridge from this world to the next—a bridge he will walk even if there is no other shore. Prayer and poetry alike depend upon the unknown, although the poet's explorations belong to the temporal order while the monk fights for eternity. My faith now was in the invisible world, in the communion of saints, in the promised land that lies beyond the final silence. St. Clement of Alexandria (c. 150–215) wrote: "We fling ourselves upon the majesty of Christ: if we then advance through holiness towards the abyss, we shall have a kind of knowledge of God who contains everything, knowing, not what he is, but what he is not." During the siege of Sarajevo it was said that an abyss had opened between one world order and the next. But from the edge of another abyss I saw that the war was but a moment in history, which left me thinking about last things. "For now we see in a mirror, dimly, but then face to face," said Paul. "Now I know in part, but then I shall know just as I also am known" (1 Cor. 13:12).

THE STONE WALLS OF GREAT LAVRA SEEM IMPREGNABLE — TALL grey façades straggling to the bluff, connected by a series of towers. The oldest and largest Athonite monastery, which dominates a spur of land on the mountain's eastern slope, two hundred meters above the sea, had withstood attacks by pirates and Crusaders, earthquakes, and the usual fluctuation of fortunes. Seven hundred monks lived here in the eleventh century; by the seventeenth century there were only five; now there were fifty, with three hundred more living in Great Lavra's dependencies — the *sketes* and settlements in the desert of Eremos. Through a portico of stained-glass arches I entered the courtyard and climbed a set of stairs on the north side. At a long table on the balcony the elderly guestmaster was entertaining the trio of pilgrims who had preceded me on foot from Karyes. I polished off a guest tray, including two glasses of raki, and was starting on another when one of the pilgrims, an abrasive disc jockey from Athens, struck up a conversation.

He said he was searching for direction, having quit his job, cast off his wife and daughter, moved out of his apartment, and shaved his head. Will you become a monk? I asked. No way, he said with a leer. I love women. That's the problem. He was also suffering from angry red blisters on his feet. The guestmaster, offering to examine his hiking boots, was not surprised to discover that they had been manufactured in Israel: the raised soles were shaped like crosses. Typical, said a pilgrim dressed in combat fatigues. The disc jockey was aghast: to think he had walked all day on crosses! His arrogance dissolved in a flash. He pleaded with the guestmaster for help. The monk obliged, using his penknife to slice the arms off each cross.

Anti-Semitism is rife on Athos. Some monks will tell you that Coca-Cola is flavored with the blood of Christian children slain by Jews; others decry Jewish bankers, praise *The Protocols of the Elders of Zion* (a nineteenth-century Russian text, fabricated by the czar's agents, spelling out a Jewish conspiracy to take over the world), and proclaim the advent of a false Messiah, a Jewish Prince of Darkness, all of which flies in the face of Isaiah's prophesy that Israel was to be "a light to the nations" (Isaiah 42:6); of Christ's injunction to love thy neighbor as thyself; of Paul's witness: "For by one Spirit we were all baptized into one body—Jews or Greeks, slaves or free—and all were made to drink of one Spirit" (1 Cor. 12:13). This revolutionary commitment to equality before the Lord presages the founding documents of every democracy. But tell that to the monks who call democracy *demonocracy*.

The sorry history of Christian-Jewish relations, a burgeoning field of scholarly inquiry, has focused mainly on the Vatican's perfidy toward the Chosen People, from the Inquisition to Pope Pius XII's silence about the Holocaust. But Jew hatred is hardly confined to Western Christendom: witness the history of pogroms in Russia. And the viciousness of, say, the Romanian Black Guard, a fascist movement that included among its early sympathizers Mircea Eliade, one of the most profound modern Christian thinkers, is an emblem of the unholy alliance between nationalism and religion endemic to the Eastern Church, the victims of which are often Jews, who in the minds of anti-Semites stand as an affront to Christianity.

This is an old story. It was John Chrysostom who said "the

demons are the Jews" and the synagogue "is not only a whore-house and a theater; it is also a den of thieves and a haunt of wild animals." In Antioch, in 386, when Christians were reeling from Julian the Apostate's efforts to restore paganism and sow dissension in the Church, Chrysostom delivered the first in a series of homilies against those whom he viewed as the real enemies of the new dispensation — Judaizing Christians, whose observance of the Law suggested that Judaism was truer than the Christian faith into which they had been baptized. Christianity's hold on the public imagination was tenuous, with pagans and Jews also vying for the spiritual welfare of the empire; any heresy was viewed as a mortal threat. In *John Chrysostom and the Jews,* a study of the sermons that helped to shape Christian attitudes toward the Jews, Robert L. Wilkin concludes that "by keeping the Law, by celebrating Jewish festivals, by seeking out Jewish magicians, the Judaizers proclaimed that Judaism was spiritually more potent than Christianity. What greater proof of the truth of Judaism than for the followers of Christ to observe Jewish law?" This, then, was for Chrysostom a matter of life and death. What hatred spilled from the mouth of the golden-tongued saint: "No better disposed than pigs or goats, [the Jews] live by the rule of debauchery and inordinate gluttony. Only one thing they understand: to gorge themselves and to get drunk. When animals have been fattened by having all they want to eat, they get stubborn and hard to manage. . . . When animals are unfit for work, they are marked for slaughter, and this is the very thing which the Jews have experienced. By making themselves unfit for work, they have become ready for slaughter." It was not long before Christian mobs attacked Jews and destroyed their synagogue.

Invective was the order of the day, and the young presbyter, believing he was fighting for the soul of the Church, employed the harshest rhetoric, which survived the politically charged atmosphere of his time. Indeed his words took on a life of their own: excerpts incorporated into the Byzantine liturgy for Holy Week taught generations of Christians to loathe the Jews; an eleventh-century Russian translation coincided with the first pogrom in Russia. And by the time Martin Luther published *The Jews and Their Lies* (1543), using the same fervid language as Chrysostom to advocate the razing of Jewish houses and synagogues (he advised rulers of Jewish subjects to "act like a good physician who, when gangrene has set in, proceeds without mercy to cut, saw, and burn flesh, veins, bone, and marrow"), Judaism was no longer a rival to Christianity and the Jews were a vulnerable minority subject. Did Chrysostom help to lay the groundwork for the lethal anti-Semitism that culminated in the Holocaust?

Certainly he provided arguments that, in different circum-stances, inspired violence against the Jews. And while it is unfair to read his work free of the context in which he wrote, I subscribe to the notion that writers are responsible for their words, now and in the future. Milosz cautions poets to "hope / that good spirits, not evil ones, choose us for their instruments." The same holds for theologians. Caught up in a political fray, Chrysostom wrote with vengeance toward his enemies, not love; his homilies carry the stench of politics instead of the fragrance of eternity, because he made precisely the kind of accommodation with the temporal order that sent other fourth-century divines into the desert in search of God. History's verdict is just: the glory of his Divine Liturgy, commentaries, and prayers must be balanced by the bru-tality of his homilies against the Jews, the legacy of which endures throughout Christendom.

I was acquainted with some of the dangers of confusing earthly and eternal needs. My journey to the Holy Mountain was inspired in part by my sense that documenting a distant war had dulled my perspective about what was closest to me. In my imag-ination Athos was a place outside history to reflect on what I had witnessed and how I had behaved, in the war zone and at home. Taken out of context, the pages I had written about the Serbian aggression might be read as an anti-Christian screed, which I in no wise intended. Nor could the angry words I had spoken to Lisa in argument be taken back. The history I sometimes wished to escape, political and personal, demanded a truer accounting from me. I had written and spoken intemperately; if I did not labor under the illusion that my words would outlive me, nevertheless I often failed to act with sufficient fear of God. In this I was no different from other Christians, whose spiritual lives have been shaped, for better or worse, by a saint who did not always write in the spirit of eternity.

And yet, and yet. Chrysostom died in exile, far from Constantinople, where he had risen to the post of bishop. His life had come full circle, his ecclesiastical career having begun in earnest only after a voluntary withdrawal from society, a trial worthy of the desert fathers: four years of prayer, fasting, and study in seclusion with an older ascetic, followed by two years of standing continuously in a cave, during which he memorized the Old and New Testaments, rarely sleeping. Not until he had ruined his health did he return to Antioch to embark on a public career, which culminated in his appointment to the bishopric in Constantinople, the highest ecclesiastical office in the empire. His was a rocky tenure: his zeal alienated the empress, who imagined herself to be the target of his reforms; his fall from grace was precipitous. He died en route to a distant port on the Black Sea, worn out from a forced march in bad weather.

Chrysostom thus embodies a crucial question for the faithful: how to live in the world in the spirit of Christ, making difficult decisions presumably subject to eternal scrutiny? His record was by all accounts exemplary, apart from his homilies against the Jews. And perhaps it was in the spirit of his last words — "Glory to God for all things" — that a modern Greek bishop named after the saint acted with such courage to save Jews from the Nazis that he was honored by Yad Vashem as a "Righteous Among the Nations." The story goes that in 1944, when the Germans occupied the Ionian island of Zakynthos, the mayor and the bishop were ordered to compile a list of local Jews to be rounded up and deported. Bishop Chrysostom said the Jews had lived there peacefully for centuries. He had no wish to see them disappear. The three men began to argue, and then the German commandant said, "No more discussions. Just give me the list." The bishop took a blank piece of paper, wrote his own name, and handed it to him. "Here is your list of Jews on the island of Zakynthos." The officer was livid. "You may go now," he said, "but this will not be the end." But the mayor and bishop urged the Jews to flee into the hills, where Christians and partisans hid them until the Nazis withdrew from the island. Zakynthos was the only community in Greece whose entire Jewish population was spared in the war.

And now the disc jockey was begging the guestmaster for mercy. The monk blessed his boots, then kissed his hand. There was much nodding and murmuring among the pilgrims. The one in combat fatigues turned to me.

"What do you expect from the Jews?" he muttered.

ATHANASIOS, GREAT LAVRA'S FOUNDER, DIED IN THE ACT OF placing the last stone into the arch of the church apse. He was almost eighty years old when the dome collapsed, killing him and six others; and since his life is the stuff of legend it is tempting to read his death in symbolic terms as well: his work on earth was incomplete, like any Christian vocation.

He took his name from St. Antony's biographer, and no doubt the life of the anchorite who helped to inspire the original monastic retreat to the desert strengthened his calling. It was in the spirit of a desert father that Athanasios settled on Athos, refusing worldly honors—he had been appointed confessor to Emperor Nikephoros—to follow the eremitical life. But the emperor would not leave him alone. First he arranged for him to have a special cell near Karyes, then he asked for his blessing to reconquer Crete, and then he commissioned him to build the monastery that fundamentally changed the character of the Holy Mountain. Demons undermined his efforts, however, and when he had exhausted his money and materials he set off for Karyes, perhaps to leave Athos. After walking for two hours, though, he met a woman who claimed to be the Virgin Mary. He asked for proof. She told him to make the sign of the cross over a rock embedded in the hillside, then strike it with his staff. Like Moses in the desert, Athanasios split the rock apart, and a stream of water gushed out, which emboldened him to complete his project. He retraced his steps to the building site, armed with Mary's promise of help and protection—both of which ran out, it seems, before he could complete his work.

From the porch overlooking the courtyard, where the guest-master and several pilgrims sat at a table filling matchboxes with incense to sell in the shops, I could see the ill-fated dome glinting in the last light of the day. I was reading a treatise on prayer by Pseudo-Dionysios the Areopagite, which I had discovered in a cabinet of books outside the guest quarters. "But see to it that you do not betray the holy of holies," he instructed clergy. "Let your respect for the things of the hidden God be shown in knowledge that comes from the intellect and is unseen. Keep these things of God unshared and undefiled by the uninitiated. Let your sharing of the sacred befit the sacred things: Let it be by way of sacred enlightenment for sacred men only." This is one reason why the iconostasis conceals part of the liturgy. "Guard the doors, the doors. Wisdom. Attend," the priest chants just before Communion. Indeed the doors are closed to unbelievers as well as to those who may partake of the sacramental mysteries. Perhaps this is how Orthodoxy inherits the Judaism of Jesus's day, when temple worship was restricted to priests, males, and the clean; only the high priest could enter the Holy of Holies on the Day of Atonement. I understood the impulse that, as the Blessed Theodore wrote, "holy things must not be given to the profane," even if it seemed to me that Jesus intended to show us precisely the opposite: that God is accessible to everyone—and that the things of the hidden God are hidden from us precisely because of our limitations, our inability to see. "Behold, You desire truth in the inward parts," the Psalmist sings, "and in the hidden part You will make me to know wisdom" (Ps. 51:6).

This is also true of great poems, which hide as much as they reveal; hence our desire to return to them, learning more about their secret depths, and ours, with each reading. And once we know a poem by heart it works on us in subterranean ways, like prayer. Whatever remains vital about the mystery of life lies in a certain inaccessibility. Heretic that I am in the eyes of the Orthodox, I realized that in the uneasy tension between what I might learn on Athos and what would always be kept from me I had discovered a metaphor for our walk in the sun. The Orthodox believe the gift of seeing the unseen comes from inner renewal in Christ: "we do not look at the things which are seen, but at the things which are not seen. For the things which are seen are temporary, but the things which are not seen are eternal" (2 Cor. 4:18). The icons, frescoes, illuminated manuscripts, liturgy, incense— these are the things of the hidden God. And the rusks of bread left out for the Twelve Invisibles, the hermits no one has seen for years: apostles of the invisible world, the world of the spirit first witnessed by Christ's apostles. And the hermitages built into the cliffs. Creation itself has many faces, most of them hidden, including—to my dismay—the desert of the Holy Mountain, which was knee-deep in snow. I would not be able to hike from Lavra around the southern end of the peninsula, so the next morning, after breakfast, I joined the other pilgrims in taking the taxi back to Karyes.

"THE LIFE OF A MONK OUGHT TO BE A CONTINUOUS LENT," SAID St. Benedict, counseling monks to pay particular attention during this season. The same holds for pilgrims. And I hiked from Karyes to Daphne with a heavy heart: something essential had eluded me. It was the first day of spring, the sky was overcast, and on my descent toward the sea, with a nerve flaring in my neck, I grew despondent. The pilgrims in the port, waiting for the ferry, wandered through the shops, buying icons, incense, and ouzo. I picked out a prayer rope made by a hermit and continued southward. The dirt road, which corkscrews up a sharp incline, then curls around the mountainside, weaving in and out of canyons, rising toward the peak, ends at Simonopetra, a monastery dedicated not to Simon Peter (as its name—Simon of the Rock—might imply), whose betrayal of Christ three times the night before His Crucifixion was weighing on my mind, but to our Lord's Nativity.

A week in the cradle of Orthodoxy had taught me that the birth of belief in God is but the first step in the religious life. Peter's denial of his apostleship I understood: afraid for his own life, perhaps dubious of Jesus's claim to be the Son of God, he was like any believer—well-intentioned, weak-willed, prey to grief. Which was why Jesus appointed him to be His vicar on earth: "And I also say to you that you are Peter, and on this rock I will build My church" (Matt. 16:18). Contrite, Peter went on to preach the good news of the Redeemer, for which he too was crucified— upside down, according to tradition, because he did not believe he merited the same treatment as the Lord. Against his momentary failure of nerve and martyrdom I set my habitual denials of faith and my aching shoulder. The pettiness of my concerns only deepened my despair. Nor did I take comfort in the knowledge that Christ built his Church on the rock of such wavering believers as me. Indeed I was praying for mercy when, rounding a ridge, I saw, across a steep ravine, perched on top of a cliff rising hundreds of meters from the sea, the monastery named after St. Simon the Myrrh-gusher, a thirteenth-century hermit whose relics produced myrrh.

Legend has it that one Christmas night this cave dweller was instructed in a vision to build a church where a bright star fell from the sky and burned into the cliff. He called his church New Bethlehem—although construction of the monastery, a seven-story architectural wonder tethered to the mountain by a stone aqueduct, did not begin for a hundred years, when a Serbian king's prayers for Simon's help in healing his sick daughter were answered. But neither its lofty setting nor the saint's intercession-ary powers could spare Simonopetra from burning down three times, most recently in 1891; charred timbers remain in the ceiling of the greeting area, where some Greek pilgrims had just finished off a tray of *loukoumi* when I arrived. I followed them out to the balcony hanging over the cliff and saw, far below, terraced gardens, an endless fall to the tower at the port, and the sea, dark blue in the emerging sunlight. Two hundred years ago an English pilgrim called this view "one of the most awful and terrific that can be conceived. The spectator looking down feels as if he were suspended over a gloomy abyss"—a feeling accentuated for me this afternoon by the smoky haze of pilgrims avid for tobacco.

I had not reserved a place for the night, but the guestmaster let me stay just the same. Nor did the fast keep him from serving a large lunch (roasted potatoes, pickled vegetables, bread, and olives), after which I went for a walk. The sun had come out, laborers were hammering and pouring cement in a new stone dormitory draped with scaffolding, and wheelbarrows lined the cobblestone mule path to the grape arbor below the monastery. Two monks weeded around the edges of one garden as I went down the switchbacking trail toward the sea. A spry Russian monk in a grey work habit was staking up cypress seedlings near a covered shrine.

"This is paradise," he said, "if you live a good monk's life."

He gathered his tools, leaped over a stone wall to tie up an olive seedling, and then ambled down the trail. I followed a narrow path behind the shrine, which led into the next canyon, and descended to a *kellí* set back from the sea. From here the trail rose along the coast, lined with prickly pears and purple irises. The air was sweet with nectar, the cliffs yellow with broom; song sparrows flitted in the olive groves and stands of madrona. In the sunlight I was sweating as I marched up and over a long hill. Around a corner I saw, across an emerald cove, the monastery of Grigoriou, one of the most dynamic on the Holy Mountain. Alas, I had no time to visit it, which pained me, for now I imagined I might find some solace there.

The poet John Ashbery once said he was more interested in the experiences he missed than in the ones he had—a fair description of my pilgrimage. Paul wrote: "Now faith is the substance of things hoped for, the evidence of things not seen" (Heb. 11:1). What to do? In grief I gazed at Grigoriou and the mountain beyond, streaked with snow. What all I had missed!

Clouds rolled in, and on the hike back to Simonopetra I began to shiver. And I shook with cold through vespers and after dinner, when I lingered in the darkening hallway outside the guest rooms, listening to a monk counsel pilgrims. They were sitting under a hole burned in the ceiling by the last fire, and I wished the things of the hidden God did not include this monk's words. I needed his wisdom. Yet even as I was feeling sorry for myself another sin rose in my memory: a speech I had recently delivered about my experiences in Bosnia to Pax Christi, a student peace group at Holy Cross. After my remarks the chaplain asked if I had prayed in the war zone. I said something about my faith in literature: how poetry had sustained me in difficult circumstances. Which was true. But I *had* prayed—at border crossings and in hotel rooms, avoiding snipers on street corners, under shellfire in crowded basements: every morning, every night. Flying into Sarajevo on military transport planes, I had recited Donne's "Holy Sonnets" as well as the Lord's Prayer. Now I saw my failure to speak the truth to the students not only as cowardly but also as sinful. I had denied my faith, as I had at so many turns in my life. My journey to Mount Athos had inspired in me dread—and a spirit of penitence. It was time for me to atone.

part two

PURIFICATION

G REECE WAS BURNING. IT WAS THE HOT-test summer on record, and hundreds of wildfires raged across the country, some set by developers to clear the last forested stretches of public land. The air tasted of smoke, the horizon was black, firefighters from all over Europe joined the annual influx of tourists. On the eve of my second pilgrimage to Athos, in my hotel room in Thessaloníki, every television channel was taken up either with footage of the fires or with advertisements for phone sex, featuring a seemingly endless variety of stripteases and orgies. I barely slept. On the crowded ferry to Daphne, seated by a monk hunched over a catalog for data-logging instruments, I saw the gutted *skete* around the first promontory in a new light. The dry woods reminded me of the long history of fire on the Holy Mountain, some monasteries razed as many as three times; in 1990, thousands of acres had burned. And on the road to Karyes the dust was six inches deep. The heat left me nauseous. I wondered what I was doing here.

"Athos has a mysterious pull on people," a pilgrim told me. And something was drawing me back. All spring I had tried to sort out my feelings about my Lenten pilgrimage—regret for my estrangement from the monks, surprise at my longing for this place apart, fear of the obligations entailed in the Orthodox life of the spirit. I bought an English translation of the Divine Liturgy, hung a small icon of the Virgin in my study, and recited the Jesus Prayer. I dreamed of Athos—the mountain and the sea, the footpaths and cliffs, the chanting, the bells. Intrigued by what I had not seen of the peninsula, I wondered if I would ever visit it again. Then, at Pentecost, when plans to write about a journey with the Café Europa fell through, I decided to pay a penalty to reroute my nonrefundable plane ticket and planned my return to the Holy Mountain for the Dormition of the Mother of God, the last major feast of the liturgical calendar.

My first night on Athos I spent at Iveron, where the guestmaster who had sketched out my itinerary at Great Lent now advised me to journey to the desert. I did not have the heart to tell him I had forgotten the map he had given me, and after my long flight I was too weary to walk to Great Lavra in one day. So on the morning of Transfiguration in the West I headed south along the ridge above Iveron, in a chestnut forest, looking for the red-and-white hand-lettered signs to the inland monastery of Philotheou. Neat piles of wood were stacked beside the dirt road, which turned into a rock path littered with dead leaves. In a clearing, some monks were drinking ouzo on the porch of a *kellí*, and their merry voices followed me back into the woods, where just days before a fire had been extinguished before it burned out of control. One spark from the chain saw a laborer was using higher up on the ridge could easily set off another fire.

Two hours of hiking brought me to a long rock wall, which descended by a tumbledown *kellí* to a wooden footbridge. Halfway across was a stone shrine propped on a massive slab of ivy-covered cement; from a deep recess of shade a waterfall spilled into a pool. And from the top of the next steep rise I could see, tucked into the eastern slope of Athos, ringed with gardens and orchards, Philotheou, a tenth-century monastery dedicated to the Annunciation of the Virgin.

The history of Philotheou, twelfth in the hierarchy, is part Slavic, part Greek—that is, complicated. Inhabited for centuries by Serbs and Bulgarians (who once chased a Greek abbot off the Holy Mountain), the monastery did not flourish until it came under Greek patronage. Even so a devastating fire in 1871, which spared only the *katholikón*, refectory, and library, inspired an unsuccessful Russian attempt to take over the monastery. The colors of the rebuilt entrance, a tall four-sided archway, seemed to reflect the clash of ecclesiastical cultures: green columns, a stark white façade, red borders for the windows and cross. And red was central to the color scheme inside the monastery—the bricks, the walls and domes of the *katholikón*, the arches above the guesthouse, where the guestmaster served me water and ouzo. From there I went to the refectory for a substantial meal of fish soup, fava beans, tomatoes, cilantro-and-onion salad, and red wine. The frescoes, perhaps by masters of the Cretan School, needed restoration. And I needed a nap. So I retired with some pilgrims to a stifling guest room and fell into a leaden, sweat-soaked sleep, from which I did not stir until the *sémantron* sounded hours later for vespers.

The frescoes of the Apocalypse above the church entrance—one miserable soul was being devoured by a sea monster—were balanced, just inside the door, by two frescoes of Christ: in the first He is seated in a gold chair, with an open book in His hands, surrounded by twenty saints playing harps; in the second He delivers the Revelation to St. John, a swordlike light pouring out of His mouth. Every wall of the church was covered with soot-stained murals, and when I had tired of looking at them I went out to the courtyard, where a hot wind gusted over the grass. Potted plants—hydrangeas, geraniums, peonies—lined the steps and walls; in the flower beds were roses, hosta lilies, and marigolds. A middle-aged man clutched a gold cross, tears streaming down his cheeks. A younger man left the church to check his cell phone for messages. A Peloponnesian in a wheelchair, a cerebral palsy victim who summered at this monastery, was trying to say something to a monk. At the conclusion of the service, when everyone filed into the refectory, the monk told me to stay behind with the Peloponnesian.

"It is because the Orthodox are not allowed to pray with unorthodox," explained Nicodemos, the affable baker. "It is only because of the prayer."

When the reading and clanging of silverware commenced, Nicodemos spoke of his many friends in America, where Philotheou's former abbot had founded ten monasteries. He himself had come to Philotheou at the age of sixteen. He had always worked in the kitchen.

"The life is very beautiful here," he said, "and poor. Silent."

The bell rang. The monks and pilgrims returned to church for compline. Nicodemos ushered us into the refectory to eat with the Greek and Albanian laborers, promising to meet me after the service. But it was a short, nasty monk who took me into the nave to see the relics—a piece of the True Cross, the right hand of St. John Chrysostom, martyrs' skulls. The monk was telling me why the Reformation was even worse than the schism. Yes, the Protestants had properly dispensed with the papacy, but they had also removed the mystery from the Church.

"There is only one true faith," the monk repeated several times, but since he could not pronounce his *r*'s I heard him say "two faiths."

"What's the other faith?" I said.

He gave me a puzzled look. "Only one two faith!" he cried.

"Yes," I said. "I see."

"Do you have any questions about the Church?" he said, sneering at the old men who offered crosses and rosaries to be blessed by the priest displaying the relics. An exercise in futility, he seemed to say. "Is there something you want to know?"

I thought for a moment. "What's your name?"

"Do you need to know?" He grimaced. "What is yours?"

"Christopher," I said, extending my hand.

"Nice name," he said, then slapped my hand and walked away.

"[T]HESE MUTTERING, MISERABLE, MUTTON-HATING, MAN-avoiding, misogynic, morose and merriment-marring, monotoning, many-mule-making, mocking, mournful, minced fish and marmalade-masticating Monx," Edward Lear wrote during a pilgrimage to Athos, in 1856. The landscape painter and poet of sublime nonsense might have been speaking of the monk who strode into the courtyard at Philotheou and glared at me as I sketched the red-and-white striped haloes around the arches bordering the staircase to the refectory. Closing my notebook, I went out the gate to a low stone wall, where monks and pilgrims gathered at dusk to talk. The sea was calm in the distance. In the garden were tomatoes staked like crosses and rows of onions and cabbages. An old monk trudged up the road with a bundle of herbs slung over his back. Crickets chirped in the woods, where someone was hammering.

In the guesthouse I had discovered some books by Nicodemos the Hagiorite (1748–1809), an essential theologian, and in the cool of the evening I read, "God is the fire which consumes evil." This line came from the prologue to *The Philokalia*, the multivolume collection of ascetic and mystical texts central to Orthodox practice. From Athonite monasteries Nicodemos and Makarios of Corinth gathered writings, dating from the fourth to the fifteenth centuries, to show how the intellect may be purified. First published in Venice, *The Philokalia* (literally, "the love of what is beautiful") forms what Nicodemos called "a mystical school of inward prayer"—a school I was attending in a fitful manner. Unsettled by my Lenten pilgrimage, I turned for comfort and instruction to patristic literature, and what I discovered was imaginative writings of the highest order, works by men blessed with a gift for metaphor: God transformed into fire.

Indeed the Greek word for God, *Theos*, derives from a verb whose meanings include to burn, to run, and to see—active verbs, Orthodox theologians note, which point to God's energies, not His essence. In the apophatic tradition, God is unknowable in His essence; only His divine energies, His power and grace, are revealed in the things of the world. "Creation is the task of energy," says Cyril of Alexandria. And our task is not only to recognize this energy but to partake of it through the sacraments. Deification— *theosis*—is the word the Orthodox use to describe the mystical union between man and God; through prayer, liturgy, service, and grace we may be united with God. *Theosis* is how man participates in the divine energies. Sacrificing the self to God is one way to avoid the trap of narcissism. Which is why monks give up their names at tonsuring. Nor do they wish to be remembered: freed from the tyranny of the self, they search for eternal peace by focusing on that which lies beyond themselves, just as new parents find a certain relief in placing their children's needs above their own.

"Absolutely unmixed attention is prayer," writes Simone Weil. This first step in the spiritual life I took through poetry. The story about Rilke's discovery of the poetic potential hidden in things—what to the Orthodox are the divine energies at work in the world—made a lasting impression. When Rilke served as Rodin's secretary in Paris, he admired the sculptor's steady craftsmanship and concentration: how he made things without relying on flights of inspiration. One day Rodin asked Rilke what he was writing. Nothing, said the poet. The sculptor advised him to go to the zoo and study an animal until he could make it spring to life on the page. Rilke was dubious, but after his first exercise in disciplined observation yielded a signal poem about a panther pacing in its cage, he drew up a list of hundreds of subjects and began to write on a regular schedule; his *New Poems*, published in two volumes in 1907–8, inaugurated the tradition of thing-poems. William Carlos Williams, Francis Ponge, Pablo Neruda—these poets also discovered the urgency of elevating attention over inspiration; their thing-poems restored to literature a measure of mystery. Here were poetic accounts of the divine energies praised by St. Basil: "I want creation to penetrate you with so much admiration that wherever you go, the least plant may bring a clear remembrance of the Creator. One blade of grass or one speck of dust is enough to occupy your entire mind in beholding the art with which it has been made." For just as Christ is the Word or Logos of God, so each thing contains a divine spark, the source of its uniqueness, which orients it toward God. The faithful are thus obliged to recognize God's Logos in everything, which is why in the liturgy the priest repeats, "Wisdom. Attend." Adam's naming of the animals, the Psalmist's praise of Creation, priestly admonitions to pay attention—these are of a piece with the poet's meditations on the things of the earth.

A full moon was rising over the hills when I went to the guest

quarters. Jet lag, snoring pilgrims, a bat circling the ceiling—
I could not sleep. So I turned to Nicodemos. Orthodoxy has no
Summa Theologica, only manuals of prayer, like Nicodemos's
Handbook of Spiritual Counsel, which he wrote in self-exile on a
barren island off the coast of Athos. This I read by flashlight, and
again in the morning, during the liturgy, when it grew light
enough to sit in the courtyard. Nicodemos argues that the world
deceives us: "We call the good evil and the evil good, like being in
a house filled by smoke, where we cannot see clearly either the inside, or the outside of the house; so we know the present things
poorly and the future worse." And death is "the end of deceit."
Meanwhile Nicodemos offers instructions for guarding the senses,
imagination, mind, and heart, as preparation for experiencing
true spiritual delight, here and in the afterlife. Needless to say, I
found his course of study difficult to follow.

For example, after breakfasting on bread, olives, and tea, I had
no sooner set off for the monastery of Karakallou, an hour's walk
downhill from Philotheou, than I began to daydream about every
woman I had ever loved—and some who belonged to my imagination. In the heat and haze I followed a narrow rock walkway
through the woods, past the ruins of *kelliá,* lost in erotic reverie.
Jays squawked overhead. Sounds of the sea came riding on the
wind. How to control my thoughts? I remembered St. Augustine's
advice: "It is solved by walking." But it was only the sight of the
stone tower at Karakallou that brought me to my senses.

Karakallou was not a popular destination for pilgrims. Raiding
pirates and Crusaders had kept the monastery from prospering
until the eighteenth century; in the next century it suffered a cata-
strophic fire and a Russian takeover attempt; in our time it was too
small and remote to draw much attention. Still I was anxious to
visit Karakallou, eleventh in the hierarchy, because it had attracted
several new monks, including two Americans. But the guestmaster
said the Americans were asleep. Moreover, the abbot did not allow
heretics to attend services or take meals with the faithful. I settled
for ouzo, water, and a quick tour of the *katholikón.*

Among the frescoes was another version of the Revelation that I had meditated on at Philotheou. The flaming light of prophesy beaming into the ear of John the Divine seated at his writing desk points to the centrality of fire in the Christian imagination. The fire-and-brimstone imagery of Revelation is rooted in a historical event: the great fire, in the summer of 64 CE, that destroyed much of Rome. It was rumored that Emperor Nero himself set the blaze to clear space for new building projects, then climbed a tower, in stage costume, to recite *The Sack of Ilium*; hence the image of Nero fiddling while Rome burns. To quell these rumors he scapegoated an obscure sect of monotheists: some Christians were crucified, some were dressed in animal skins for wild dogs to tear apart in the arena, some were torched in the Vatican gardens. Historian A. N. Wilson suggests that by targeting a little-known movement Nero gave Christianity "two vitally important privileges: a public name and a number of dead, who could be seen instantaneously as martyrs"—including, perhaps, Peter and Paul, the saints to whom Karakallou is dedicated (in the *katholikón* was a splendid icon of the saints cheek to cheek, in the kiss of peace). He also inspired a work of poetic genius. John the Divine was fortunate to escape the persecution, and on the island of Patmos he composed the Revelation, fueling the apocalyptic imagination down to the present, especially in a hot summer like this one, on the eve of the new millennium.

A vision of the risen Christ instructs John the Divine to write a letter to the seven churches of Asia, bolstering the faithful while warning sinners that the end time is at hand. The Seer likens Rome to the doomed city of Babylon; to a harlot drunk on the blood of saints; to "a beast rising up out of the sea, having seven heads and ten horns, and on his horns ten crowns, and on his heads a blasphemous name." And Nero, who "had two horns like a lamb and spoke like a dragon" (Rev. 13:1, 11), is code-named 666 (from the Greek spelling of his name translated into Hebrew letters, which also function as numbers), a favorite number on Athos, where paranoia is rife and literal interpretations of Scripture are common. Did you know the first Apple computer sold for $666.66? a monk once asked me. I shook my head. And if you translate Microsoft Windows into ASCI it adds up to 665, he assured me. Missed it by that much, I said, imitating an old Maxwell Smart joke. The monk was not amused. Nor did John the Divine imagine that two millennia would pass without any sign of the Second Coming.

Nero committed suicide (his last words: "What an artist the world is losing in me!"), but Rome did not fall for 350 years—after becoming Christian. Indeed the doomed city at the time of Revelation's composition was Jerusalem, which the Romans besieged in 66 CE to put down a Jewish revolt; when the temple was destroyed four years later, the writer of the Epistle to the Hebrews seemed the better prophet, having announced that "our God is a consuming fire" (Heb. 12:29)—though he surely did not expect Jerusalem to go up in flames, a catastrophe that continues to shape the world. Church history, for example: not only were any records about Jesus destroyed but also His hope of reforming Judaism from within; the Jewish diaspora ensured that He became the Messiah not of the Jews but of a new religion taking root among the Gentiles, thanks in large part to Paul's missions to Asia Minor and Greece.

The apostle's message resonated among the downtrodden of the empire. "Paul's epistles are extracts from the handwritten journal of a revolutionary work-in-progress—a collection of passionate notes from the underground," write the biblical scholars Richard A. Horsley and Neil Asher Silberman. And it seemed to me these notes acquired new meaning in the postmodern world, in the wake of the carnage inspired by the poet-priests of revolution, the political ideologues who transformed Christianity's radical egalitarianism into hellish versions of earthly paradise. Paul's counsel is sobering: "Among the mature we do impart wisdom, although it is not a wisdom of this age or of the rulers of this age, who are doomed to pass away. But we impart a secret and hidden wisdom of God" (1 Cor. 2:6–7).

This was the wisdom I sought when I strolled out of the church, a little drunk, and headed for the woods. The sun blazed, although the mountain was shrouded in clouds, and the path was covered with dry leaves, which crinkled underfoot. The effects of the ouzo had worn off by the time I gained the dusty road to Great Lavra. A familiar pain coursing through my shoulder and neck, which on my first pilgrimage had nearly crippled me, now brought to mind an Anglican priest's sermon on the Beatitudes, in which he suggested that the blessings bestowed by Jesus on His disciples — "Blessed are the poor in spirit, for theirs is the kingdom of heaven," and so on (Matt. 5:1–12) — be translated as congratulations. Congratulations on your suffering, which may open you to God's healing vision. Jesus leads His disciples up the mountain to tell them that salvation lies in humility, not pride. Nicodemos said that when God wants to lead the proud to the path of perfection he sends them afflictions, a test that "immediately shows what is hidden in their hearts, and how deeply they are corrupted by pride. For whatever affliction may visit them, they refuse to bend their necks to the yoke of God's will and to trust in His righteous and secret judgments." Too proud to trust entirely in God, still I had returned to the Holy Mountain, and now I realized that even a flaring nerve could lead to spiritual progress.

The road entered the shade of chestnut trees. In the dust were the loping paw prints of a wolf, the last of which had supposedly died out on Athos in the 1980s. All at once I was alert — and scared. I followed the wolf tracks for a hundred meters before they disappeared into the woods, which now seemed to throb with mystery, and then they reemerged at a bend in the road, continuing as far as the eye could see. I was walking with God, in the shadow of a wolf.

THE SHRINE COMMEMORATING THE SPRING OF ATHANASIOS LIES up a small hill off the road, halfway between Karakallou and Great Lavra. A set of steps leading to a cave separates a locked stone building from a gazebo, where pilgrims can sit at a wooden table and reflect on the strange career of Great Lavra's founder, the hermit responsible for turning Mount Athos into a city of monks, in the words of his biographer, in the same way that "the desert became a city" under the tutelage of St. Antony of Egypt. Athanasios wanted nothing more than to praise God in solitude. But the emperor had other plans for him. Athanasios labored for forty years to build his monastery and create the cenobitic system, deciding along the way that monks should struggle "like athletes and martyrs." And his struggle was mighty. It was here that, walking in despair over construction problems at Great Lavra, he was vouchsafed his vision of Mary instructing him to strike a rock from which flowed the water I knelt to drink—water that was clear, cool, and sweet. Athanasios, heartened, returned to the task of building Great Lavra, which was my destination. Not long after I resumed hiking, a monk from the monastery offered me a ride in a Land Rover. Soon we came upon three backpacking pilgrims, who reluctantly joined us.

The pilgrims—a Greek doctoral candidate who was completing his studies in Vienna, an elderly, red-faced Austrian and his son—had arrived in Daphne the day before and hiked until ten at night. Their attempt to summit Athos had ended in failure due to bad weather above the tree line, and they had spent this morning lost on the ridge. Now they planned to cross the desert in time to catch tomorrow's ferry to Ouranoupolis. They had camped out last night and expected to do the same tonight. They had visited no monasteries. The Greek, a lean, unshaven young man with brilliant white teeth, was a student of sports psychology. He specialized in motivational strategies, but he took an odd approach to his discipline. When he learned that I also hoped to cross the desert he urged me, repeatedly, to think again.

"You must sign up for the bus to Karyes," he insisted in German-accented English. "There is a problem with water. We have four liters apiece."

I showed him my water bottle, which held a liter and a half.

"I don't know how much you need," he said gravely.

I told him I would refill it at the Romanian *skete* south of Great Lavra.

"But maybe they won't be there," he said. "Then you'll have to go in and take it yourself."

The older Austrian nodded. He unbuttoned his shirt and fanned himself with his straw hat, a sight that seemed to upset the monk, who raced along the cliff, spinning his tires in the dust. The monk was a spiritual athlete (the root of asceticism is *askein*: "to work, to train the body") whose course of training was more rigorous than anything a sports psychologist might devise. In his fourteenth-century text, *Life in Christ*, the Byzantine theologian Nicholas Cabasilas writes, "He makes us His athletes; He trains and anoints us; He runs beside us in the race." These pilgrims were no athletes of Christ. The monk, who must have performed hundreds of prostrations every night in his cell, probably took the same dim view of me. But I was hoping that my training on the soccer field had prepared me for the harder regimen of faith.

Soccer was the lodestar of my adolescence. I traced this to a rented cottage on the hill behind the Congregational church in our village. The construction of my parents' dream house had fallen behind schedule; my father was confined to bed with a mysterious ailment; my mother was often angry. I spent my free time outside, kicking a soccer ball against the cement wall next to the garage. Out of the corner of my eye I could see, fifty meters away, the church steeple, level with the wall; as I juggled and kicked and trapped the ball I sometimes imagined I could leap from the hill into the steeple to ring the bell. I was developing peripheral vision, as an athlete and in my relationship to matters of the spirit. Our lives were in limbo—precisely the state in which great changes, even revelations, may occur, as well as lasting heartache; juggling a soccer ball, in sight of the church, was a form of solace, a kind of charm, like counting beats in a line of verse, which improved my touch, preparing me for literary work—and the work of the spirit.

St. Clement of Alexandria believed in the merits of exchanging the rigors of one discipline for another: "Just as there is one way of training philosophers, another for public speakers, and another for athletes, a certain character results from the training of Christ." This character or quality of vision, which I cherished in the poems of Donne and Herbert, Hopkins and Milosz, was what I hoped to discover in myself, with Christ's help. He is the Divine Instructor, according to Clement, who "devotes himself to watching for the favorable moment, reproving evil, exposing the causes of evil affections, and striking at the roots of irrational lusts" — instruction I badly needed. It was time for me to unite the spiritual and physical sides of my being in such a way as to hear His voice. Easier said than done, even on the Holy Mountain.

An icon of Christ swung from the rearview mirror as the monk wheeled around the corners, frequently crossing himself. The drop-off to the sea was dramatic, and while the Greek student joked with his companions about their upcoming hike I recited the Jesus Prayer. St. Basil described monastic life as "an arena of athletics, a method of traveling forward" — a far cry from our reckless drive down the peninsula. An unbridgeable gap seemed to lie between us and the monk; and when we arrived at Great Lavra he walked off without a word. The hikers stayed just long enough to refresh themselves, then set out, in the heat of the day, for the desert.

FROM THE ARSANAS THE ROUGH WATER GLITTERED IN THE MID-day sun. The watchtower had a new coat of cement, but the staircase was rotting, and so I had to climb around the holes in the timbers to get a better look at the island on which Nicodemos wrote his *Handbook of Spiritual Counsel*—though on closer inspection the dark shape in the distance turned out to be a freighter. Smoke was on the wind; the outbuildings along the quay were falling apart; grass grew around the rusted oil barrels in the roofless boathouse. An overturned rowboat lay in the sand, not far from an older pilgrim who was hard at work untangling a fishing line. The monk who had given me a ride fished from the jetty. Through the afternoon I took notes on Nicodemos and *The Philokalia.*

Blessed with a capacious mind, Nicodemos borrowed liberally from Western theologians. His *Handbook* expanded on St. Ignatius of Loyola's *Spiritual Exercises;* his adaptation of *Unseen Warfare,* a sixteenth-century text by a Venetian priest, is sometimes printed as an original work. Indeed he revised key elements of the Venetian's argument, offering a vision of prayer in keeping with Orthodox tradition. Hesychasm, which he called "the flame of grace," was the cornerstone of his thought; his efforts to revive the discipline of "God awareness" (the phrase is Bishop Kallistos Ware's) spurred Orthodoxy's nineteenth-century revival; his advice, in *Unseen Warfare,* to collect "the mind into the midst of the heart," helped me to imagine the work ahead.

The war of the heart was what engaged me in the wake of the Balkan Wars. If in Sarajevo the challenge had been to control my nerves under siege, the danger now was of a different order. Once I had recorded war stories, in the hope of capturing the essence of change and tragedy; now I listened to the secret directives of my heart, in the hope of redeeming my walk in the sun. If the first step in the spiritual life is what theologians call *metanoia*— a Greek word with a number of meanings: to repent, to turn toward God, to make the sign of the cross—then purification is necessary to continue the journey. Purity, which St. Diatokos of Photiki (c. 400–486) defined as "unwavering perception of God," is thus another way of describing the stillness of the heart that hesychasts seek in ceaseless prayer—perhaps the prayer of the monk fishing from the jetty.

At the start of His ministry Jesus invited Peter and his brother Andrew, and James and his brother John, to leave their fishing nets by the sea and become fishers of men (Mark 1:16–20, Matt. 4:18–22, Luke 5:1–11). And it seemed to me the serenity of the monk reeling his line through the shimmering water could turn a man toward God. He was, I thought, a witness to the power of prayer to purify the heart and mind—the central theme of *The Philokalia*, Nicodemos's major work. It was not by chance that he and Makarios reserved the greatest number of pages in their compendium for the writings of St. Maximos the Confessor (c. 580–662), a prolific theologian who underscored the connection between dogma and prayer: how the one fortifies the other; how both must be lived; how theology without action (penitence, purification, prayer) is a demonic exercise. And Maximos certainly lived and died for his faith. An aristocrat from Palestine, he gave up a career in the civil service to enter a monastery near Constantinople—which did not spare him the ravages of history. The Persian invasion of 626 sent him into flight, first to Crete and then to Africa, where he got caught up in the continuing battle over Christ's nature.

The controversy dated back to the Gospel accounts of Jesus's baptism in the Jordan River, when "a voice came from heaven, saying, 'This is my beloved Son, in whom I am well pleased' " (Matt. 3:17). If this was indeed the voice of God, then Jesus belonged to the Godhead. But in what form? The question vexed theologians of the early Church; some of their answers were later deemed heretical. For the religious imperative of the first six ecumenical councils was to define Christ's nature; the doctrines of the Incarnation and the Trinity resulted from the development of arguments to combat the heresies denying the belief that Christ was at once God and man. Arians argued that He was not divine, Nestorians thought He was two persons, Monophysites said He was not fully human, and so on. It takes a leap of faith to embrace the dual nature of Christ, the contradiction at the core of Christianity, and in Maximos's day the Monothelites proposed that Christ had two natures but one will—which thus diminished His human nature. Maximos could not convince the imperial authorities to reject this argument, hampered by an emerging threat that would eventually destroy the empire. Islam was on the rise; Byzantium was losing territory—Syria, Palestine, Egypt, which left the patriarchates of Antioch, Jerusalem, and Alexandria under infidel control; the emperor treated dissenters harshly. Arrested and transported to Constantinople, Maximos was tried and punished—flogged, mutilated (his tongue torn out, his right hand cut off), and exiled to the Caucasus—only to be exonerated at the sixth ecumenical council, twenty years after his death—the date of which is celebrated two days before Dormition.

His interpretation of the Incarnation guides his understanding of prayer. Even as Christ emptied Himself (*kenosis*) into human form, so man, emptying his heart and mind of everything save the presence of God, may become pure enough to participate in His divinity. This is what Orthodox theologians mean by deification: through Jesus we may partake of God's glory, insofar as we align our will with His; through prayer and the sacrament of Communion we are deified, made Christ-like, and receive the first fruits of eternity. Maximos regards prayer as the foundation of a life in Christ. In *Four Hundred Texts on Love*, which is divided into centuries of meditations corresponding to the four Gospels, he describes the means by which prayer leads to love, a holy state. "He who truly loves God prays entirely without distraction," Maximos writes, "and he who prays entirely without distraction loves God truly. But he whose intellect is fixed on any worldly thing does not pray without distraction, and consequently he does not love God."

How to pray without distraction? Maximos believes that love is engendered by dispassion, which has four stages: abstaining from sin; rejecting evil thoughts; contemplating the essences of visible things; and contemplating what he calls "passion-free" images. It is not enough to practice the virtues and push aside sinful thoughts. The penitent must see in the things of the world God's energies, and then, in the prayer of the heart, concentrate on the presence of God to the exclusion of everything else. Simone Weil follows Maximos and Nicodemos in distrusting the imagination, which will furnish the mind with images contrary to the higher reaches of the spirit. "The imagination is continually at work filling up all the fissures through which grace might pass," she writes.

It is only in a state of emptiness that we may come to know God. And prayer can foster a kind of openness in which to listen to the divine emptiness.

The question then is what will fill that space. It is like fishing: you cast your line into the sea and wait, praying for good luck. But every monk, every fisher of men, knows how the mind strays from reflections on the eternal to the mundane. Maximos suggests psalmody to rid the mind of unwelcome thoughts. And surely the monk on the jetty, who hoped to catch a fish and perhaps the voice of God, chanted psalms to himself. Just so a poet is receptive to the slightest stirrings of the language, waiting for a nibble — a rhythm, an image, a word rich with meaning. The difference is that the poet depends upon the imagination to set fire to the language; what rises to the surface of the mind may carry meaning — sacred and profane.

The older pilgrim was gone when I gathered my notes and headed for the steep dirt road up to the monastery. The freighter had not moved. Nor the monk, except to cast his line. He had not caught anything all afternoon. He looked perfectly content.

AMONG THE FRESCOES IN GREAT LAVRA'S REFECTORY IS A CURIous rendering of the death of Athanasios: the haloed saint lies on a golden bed, with grieving monks assembled around him in the shape of the very dome that collapsed on him. Was this visual pun a conscious allusion to the tragedy, or had God steered the iconographer's hand unbeknownst to him? A monk blessed the food, and then I took my seat on a marble bench curling, like a horseshoe, around a circular table, between a bassoonist from Athens and a curtain maker from Mount Sinai. The bassoonist, a fidgety man who kept whispering that he needed to relax, picked at his food with a scowl that reminded me of my own misgivings about the food during my first pilgrimage. But now I devoured the meal of tomato-and-rice soup, tomatoes, bread, olives, white wine, and water.

After the benediction I followed the curtain maker out to the courtyard. He was a pudgy newlywed proud to tell me that his birthplace was the Monastery of St. Catherine—the traditional site of God's appearance to Moses, in the form of a burning bush (Exod. 3:1–4). This was where God not only promised to deliver the Israelites from their bondage in Egypt, foreshadowing the liberation from sin and death that Jesus offered to mankind, but also revealed the Law, which was fulfilled in Christ (Matt. 5:17, Rom. 10:4). St. Catherine's and its dependencies, which form the autonomous Church of Sinai, the smallest Orthodox church, thus serve as a visible connection between the Old and New Testaments. The sacred bush growing near the monastic church is at once a memorial to the Mosaic covenant and a symbol of Mary's perpetual virginity—"the bush was burning, yet it was not consumed" (Exod. 3:2).

Mary is sometimes described as the link between the human and divine, the Old and New Testaments, Jews and Christians, Christianity and Islam. (An entire chapter is devoted to her in the Qur'an.) Tradition holds that a pair of miracles brackets her life: born sinless, at the end of her days she ascended into Heaven. If Christ was the new Adam sent to redeem fallen man, some church fathers argued, then Mary must be the new Eve. Immaculate conception thus reversed God's promise to the mother of mankind: "I will greatly multiply thy sorrow and thy conception" (Gen. 3:16). And the story of Mary's Assumption, which dates from fourth-century New Testament apocrypha, offers a singular exception to God's judgment on man: "for dust thou art, and unto dust shalt thou return" (Gen. 3:19). If she was taken body and soul directly into Heaven, then the terrible sentence of death had been commuted.

These miracles, which are no more rooted in fact than the story of her ship being blown into the Bay of Iveron, testify to the need for some human presence in the divine order, a need that grew with the postponement of the Second Coming. Legends accumulated around Mary, balancing the Trinity of Holy Writ; the development of Christian practice, in all its variety, is rooted in this tension between the human and divine, female and male angles of vision, tradition and Scripture. And in my mind there was a connection between the way that an unknowable God inspired a human counterpart, a woman to whom the faithful could pray for intercession, and the way that the elevation of Christianity to official status in the Roman Empire gave rise to the desert fathers. The dialectics of Holy Writ and Mariology, of state religion and monasticism, laid bare the nature of Christian truth—how it oscillates between the edicts of authority and folk belief, the claims of this world and the next, things seen and things unseen.

Mary lies on the side of mystery, since the New Testament contains little information about her—no more than a few pages. Nor did the absence of hard evidence prevent her from becoming the best-known woman in the history of the world. At the Council of Ephesus (in 431) she was proclaimed Theotokos, God-bearer or Mother of God; the liturgy contains a number of short prayers to her called *Theotokia*, symbols of the division between Scripture and tradition: "True Theotokos, we magnify you." In the Gospels we learn why: what Mary, the first believer, bore in her womb we may bear in our hearts.

It is at the wedding at Cana (John 2:1–11) that we gain the clearest view of the interplay between the human and divine, the physical and spiritual. The first of Jesus's seven signs is the most domestic: the wine has run out at a wedding feast. Mary's anxiety provokes a reply from her Son that, at first blush, sounds like that of any exasperated young man: "Woman, what does your concern have to do with Me? My hour has not yet come." But Jesus uses the term "Woman" as an honorific; what really concerns Him is the promise of Heaven, grounded in the quotidian, to be revealed at the time of His glorification. Yet He defers to Mary, as she knew He would: "His mother said to the servants, 'Whatever He says to you, do it.' " On Jesus's orders the servants fill six stone water pots set aside for purification, and when He changes the water into wine the old dispensation gives way to the new, anticipating the transformation of bread and water into His Body and Blood at the Last Supper and in the Eucharist. If Old Testament weddings symbolize God's union with Israel, the wedding at Cana in Galilee, a predominantly Gentile area, suggests the universal reach of Christ's message, which seeks to wed God to all of mankind.

The Gospel story also points to the sacredness of marriage, which is why it is read in the Orthodox wedding service, a far more serious ritual than the ceremony that Lisa and I devised for ourselves. Ours was a study in artifice: we wore wedding suits from a vintage clothing store to a Victorian mansion in Seattle, where a string quartet played Mozart. The ceremony began with a former rock-and-roll musician, now a doctoral student of Sanskrit, reading a nuptial essay laced with quotations from the philosopher Martin Buber. I recited a sonnet, wrongly attributed to Shakespeare, praising the marriage of music and poetry; the Congregational minister read from Paul's First Epistle to the Corinthians; Lisa cried so hard that her mascara blackened her cheeks.

My mother did not hesitate to voice her displeasure with the event. She is a strong-willed, outspoken woman, and I cringed as she explained to the minister, a formidable figure herself, why she disapproved of women of the cloth. My mother possesses a clear sense of propriety—she was the one who taught manners to my sisters and me, enrolled us in ballroom dance classes, took us to church while my father slept in—and a wariness of anything different. Which may explain why I cherish open-mindedness. Yet I am continually surprised to discover how much of my mother's skepticism I have inherited, including her suspicion of things Catholic. Protestant hostility toward the papacy and Mariology endures. And if at a Jesuit college I could hardly ignore the papal announcements that might bear on my employment, still I had given Mary little thought before coming to Athos. She had not figured in the lessons drilled into me during confirmation class. I grew up knowing nothing about her Immaculate Conception or Assumption.

Then again, neither does Orthodoxy recognize the doctrines of Immaculate Conception, proclaimed by Pope Pius IX in 1854, and Assumption, which Pope Pius XII elevated from liturgical observance in 1950. But these are murky waters. In the first instance Orthodox theologians argue that Mary is the most righteous Old Testament figure as well as "the hidden heart of the Apostolic Church," in Bishop Ware's phrase; Immaculate Conception severs the link between the Old and New Testaments by placing her squarely in the New, even if in Orthodox texts she is described as immaculate or all-holy (*panagia*). The argument against Assumption is that it is derived from papal decree, not ecumenical council. Indeed Orthodoxy affirms that Mary was taken body and soul into Heaven, where she awaits the faithful. But this belief belongs to what the theologian Vladimir Lossky calls "the mysteries which the Church keeps in the hidden depths of her inner consciousness." Christ must be preached to the world, the mystery of His mother revealed only to the faithful. The dispute, then, is over public and private forms of worshipping the same thing.

Mary lies at the heart of the differences among many Christian denominations. For she is a figure of both unity and division, a contradiction echoed throughout Christianity. Jesus is human *and* divine; in death the believer lives; and so on. Simone Weil defined contradiction as a lever of transcendence; and what is more contradictory than the idea of a virgin mother? Presumably in the Age to Come every contradiction will be resolved. Meantime the monk at Philotheou was right: Protestantism *had* dispensed with mystery, the chief symbol of which is Mary. Curiously, the Reformers accepted the development of doctrine by which the Trinity was enshrined in the Nicene Creed, but not the tenets of Mariology. Was a female presence in the divine order threatening? In this I glimpsed some of my own tangled history of relations with women. For all of my praise of mystery, in poetry and spiritual matters, in a marital spat my first resort was to logic. Which Lisa refused to consider. Which led me to offer more vindicating proofs. Which made her angrier . . . It was a vicious circle. I wanted to be right, she wanted to know I loved her. A marriage will founder on the reef of logic and certainty.

But love, like poetry, like faith, is rooted in uncertainty. Indeed my mother had taught me this lesson long ago, when she said that even though my father was the most predictable man she knew—in his devotion to order, for example, he filled our house with clocks, which chimed and tolled the hour, creating a cacophony—he was capable of surprising her at any moment. When I told this to a friend, he replied, "She's still in love with him, isn't she?"

Marriage depends upon cultivating that sense of mystery—and discipline, which Orthodoxy likens to the discipline of monasticism. Just as a monk is betrothed to the Divine Bridegroom, so a man marries a woman. The only difference is that married couples can make love.

Above a garden of roses, dahlias, and lime trees was an open-air belfry, which resembled a fire tower. "It's important to see different ways of worshipping God," said the curtain maker, as the guestmaster ascended the stairs to the belfry, "except that on Athos they've been doing it the same way for more than a thousand years."

Under the red roof of the belfry were thirteen bells, connected by a series of strings, which the guestmaster tugged to create a complicated run of notes, calling us to a special service in the Virgin Mother's honor. I followed the curtain maker to the *katholikón*, which is flanked by a pair of cypresses said to have been planted by St. Athanasios himself. If John Donne believed that bells tolled to remind you of your mortality, I heard them calling me now to a new way of thinking about marriage, in the form of an ancient discipline. Into the church I went.

I LEFT GREAT LAVRA BEFORE DAYBREAK, PICKING MY WAY SOUTH-ward along a rock path through scrub woods, pursued by horse-flies—which, according to an Athonite joke, were made *after*

Adam had named the animals. The path met up with a dirt road, and soon two monks passed, nodding their greetings. The sun rose bloodred over the sea; the mountain loomed overhead. Presently the Romanian *skete* of Timiou Prodrómou came into view, a rectangular complex of buildings set on a hill above the sea. Following a stone wall down to the gate, I entered the empty courtyard, in the center of which was the *kyriakon*, the common church of the *skete*, dedicated to St. John the Baptist, with four tall cypresses standing on either side of the entrance, locked at this hour. Only ten cenobitic monks lived in Timiou Prodrómou, which had but lately begun to recover from the Church's years of persecution in Communist Romania. The liturgy was thus being sung in a small chapel, where the sun blazed through the windows next to the altar. An old monk was on his knees before a chair, his head buried in his hands. Two bearded laymen in dress shirts assisted the priest. I slipped away, feeling as if I had intruded on an intimate scene.

In the hall outside the chapel, though, a suite of icons caught my eye. What intrigued me was not so much their draftsmanship as the fact that they were new: green shoots on the edge of the desert. They brought to mind the works of the contemporary Romanian neo-Byzantine school of artists. Once, in Bucharest, an art critic from the Café Europa took me to visit the group's impresario, Sorin Dumitrescu, a tempestuous, white-bearded artist who had won fame in the early 1980s for challenging the prevailing socialist realism to create space in his work for spiritual matters. While the dictator Nicolae Ceauşescu was destroying churches and implementing the austerity measures that would lead to his downfall, Dumitrescu and his friends turned to iconography for inspiration. Influenced by *The Philokalia*, a Romanian translation of which had been published in Bucharest in 1946, they expanded their artistic vocabulary to include banished forms and subjects—Noah's ark, the pietà. Dumitrescu painted close-ups of the Archangel Gabriel's hand, carved wooden reliquaries, and produced icons for the patriarch. In one church I saw his swirling vision of the Revelation, a brightly colored icon in which Christ and the Seer form a circle. From a black triangle in the upper left-hand corner streams a silver light, which forks above Christ's shoulder; the Seer's head is bowed as he takes down His words.

The artist's studio, which took up several dimly lit rooms of an old flat, was teeming with new projects in various stages of completion. He had just returned from an interview at the radio station, in which the journalist, also an apprentice iconographer, had asked him why her icons lacked life, despite her prayers and fasts. Better to be enthusiastic about your work, he told her, than to slavishly follow rules, for enthusiasm means to be filled with God (*en + theos*). And he was truly enthusiastic about the artists affiliated with his Catacomba Gallery. In his lavish catalogs he praised them in hagiographic terms; their latest exhibition, he declared, *Versions of Transfiguration*, had opened to wide acclaim in Budapest.

"Tell me," he said, fixing his eyes on mine, "have you ever forgiven an enemy?"

I replied, glibly, that I had.

"Then you must be a saint," he said with an ironic smile.

Ashamed, I followed him over to the wall facing his desk to see the plans for his most important commission to date: the iconostasis for the Church of St. John Cassian in Rome; the pope and the Romanian patriarch would celebrate its installation at Easter. The scale drawing of the altar tacked to the wall seemed to me to be a blueprint for the reunion of the churches. If *The Philokalia* had made a chink in the armor of the Ceauşescu regime, then Dumitrescu's icons might help to tear down the more durable wall between the Orthodox East and the Latin West. It was a Romanian monk, after all, who had arranged the ceremony in Jerusalem, in January 1964, between Pope Paul VI and Patriarch Athenagoras (the first such meeting between a pope and an ecumenical patriarch since the Council of Florence in 1438) in which they agreed to revoke the anathemas of 1054. And Romania was the first Orthodox country that Pope John Paul II visited in his bid to reunite Christendom. The Romanian Church, the world's second largest Orthodox church, is Latin in its national identity and orientation; at the crossroads of Byzantium and the Slavic lands, it has a more universal outlook than other branches of Orthodoxy—despite its own internal divisions. Romania has a large Uniate population who, under the Communists, were forced to unite with the Orthodox Church; their efforts to recover church property complicated the theological picture. In the meantime a flourishing movement of Old Calendarists, who had suffered more under the prewar Romanian government than under Ceauşescu, locked horns repeatedly with the official Church. The Freudian idea of "the narcissism of minor differences" was in full force in Romania: the pope's last best hope to begin his campaign for reunion.

The curator of *Versions of Transfiguration* described the Catacomba artists' aesthetic program as a marriage of the avant-garde and Orthodoxy, a radically conservative effort, "under the sign of the Icon . . . to transcend the conflicts that appear in daily Romanian life involving religious, ethnic, and national minorities." Dumitrescu's contributions to the exhibition included an unearthly landscape inspired by his single pilgrimage to Athos: a ghostly canoe, a tear lodged in a mouth or an eye, a golden background of mountains or waves. Here was an essay in light, which in the curator's words obeyed the principle of *inverted perspectives*—a surrealist principle, I might add. Dumitrescu's pilgrimage had marked him. Disdaining Athonite austerity, he nevertheless gave up his three-pack-a-day cigarette habit in honor of the Virgin. Accordingly she granted him not one but two miraculous visions, the substance of which he refused to divulge but which he gave me to understand informed his current work. It was in the spirit of his silence about that sacred mystery that I left the Romanian *skete* and continued toward the desert.

THE MONKS SAID IT WAS TOO HOT. MANKIND HAD DONE GRIEVOUS wrong to the planet—an issue dear to Ecumenical Patriarch Bartholomew, the so-called Green Patriarch. His All Holiness is indeed the most active environmentalist among world religious leaders. He proclaimed September 1, the start of the liturgical year, as a day of prayer for the protection of the environment; on Patmos, in 1995, he used the 1,900th anniversary of St. John's recording of the Apocalypse to convoke an international symposium on the health of the oceans; at the Monastery of the Holy Trinity, on the island of Halki, he regularly convened seminars on environmental justice, ethics, and education. The Communist legacy of toxic industrial practices was destroying the health of his subjects; defending Creation, a theologically sound and politically astute decision, might heal a church riven by nationalist sentiments, in the same way that the Turkish yoke had once helped to unify Orthodoxy. The new infidel was the Industrial Revolution, whose ravages were everywhere on display in the fouled rivers, lands, and air of the Eastern bloc.

It was little better in Greece, where the tradition of setting forest fires to clear public land for private development, a practice tacitly approved by the government, left the skies hazy and the wind tasting of smoke. It was said the wolves had returned to Athos to escape the flames on the mainland, and on my climb to the ridge dividing the mountain's eastern slope from the desert I kept an eye out for their tracks. But there was only a jackrabbit at the saddle, marked by a cross propped in a cairn of rocks. I gazed westward at a wide scree field and cliffs dropping hundreds of meters to the sea—the ascetic heart of Athos. Without a map to consult, I set off on what I later learned was the high trail across the desert, the steep, sparsely inhabited southern slope of the mountain, sometimes following a black plastic pipe that carried water from a spring. But there were no spigots on the pipe. Even in the shade the air was stifling.

The question of right relation to the earth is troubling for

Christians, who have a long history of interpreting God's command to "have dominion over the fish of the sea and over the birds of the air and over every living thing that moves upon the earth" (Gen. 1:28) in literal terms. The patriarch blamed the ecological crisis on our refusal to see life as "a sacrament of thanksgiving"; our treatment of the earth, he argued, defines our relationship with God and with others. We must be stewards of His Creation; in the bread and wine of the Eucharist we may offer Creation back to the Creator—and to one another: the living presence of God is a blessing and a summons to reimagine our place in what the patriarch calls "a complex web of relationships that extend throughout our lives, our cultures and the material world."

Asceticism provides a model for living in harmony with nature, teaching us to be mindful of limits. "Excessive consumption leaves us emptied, out of touch with our deepest self," writes the patriarch. "Asceticism is a corrective practice, a vision of repentance"—which carried particular meaning for someone traveling from the most profligate nation on earth. The vertical desert of Athos was a tonic to a culture predicated on materialism. "All nature from beginning to end constitutes a single icon of God," writes the poet and theologian Philip Sherrard; and what is more iconoclastic than modern industrial society, which has ravaged the earth?

In the heat I realized how far I had strayed from my deepest self, having forgotten what was once an article of faith: the intimate connection between the conservation of the earth and a good marriage—how each depends upon recognizing limits. I remembered how Lisa and I used to spend our free time in the wild. We hiked in the deserts and mountains of the West, learning the names of wildflowers, trees, and birds: emblems of how we named each other anew, acts of attention that sometimes led to poems. But the added responsibilities attending our move to New England left us little time to explore our surroundings; we were too busy even to plant a garden. The farmer-writer Wendell Berry, noting that "heal," "whole," and "holy" come from the same Indo-

European root, suggests that the planet's health demands a healing vision, which preserves in us "the spirit and the breath of God." My stiff neck and broken marriage, my hiatus from poetry and lost connection to the earth: they were of a piece. Nor would I become whole except through the grace of God. The fate of everything I loved hung in the balance.

A mule path took me to the edge of a cliff, over which lay a rope for lowering baskets of food to a hermit who lived below in a cave. The tradition is that a monk from the hermit's monastery regularly delivers provisions to him; when the basket is pulled up with its supplies intact, the monk climbs down to remove the corpse (his skull is later returned to the cave) and another hermit takes his place. Here was the hidden heart of Athos—which I could not see. The brush was too thick, the scree too steep for me to descend. In the distance I heard the tinkling of a mule's bells. A novice was perhaps carrying food to this very hermitage.

I returned to the woods and started climbing. The monks believe that just as Christ was the new Adam and Mary the new Eve, so Athos is the new Garden of Eden, a place to redeem both man and nature. Indeed much of the peninsula remains in its natural state, with more than 90 percent of the land under forest cover; and in the areas under cultivation—vineyards, olive groves, gardens—organic farming methods are practiced. Thus when the monks say that mankind is on the wrong trail they speak as inheritors of a land lovingly tended for more than a millennium. Theirs is the long view. "Patience, hard thing!" Gerard Manley Hopkins wrote. But God demands patience of the sort a monk suffering from depression revealed, when he told me he was prepared to spend the next five or ten years working out his despair.

"There are two words I understood only after coming to Athos," said the monk. "*Sin*, which in Greek means to divert. Sin is a diversion from God. Every sin takes energy away from your attempted union with God. And as one spiritual father says, 'There's no sense in seeking union with God in the afterlife. Now is the time.' The other word is *redemption*, which in Greek means a change of heart. We must not only make outward signs of contrition, Hail Marys and so forth, but also an inward change. God knew that Adam and Eve had sinned because they had deviated from His way. So what did Adam do? He blamed Eve. She blamed the serpent. Neither repented, and so they were cast out of paradise.

"But nature also fell with Adam and Eve," he continued. "And the more we stray from God's will, the more nature suffers. We're juggling too many balls: the environment, the markets, the family. We can't keep them up in the air forever. When they fall the end will be at hand."

THE *SKETE* OF KERÁSIA, A DEPENDENCY OF GREAT LAVRA, LIES IN a sloping wooded valley eight hundred meters above the sea. At midmorning, from a cornice a kilometer or so to the east, I heard, across the next hillside, tinkling bells, and spotted a monk leading a pack of mules laden with flagstones for the *skete*; the mules were feeding in the paddock by the time I arrived at Kerásia, which means cherry tree—the *skete* was once famous for the fruit harvested by the monks and for the red wine they produced. But few monks remained, and when I rang the bell minutes passed before an old monk came to the door. He gave me a once-over, then disappeared. I stood there wondering what to do until my impatience got the better of me and I resumed hiking. That the monk might have been preparing a guest tray did not occur to me until it was too late to go back. The trail wound down through a dark glen and then up to a ridge, where it divided into three: one route led to the summit of Athos, another to the settlement of Katounákia, a third to the *skete* of St. Anne. I refilled my water bottle from a spring, where someone had left a paper plate with two crusts of bread for a wandering hermit, and was halfway to St. Anne before realizing that I had crossed the desert without knowing it. If only I had brought a map! The Twelve Invisibles, the hermitages overlooking the sea, the hidden world of faith—I had missed them all.

Now I saw my life as a series of missed hints. I recalled an incident from the summer after my high school graduation, when my family moved south for my father's new job. I stayed behind to work as a teaching tennis pro—and to indulge my taste for illicit drugs. On the day the furniture movers came I drove with a friend to a park, where we smoked hashish and sat under a waterfall until dusk. My parents' dream house (we had lived in it for only five years) was empty when I returned, except for the grandfather clock, deeded to my aunt, ticking loudly in the living room. I became aware of a mysterious presence and broke out in gooseflesh—a shiver of feeling I might have interpreted as instruction in holy terror: "The fear of the Lord is the beginning of wisdom" (Ps. 111:10). But I fled the house to get high again.

When I returned the next morning, hoping to duplicate whatever it was I had felt in the night, the house was filled with the furnishings of the new owners, who did not invite me in. So I went to the back field to sit among the black walnut trees my father had planted to screen out the housing development spreading over the hill across the valley. In this field I had mowed hay, learned to drive a surplus army jeep, smoked my first cigarette. Wordsworth believed that poetry "takes its origin from emotions recollected in tranquility." The only emotion I could summon in the field, however, was remorse for having cut down so many seedlings by driving the tractor too fast. But if the poetic impulse is born of loss, then I date my literary beginnings to that morning in the field, when the sun was high and alfalfa stubble scraped my legs. The loss of a house or homeland is but a sign of our exile from the Kingdom of God—to which Christ Jesus promised to restore us in the Age to Come. Hence the physical beauty of an Orthodox church, God's house—the icon of His Kingdom in which it is ordained that we will find our true home.

A cross was raised on the bluff above St. Anne, which resembled a hill village, with some fifty *kalyvae* (mainly uninhabited) scattered over a very steep slope. My heart was too heavy for me to descend just yet, so I climbed a mule trail, lined with fresh manure, to the deserted *kellí* of St. Artemis, in the shade of a granite outcropping. The dilapidated chapel was locked; in the tiny garden were six withered cabbage plants and a rusted watering can; what looked like a fresh grave had in fact been dug seven years before—the dirt had never settled. When I started down toward St. Anne, a raven followed me from tree to tree, cawing four times, then two, then three. At a white boulder anchoring a pulley for lowering food to a hermit I surveyed the series of cliffs that define the coastline; rising from the *arsanás* far below was the sound of the ferry putting out to sea. The sky was deep blue, the trail of scree so steep I kept losing my footing. The cistern by a shrine cut into a rock archway was empty, and I was parched long before descending a seemingly endless concrete stairway to St. Anne, the Holy Mountain's oldest *skete*, the common area of which is carved out of a cliff four hundred meters above the sea.

Goldsmiths and iconographers live in this dependency of Great Lavra, and I hoped to see them at work. But the guestmaster had other ideas. Under the gazebo in the courtyard he set a pitcher of water, along with peaches, tomatoes, feta cheese, and rusks of bread. I ate and drank with gusto, gazing at the sea, until he invited me to follow him and two Greek pilgrims into the *kyriakón* (literally, "house of the Lord," from which comes the word "church"). Dry leaves skittered across the floor, and it was too dark to study the soot-stained icons. The pilgrims kissed the *skete's* holiest relic—the foot of St. Anne, Mary's mother. The guestmaster told me there was room enough to house only the Greeks—the dormitory was under renovation. At the monastery of St. Paul, an hour's hike up the coast, I was sure to find accommodations.

Along the cliff I walked, sidestepping piles of manure. Plagued by horseflies, I hurried through Nea (New) Skete, an eighteenth-century settlement renowned for the spiritual wisdom of its elders, and came to a road of white gravel, blinding in the sunlight, connecting the *arsanás* of St. Paul and the monastery, which lies under a cliff between two gorges, with the mountain rising starkly behind it. A dramatic setting: floods and avalanches have swept

away walls and buildings that were not breached by pirates and
Catalan mercenaries or razed by fire. And this was where in the
fifteenth century Sultana Maria, bearing the gifts of the Magi,
heard a voice tell her not to come closer, for this was the province
of a greater queen than an Ottoman ruler's Christian wife: the
Queen of Heaven. Thus St. Paul is dedicated to the Purification
of the Virgin. Halfway up the road is a chapel commemorating
the place where she spoke.

The narrow stone courtyard, dominated by the *katholikón*, lay
in shadow. The monks and pilgrims silently shelling peas outside
the refectory did not raise their heads when I walked by. Nor did
the novice writing verses in the waiting room on the second floor.
He was seated by the west window, in the afternoon sunlight, with
a notepad on his knee. I envied him for his concentration: once I
had worked with the same fervor of attention. And when I peeked
in the room on my way to vespers three hours later he was still
hard at it.

"All that I have written is straw," Thomas Aquinas told a fellow
monk, thousands of pages into his effort to prove God's existence
by means of deductive logic. Granted a vision, the details of
which he kept secret, the father of Scholasticism did not write another word. I like to think he discovered the limits of reason, although the legacy of his proofs, his *Summa Theologica*, persists in
the Western imagination. How quickly straw burns, I thought, and
took a seat on the bench curling around the outer narthex (non-
Orthodox are not allowed inside the *katholikón*). I recalled the
words of St. Symeon the New Theologian: "I who am straw receive the Fire"—the necessary attitude for prayer and poetry,
counterparts to scholastic reasoning. A monk came up to me.
"Don't cross your legs," he scolded. Then the chanting began.

A FULL MOON OVER THE SEA. THE OLD HERMIT IN THE CORNER
of the outer narthex was talking feverishly to himself. His sandals
were torn, his habit rolled up to his knees; every few minutes he

would rise to his feet, shuffle to a faucet, and run water over his head. He was what the Orthodox call a Fool for Christ, first described by St. Paul: "We are fools for Christ's sake" (1 Cor. 4:10). This monk's descent into madness had earned him an honored place among his brethren—he was free to speak the truth to anyone, including figures of authority. The Fool for Christ is thus the truest revolutionary: the cross he bears is madness, which points up the deficiencies of reason, upon which most political structures and institutions are based.

Paul defined the role of foolishness in Christian belief:

> For the word of the cross is folly to those who are perishing, but to us who are being saved it is the power of God. For it is written, "I will destroy the wisdom of the wise, and the cleverness of the clever I will thwart." Where is the wise man? Where is the scribe? Where is the debater of this age? Has not God made foolish the wisdom of the world? For since, in the wisdom of God, the world did not know God through wisdom, it pleased God through the folly of what we preach to save those who believe. For Jews demand signs and Greeks seek wisdom, but we preach Christ crucified, a stumbling block to Jews and folly to Gentiles, but to those who are called, both Jews and Greeks, Christ the power of God and the wisdom of God. For the foolishness of God is wiser than men, and the weakness of God is stronger than men.
>
> [1 Cor. 1:18–25]

Foolishness is integral to belief (also to poetry and marriage). This is what Kierkegaard means by a leap of faith: to obey God's will, even against the evidence of our senses and reason, as Abraham was ready to sacrifice Isaac, his only son, because God told him to. This leap of faith defies the logic of the world, a divine contradiction the holy madman grasps better than anyone but the poet and the lover. Poetry and love are indeed the levers of transcendence we know best: a poem balances opposing forces, lovers glimpse eternity in their lovemaking. And my literary apprenticeship was predicated on one of William Blake's "Proverbs of Hell": "If the fool would persist in his folly he would become wise." The same holds for marriage and faith.

The Fool for Christ running water over his head had come from his hermitage for the vigil in honor of St. Paul's founder. If the monastery was not named after the apostle, though there is a tradition that he lived as a hermit in Macedonia, the vigil still embodied his belief that "our citizenship is in heaven, from which we also eagerly wait for the Savior, the Lord Jesus Christ" (Phil. 3:20). Matins gave way to the liturgy, the sun came out, the chanting resumed. It was 9:30 before we went to the refectory. A monk led me to a table apart from everyone else, except for the hermit, who sat alone behind me, talking to himself until a monk came by with a sweet to commemorate the founder. The monk was spilling crumbs into my napkin when the hermit hissed, in English, "Not Orthodox!" The monk scooped up the crumbs and shook his head.

After the meal, a pilgrim caught my arm outside the refectory. I had hoped to speak with an American monk, who was escorting two EU officials up the stairs, but the pilgrim would not let me go. He mourned the changes fostered by the infusion of EU money.

"All this technology!" he cried. "The monks didn't want electricity, which only came a few years ago, and now they love it. This used to be a medieval place. No more."

But at the sight of the Fool for Christ the pilgrim was filled with pity.

"To be a hermit," he said, "you must either be very religious or very disappointed."

ARISTIDES WAS IN A FOUL MOOD. THE COMPUTER SCIENCE GRADuate student fell into step with me on the shore below St. Paul, near the ruined tower, and it was not long after we started up a narrow path along the cliff that he began to complain. The prospect of falling into the sea terrified him, the trail circling the ravine seemed to go on and on, and when after an hour we arrived at the monastery of Dionysiou the guestmaster offered only water. Aristides' plea for ice was met with stony silence. Off we went to the *katholikón*, where a layman on a scaffold was restoring a fresco, wiping off the grime around the Madonna's halo; a novice used an acetylene torch to clean the candlesticks. Aristides asked the supervising monk to display the sacred relics. He wanted to reverence the right hand of St. John the Baptist. I was keen to see the tusk of St. Christopher (c. 250), who was born with a dog's face; it is said that upon his conversion he was bestowed with such beauty that he converted forty-eight thousand pagans, including the pair of courtesans the emperor sent to seduce him. (There is another version of the saint's story: born beautiful, he prayed to God to give him a brutish appearance so that he might be spared temptation. In either case, he died a martyr, beheaded after he was locked in a red-hot metal box, which did not burn him.) But the monk refused to show us anything. Aristides returned to St. Paul, visibly angered.

I had an ambitious plan—to hike north to Simonopetra, catch a ride to Daphne, then walk to the Russikon for the feast of St. Panteleimon. The trail, a rockway twisting over bluffs and around ravines, through dry scrub and bushes, was as punishing as the midday sun. And my first thought upon hearing a woman's voice was that I had lost my mind. Strange siren! I was standing on a cliff when a ferry sailed by, a floating monastery of women looking at the forbidden land. Over a megaphone a guide with a sultry voice was reciting the history of the Holy Mountain. How I longed to be on that ferry! But my fantasy of starting a new life with a tour guide dissolved in a sudden fear of pitching headlong into the sea, before her startled eyes.

And now she was describing the monastery of Grigoriou, which on my first pilgrimage had furnished me with a vision of a place where I might find solace. But I had not intended to stop there—

the Russikon was still many hours away—until I started down the trail and realized that in this heat a break was in order. My last husks of bread I left in a white paper bag nailed to a tree trunk for a hermit, then I hiked through an olive grove to a stone staircase descending to the monastery, perched on a cliff ten meters above the sea. Outside the gate, under an arbor thick with grapes, was a flower bed, with chest-high geraniums, hosta lilies, and roses—a glorious sight that convinced me not to go to the Russikon this day. Inside the gate was a larger grape bower, and at the far end of a courtyard lined with fruit trees in oil barrels was another archway. It was as if I had entered a set of Chinese boxes. Under a mosaic of St. Nicholas I stepped lightheartedly. And the first thing I saw inside the next courtyard was a pair of clocks, on the north wall of the *katholikón*, set at different times, Byzantine and Western.

The waiting room overlooked the sea. Supplied with a guest tray, I was resting on a bench by the open window, cooled by the salt breeze, when the cellarer or *docheiaris*, the monk in charge of provisions, asked, in perfect English, if I wished to join him for a cup of Nescafé. He was about my age, and his story—of travel, hallucinogens, and spiritual wandering—was familiar. He had worked in a variety of professions, including a stint as a music video editor in London, a job he described as trying to figure out how many jump-cuts he could fit into three minutes of footage; he regretted his contribution to the proliferation of images bombarding mankind.

"People go to bed at night punch-drunk," he said with feeling. "They can't *see* anymore."

He had enough images stored in his memory, he said, to last a lifetime; now he had to free himself from their bonds, through constant prayer and vigil, fasts and psalmody. But what St. Basil wrote after retiring to Pontus—"although I have left the distractions of the city, which are to me the occasion of innumerable evils, I have not yet succeeded in forsaking myself"—applied to this monk, too. Which was why he had not left the Holy Mountain since his tonsuring: he did not trust himself. Nor did he gloss over the difficulties of his vocation, though he preferred to speak of its attractions, because, as he said more than once, the last days were at hand, whether mankind died out in a month or three centuries from now. The war in the Balkans, the fires, global warming, plague—anything could trigger the end. The faithless had two choices: to commit suicide or to party until they dropped. He felt blessed to have found his way here.

"Orthodoxy is like a perfectly tuned car," he said. "Why monkey around with the engine? It is the only unbroken line back to Christ and the apostles. The outward trappings are different: the rituals, this habit, the buildings. But the spirit remains the same. Remember that Orthodoxy was squeezed between the popes and Muslims, who wanted to destroy it. That's why we adhered to inwardness, which was our only defense. That's how we preserve the apostolic line.

"Every moment of the monk's life must be directed toward union with God," he added, "even this conversation. Yes, this is a diversion of my energy, but you never know when a word or a gesture will open the door for someone to redirect their life toward God."

He recalled his meeting, in Karyes, with a hermit who had the charism of discernment. The hermit was counseling another monk when he arrived; only later did he realize that the hermit's warning about dabbling in Eastern religions applied to him as well. An earmark of an encounter with a holy man is that you may not appreciate the nature of the gift bestowed upon you until long after, if at all. I remembered the parting words of the guestmaster at Iveron, after my first night on Athos: "Be fruitful, and write many poems." I had done nothing of the sort.

What do you do during spiritual dry spells? I asked the monk.

"Keep physically active," he replied, "and trust that it will pass. That's why patience is the monk's greatest, and most difficult, virtue. First comes the fear of God, then the love of God."

I said it was the opposite in earthly relationships: first love, then judgment.

"First lust," the monk corrected me, "then judgment, and then, if you're lucky, love."

CHRISTOPHER. A LAME UNLETTERED MONK, AN OLD FOOL FOR Christ (*dia christon salos*), told me the story of my namesake, the third-century Canaanite who discovered his vocation when a hermit offered to teach him God's truth. The hermit's job was to guide travelers across a river, and when Christopher replaced him he elected to carry people to safety on his shoulders. One day he carried a child who grew heavier with each step, and he had nearly sunk before the child revealed Himself as Christ—bearing the weight of the world. Christopher (Christ-bearer), patron saint of travelers, was thus entrusted with bringing people to God. He died a martyr.

Vespers was ending. The monk leaned on a makeshift crutch outside the *katholikón*, and when the cellarer had translated his story I joked that my name was too great a burden to bear. The monk pointed his crutch at me like a gun, and laughed. I felt a pang of conscience. He told me to write to the cellarer when I got home, he wanted to keep track of my progress.

The cellarer waited until the monks and pilgrims had left the church before leading me in to see the artwork. In the narthex I adjusted my eyes to the darkness—which should remind me of the darkness of the womb and the tomb, said the cellarer. He crossed himself, then kissed the large frescoes of the archangels Michael and Gabriel, who stand for judgment and love, respectively. He lit a candle and placed it in a circular stand. Into the nave we went.

Three times the monastery had burned down since its founding in the fourteenth century, most recently in 1761; hence the monk first showed me a fresco, on the south wall, of two saints, Grigoriou the Founder and Ioakeim the New Founder, carrying a replica of the monastery. The story goes that after the last fire the monks begged a hermit named Ioakeim to leave his cell and raise the money to rebuild the monastery. Are you crazy? he said. I've been in the wilderness too long. Only if my beard grows to the floor will I undertake such a thing. By the next morning, though, his beard reached the floor, so he set off for Constantinople, hailing a ride with a pasha, who donated a box of gold coins toward his cause. But Ioakeim used the money to redeem Christian slaves and had to go back to the pasha to ask for more. What? said the pasha. If you had been among the slaves, said the hermit, I would have done the same for you. The pasha gave him another box of coins with which the new church was raised. In the fresco Ioakeim's beard hangs from his chin like a vestment and pools around his feet.

Icons of Christ and Mary; biblical scenes; portraits of prophets and apostles, of evangelists and saints—every inch of the *katholikón* was covered, in vivid reds, blues, golds, and whites. The painters worked in cycles (the Christological cycle, the lives of Mary and John the Baptist), in simpler forms and compositions than Byzantine artists; their freshness of vision (which Greek scholars, ever wary of Western influences, label as degenerate) I attributed to the eighteenth-century spiritual renaissance on Athos, which culminated in the publication of *The Philokalia*; the violence of some of the imagery and the fact that in the nave portraits of warrior saints outnumbered those of monks were for me signs of Orthodoxy's growing defiance of Ottoman rule, which soon led to risings against the Turks. The cellarer kissed a portable icon in which the Madonna and Child had their eyes fixed in different directions—shining from within, he said. For icons point to the invisible world, even as the senses, in Nicodemos's words, are portals to the beyond: they complement the Jesus Prayer, which directs our inward gaze toward God.

"It's like climbing a ladder," said the monk. "The higher you go, the more rungs fall away until you near the top. Then death is just a door to the Heavenly kingdom. The great monks live in this world as if they were already in the next. This is why we wear black: to signify our death to this world. Death is for us the way to climb the ladder toward union with God."

But if the monk's figure for the spiritual journey suggested a kind of simplification, another progression was at work in the *katholikón*: elaboration. From the narthex to the sanctuary the paintings grow more complex, because, the monk explained, Orthodoxy offers many routes to the sacred: when your soul needs to feed on beauty, you can look at icons or listen to the liturgy; and when your attention drifts you can say the Jesus Prayer—which is not as simple as it seems: the prayer of the heart reveals infinite depths in the presence of eternity. You may lose your way, said the monk, but if you're grounded in tradition you will eventually return. And here was a pair of icons saved from the last fire— a wonder-working icon of the Madonna and Child and an icon of St. Nicholas, which had inspired the iconographers of the new church. Their scenes from the life of St. Nicholas, to whom the monastery is dedicated, run in a band around three walls of the nave. Here is the patron saint of the sea with waves for a beard, lips like a boat, and a nose and brow curving into an anchor. Now he heals the sick, now he saves a drowning sailor, now he stops the executioner's sword from beheading an innocent man.

Half in jest, I told the monk I owed the saint an apology. An ancestor, Clement Clarke Moore, wrote "The Night Before Christmas," a founding document in the commercialization of the holiday. The children's poem turned Nicholas into the patron saint of shopping.

"This is why we believe the slightest deviation from tradition can wreak havoc," the monk replied. "You never know what the consequences of any change will be."

I recounted a conversation, on a transatlantic flight, with a physicist who built atomic clocks for the geographical positioning system. If one clock is off by a fraction of a second, the physicist said, the entire system will fail, threatening planes, ships, even hikers.

The monk smiled. "Don't worry," he said. "Nicholas forgives you for what your ancestor did. If it wasn't him, someone else would have come along to turn Advent into money."

It was but a few steps from a portrait of St. Christopher clutching a sword, flanked by two warrior saints burned alive, to the Scales of Justice painted above the doorway dividing the fresco of the Second Coming into scenes from Heaven and Hell. On one side is St. Peter turning the key in the golden door to a walled garden in which Abraham, holding the souls of the righteous, awaits the faithful; on the other, a fiery river bearing the damned down into the jaws of a silver dragon. Any decision can tip the scales between salvation and damnation. The monk advised me to keep my mind fixed on the doorway into eternity.

"It's a big game to prepare for," he said solemnly.

THE AIR WAS COOLER IN THE CELLARS—THE MYSTERIOUS WORLD of stone, at the bottom of a dark staircase, which the cellarer unlocked for me after everyone had gone to bed. What joy I felt in the book bindery, where monks used a letterpress to produce miniature leather-bound editions of the Gospel of Mark and the Acts for the abbot to give away. The lead type and bevels, bottles of ink and sheets of paper—these were for me emblems of a sacred order; a cure even seemed within reach for the vertigo I experienced at any intimation of mortality, the sensation that I was on a cliff crumbling into the sea. Across the room was an easel, and as I examined an iconographer's discarded efforts (an icon must be completed in one sitting, before the egg tempera dries; hence the number of failures) the monk described an art that only appears to be formulaic.

"The figure's given, the colors are given," he said, "and this gives you real freedom. You have no idea what freedom such a tradition offers. Think how much you can do with the eyes or the shading. True tyranny is a blank canvas."

Few artists escape the tyranny of the emptiness preceding creation. Rimbaud's systematic derangement of the senses, aleatory music, action painting: bold spirits will try anything to break the stranglehold on the imagination. But the monk was proposing a subtler form of liberation: to improvise within the strictures of Orthodox tradition. Which brought to mind the rhythmic effects that Alexander Pope achieved in his heroic couplets by varying the placement of the caesura, the pause in the line: "Howe'r, what's now *Apocrypha*, my Wit," he writes in his versification of one of Donne's *Satires*, "In time to come, may pass for *Holy Writ*." Thus even a comma can dramatically reinforce meaning for those who have "ears to hear," to borrow a phrase from Jesus (Matt. 11:15). But how many poets and readers can hear such fine distinctions anymore? The same holds for our responses to other art forms. Accustomed to gaudy spectacles, we miss out on the small victories of the craft, which mark a thing of beauty and quicken the spirit.

In the storerooms were plastic containers of olives harvested from the monastic vineyards on the mainland; candle-making machines and blocks of beeswax; a cement vat which would soon be filled with several tons of grapes; oak barrels in which to age the wine; a steamer for producing raki; and, between a pair of chestnut barrels, a mattress, covered with bat droppings, on which the monk slept on hot nights. He served me a glass of water, and while he spoke of the imminence of the last days I understood why Jesus chose the wedding in Cana to reveal Himself. His message is the communion of saints. What the monk offered me was the fellowship that Jesus proclaimed at the feast, drawing the guests together by changing the water to wine. Here by the vat of Communion wine I saw the Eucharist in a new light: how we celebrate the enduring miracle of His presence as well as our daily transformation from solitary individuals into a community of believers. The monk's unexpected gesture of friendship confirmed for me Simone Weil's notion that random acts of kindness can lead us toward God. "God could create only by hiding himself. Otherwise there would be nothing but Himself," she wrote. "Holiness should then be hidden too, even from consciousness in a certain measure. And it should be hidden in the world." But I had seen the inner workings of this monastery. And I could not contain my excitement.

The hour was late when the monk bid me good night. Unable to remember which room had been assigned to me in the guest quarters, I tried several doors before finding the right one. Then I undressed in the dark and lay awake on the hard bed, mulling over what the monk had said about his decision to be tonsured. He had been living at the monastery for some time when the abbot asked him if he wished to take vows. Wait a minute, he thought, then quickly agreed. What stayed with me was the casual way he told the story. For what could be more serious than the questions he had to answer before putting on the habit, the garment of gladness—questions concerning stability, obedience, poverty, and chastity? But he seemed to have discovered his vocation almost by chance. And I was thinking that what had inspired him to become a monk had also brought us together, when the *sémantron* called me to church—to praise Christ Jesus.

IN THE FRESCO OF THE DORMITION, WHICH TAKES UP THE WESTern wall of the *katholikón* at Grigoriou, the Virgin Mother is laid out on a couch, crosswise to her Son, who stands behind her, framed by an almond-shaped aureole called a *mandorla*. With one hand He blesses her, in the other He holds a child swaddled in white: a figure for His mother's soul. Haloed saints and mourning women—the body of the Church—surround Her. In the azure sky angels escort the apostles, in pairs, from their evangelizing missions; another angel stands guard below the bed, his sword raised against a Jew who, according to tradition, touched Mary; his severed hands float above his wrists, like balloons—a pictorial essay in anti-Semitism. Just so my thoughts floated off during the liturgy: now I was in the cellar tasting wine, now I was in bed cavorting with an unknown woman. After the service, when the cellarer invited me to return for Dormition, I eagerly accepted.

Evloyite, I said. Your blessing.

Tou Kyriou, he replied. The Lord's.

With uncommon energy I set out in the brilliant morning light for the Russikon. From now on I would hike with more vigor than I had felt in years, needing only water to sustain me through the heat of the day. I strode with renewed purpose by a stand of prickly pears, then up the ridge from which I had first gazed at Grigoriou. Blessed with a deeper understanding of monastic life, I charged up the switchback below Simonopetra, stopped to refill my water bottle, then continued along the road until a monk gave me a ride to Daphne. From there I tried to hitch a ride to Karyes—my *diamonitirion* had lapsed—but as I neared the monastery of Xeropotamou without flagging anyone down I realized the administrative offices would close soon. So I took the coastal trail, tramping through thorn bushes along a low cliff. There were two footbridges to cross before I came to an olive grove belonging to St. Panteleimon, which in the aftermath of its feast had the air of a college fraternity. The guest quarters by the sea—a five-story stone barracks (half of which lay in ruins), with room for thousands of pilgrims—were thick with flies and empty beer and vodka bottles. Monks and pilgrims lounged around a table in the common room, swilling fruit juice. The guestmaster whisked me into the gift shop, insisting that I buy an icon of St. Christopher and a compact disc of the monks chanting hymns to the Mother of God. Nor would he show me to my room until I had stuffed some drachmas into a box on the wall, below a hand-lettered sign requesting, in English, donations for the rebuilding of the monastery.

The guestmaster's mercantile spirit was at odds with anything I had encountered on the Holy Mountain—and especially with the example set by St. Panteleimon, a doctor who refused payment for his work. Perhaps his greed fell under the rubric of *economy,* the term in Orthodox canon law used to describe how errors in belief or practice may be excused, by the grace of the Holy Spirit, in the interest of the Church's greater good. For a tour of the Russikon (literally, "of the Russians") revealed the magnitude of renovations necessary to restore it. Around a resplendent core—banks of gleaming white façades and green roofs; refurbished onion-shaped domes, chapels, and cells; a new lawn and vineyard—lay a circle of destruction—shells of buildings, with weed-choked floors and sumac growing through the windows: a symbol, I thought, of the Church's embattled position in the modern world. I asked a monk if the monastery had received funding from the Russian patriarchate or the government.

"Unfortunately we cannot expect anything from Russia," he said wearily.

This was not always so. Any history of the Russian presence on Athos is complicated by politics, but there is no disputing the fact that the czars contributed significantly to several *sketes* and monasteries. Russian monks had settled here by the eleventh century, and in 1169, when their numbers had grown too large for one monastery on the northeastern side of the peninsula, they acquired the ruins of another, the Thessalonian, dedicated to St. Panteleimon. Its fortunes fluctuated until 1497, when Ivan III, who freed Russia of the Golden Horde, sent gifts, establishing a tradition of patronage that lasted until the Bolshevik Revolution. A certain symmetry obtained: Moscow threw off its Tatar yoke as Constantinople fell and thus inherited the Byzantine legacy; Muscovites came to believe they lived in the Third Rome (Ivan had married the niece of the last Byzantine emperor); in the Ottoman era the czars acted as Orthodoxy's protectors, dispensing alms, building churches and monasteries all over Eastern Christendom, and sponsoring national movements in the occupied lands. Tragically, no sooner were the Turkish shackles on Orthodoxy lifted than the Bolsheviks launched their attack on religion, and the Church fell captive again, this time to secular ideologues. Byzantium was lost. The patriarchates of Constantinople, Alexandria, Antioch, and Jerusalem had long since been reduced to islands in a Muslim sea. The suffering of the Russian faithful, particularly under Stalin, when the Church was driven underground and more than 150,000 bishops, priests, monks, and nuns were executed (only 200 were still active at the time of the dictator's death), was of a piece with what Christ announced in the Beatitudes and endured on the cross: "Blessed are those who are persecuted for righteousness's sake, for theirs is the kingdom of heaven" (Matt. 5:10). The Eastern rite survived in Greek parishes and diaspora communities; on Mount Athos; in the catacombs.

There was another coincidence to note: a Slavonic version of *The Philokalia* was published in Moscow in 1793—the year that the architects of the French Revolution transformed the hope of mankind into the Reign of Terror. "Bliss was it in that dawn to be alive," Wordsworth wrote of his journey to France in the first days of change. "But to be young was very Heaven!" And if the excesses of the new secular religion soon disillusioned the poet (he became a staunch Anglican—to the detriment of his poetry), there were plenty of other writers to cheer on the prophets of reason, who won the day in Russia. Now that their experiment in social engineering had run its course, though, *The Philokalia* seemed more radically egalitarian than anything proposed by Rousseau or Marx, because it describes the land of the spirit, where the most stringent form of equality is practiced—equality before God. And it was an epileptic novelist who best portrayed these competing revolutionary ideas—one rooted in mystical theology, the other in social justice—that, in an earlier age, might have merged. Not so in nineteenth-century Russia, at the end of the Christian era, as Fyodor Dostoevsky's life and work reveal.

He was a gambler whose heavy losses left him on the edge of penury, writing furiously to stave off creditors; his first masterpiece—*Demons*—was inspired in part by his decision as a young man to gamble with his soul. "I have acquired the truth," he wrote at the time, "and in the words *God* and *religion* I see darkness, obscurity, chains, and the knout." But his membership in a secret utopian society nearly cost him his life. Arrested, tried, and sentenced to death, he and his comrades languished in jail for eight months before being led to a parade ground in groups of three and set against posts to be shot: a Calvary-like scene. In what Dostoevsky imagined was his last minute of life he was filled not with terror but love for his brother and his companions. The czar's reprieve, worked out long before and cruelly withheld until the men had lost all hope, triggered the novelist's first seizure—and marked the beginning of his spiritual regeneration. In a word, he saw the light. And ten years of imprisonment and exile, recounted in *Notes from Underground*, convinced him that he and his countrymen were possessed by demons, like the man named Legion in the Gospel account, which provides an epigraph to *Demons*:

> Now a large herd of swine was feeding there on the hillside; and they begged him to let them enter these. So he gave them leave. Then the demons came out of the man and entered into the swine and the herd rushed down the steep bank into the lake and were drowned.
>
> When the herdsmen saw what had happened, they fled, and told it in the city and in the country. Then people went out to see what had happened, and they came to Jesus, and found the man from whom the demons had gone, sitting at the feet of Jesus, clothed and in his right mind; and they were afraid. And those who had seen it told them how he who had been possessed with demons was healed.
>
> [LUKE 8:32–36]

To exorcise these demons, Dostoevsky dramatized the division in his soul between his yearning to believe and his doubts. He traced a downward spiral, from the questioning of God's existence to the replacement of Him with an exalted image of mankind, to anarchy. He foresaw the dangers of translating the Christian notion of an afterlife into a paradisal future on earth (an idea imported from the West, he was at pains to remind readers) long before the Soviets established a workers' paradise. He knew from experience the ruthlessness of the revolutionaries whose real enemy was God, which is why murder forms the centerpiece of each of his major novels—*Demons*, *Crime and Punishment*, and *The Brothers Karamazov*. What better symbols of the death of God than the ideologically driven killings of a revolutionary, a pawnbroker, and a father? Liberated from the fear of God, the Communists systematically murdered millions of so-called enemies of the people—landowners, merchants, writers, artists, the faithful.

The miracle was that the Church survived, said a monk visiting the Russikon. He thought it would take at least a generation to root out the rot in its hierarchy; that the accommodations the clerics made with the Communist governments in Russia and Romania, Bulgaria and Serbia, were more damaging to Orthodoxy than anything done by the Mongols or the Ottomans. Another Byzantine legacy: if the fall of the Roman Empire sundered the relationship between political and ecclesiastical authorities in the West, in the East the tradition of close connections between the emperor and ecumenical patriarch played into the hands of atheists bent on undermining the influence of clerics. They compromised the ones they did not kill.

Dostoevsky foresaw this, too, giving voice to a prototypical nihilist in his final work, *The Brothers Karamazov*. In literary circles it is customary to read the parable of the Grand Inquisitor that doubting Ivan Karamazov tells his believing brother Alyosha as a prophecy of the looming totalitarian nightmare. But Dostoevsky will not let us forget that the murderous underpinnings of our time were furnished by the erosion of the religious imagination in his. Like the seminarians who gave up the cloth to join the Bolsheviks, prominently Joseph Stalin, Ivan wants to believe but cannot overcome his doubts about a God who will allow a child to suffer; hence his story of Christ's journey to Seville during the Inquisition, fifteen centuries after the Crucifixion. The Son of man heals a blind man, raises a child from the dead, and when a murmur goes up from the crowd He is arrested by order of the Grand Inquisitor, an old Jesuit flush with the fever of burning heretics at the stake. The Inquisitor, recognizing his prisoner, delivers a monologue (Christ never speaks) explaining why He is no longer needed. In a radical rewriting of the temptation in the desert the Jesuit taunts the Savior, saying His rejection of Satan was foolhardy. The people are hungry, he insists, avid for signs, and happy to relinquish the freedom Christ offers, since everything now belongs to the papacy, including the freedom to decide whether to believe in Him; now the clergy will bear this burden of conscience for the faithful. Christ silently accepts the Inquisitor's verdict—that as a danger to the functioning of a well-regulated society He must be condemned—and kisses his "bloodless" lips. The Jesuit shudders—the kiss burns his heart—then flings open the door and orders Christ never to return.

The Russian propensity to accept authoritarian political figures Dostoevsky interpreted as a universal need for certainty, the most potent symbol of which, in theological history, is the Inquisition, the scourge of the Jesuits for whom I worked. Certainty is what we crave in the midst of change, and Dostoevsky, writing in the shadow of the revolutions of 1848 and the first Vatican Council, when the dogma of papal infallibility drove Eastern and Western Christendom yet further apart, drew a parallel between the papal responses to heresy and to the tumult of his time. Ivan's parable, which drips with venom for the papacy, may indeed be read as a restatement of the clash between Rome and Constantinople. Papal logic, Ivan suggests, inevitably leads to the inversion of Christ's message, because it invests in a single man the Messiah's power to decide the fate of any individual. And if the freedom to choose salvation was Christ's greatest gift to mankind, then the Inquisition represents an even greater evil, since it robbed believers of their freedom, providing a blueprint for modern totalitarian regimes, secular and religious.

Which is why Dostoevsky does not grant the Jesuit the last word on freedom. For in the very next book of the novel Alyosha paints a deathbed portrait of his spiritual father, Zosima, based on the biography of St. Tikhon of Zadonsk, one of the holy men or starets who laid the groundwork for Russia's spiritual revival in the nineteenth century—the age of the starets, according to Orthodox theologians. In his hermitage, surrounded by his disciples, Zosima recalls his spiritual awakening, laying special emphasis on his rash decision, as a young military officer, to challenge a rival to a duel. That night he returned to his quarters in a foul mood and struck his orderly, who stood at attention, until he bled. And it was the memory of his orderly's composure that brought him to his senses the next morning. Ashamed, he begged forgiveness of his orderly, realizing that another man, "the image and likeness of God," should never serve him. To the duel he drove in a rapture and cheerfully faced his adversary, who took the first shot, grazing his cheek and nicking his ear. Turning the other cheek, he hurled his pistol into the trees, begged forgiveness of his rival, and resigned his military commission to enter a monastery.

What is a monk? Zosima asks his disciples. Russia's savior. For in the freedom of the modern world the starets sees only isolation, slavery, and suicide, against which he offers the figure of the monk, who wins his freedom, through obedience, prayer, and fasting, from the craving for luxury, which makes the poor envious and never satisfies the rich. In the solitude of his cell the monk clings to the purity of God's truth, which as the need arises will be "revealed to the wavering truth of the world." Indeed it is tempting to imagine a different history for Zosima's troubled land, like unto his prophecy that God will save Russia, and that salvation will come from the people, not their betters—a way of thinking that stands in stark contrast to the cynical calculations of the Grand Inquisitor and his political descendants, the apparatchiks who carried out Stalin's pogroms. It was the people, the starets believed, who would rise up against the atheists to restore Orthodox Russia. And perhaps his prophesy had come true, however belatedly: the peaceful demise of the Soviet order was widely hailed as a miracle.

But even Zosima's witness cannot satisfy Dostoevsky, whose intuitive grasp of the darker fate awaiting his countrymen is reflected in the next book, when the starets' spiritual authority is undermined within hours of his death: the rapid putrefaction of his corpse throws everyone into a quandary. How can these holy relics give off the stench of earthly corruption, not the fragrance of eternity? Some see in this a sign from God: Zosima was a secret sinner. To counter the maligners one monk advances the Athonite argument that the glorification of the saved is determined not by bodily incorruptibility but by the color of the bones after they have lain in the earth. In vain. Zosima's disciples fall silent, and what Dostoevsky calls the scoffers take over, remembering the dead man's sins: pride, abusing the sacrament of confession, and so on. A holy fool, the starets' sworn enemy, enters the cell, making the sign of the cross at each wall to drive out the unclean spirits. He accuses Zosima of gluttony, arrogance, and causing demons to breed like spiders in the corners of his cell. A monk interrupts his reading aloud of the Gospel to order him to leave. An argument ensues. The madman falls to the ground, crying like a child. Everyone rushes to his side, seized by a demonic frenzy, some even proclaiming his righteousness. Only the tolling of the bell brings the monks to their senses. They cross themselves and hurry to church.

A great change has come over Alyosha, though. He leaves the monastery without asking the abbot for permission, and by nightfall trades his innocent faith for a new understanding of his calling. He lies under a tree, mourning his beloved elder's disgrace and defamation; curses God, tormented by an "evil impression" from his conversation the day before with Ivan; then visits Grushenka, a fallen beauty (and paramour of his father and half-brother, Dmitri) determined to ruin him—to no avail. In the evening, when Alyosha returns to the hermitage to pray for Zosima, the monk who ordered the Fool for Christ to leave is reading aloud the story of the wedding at Cana of Galilee. What joy this miracle inspired in the Galileans, the poorest of the poor, Alyosha thinks before he dozes off. In a dream Zosima calls to him from the feast, where he has drunk the new wine, to instruct him to begin his work. Alyosha wakes in a rapture, walks out of the cell, his soul "yearn[ing] for freedom, space, vastness," and throws himself on the ground, sobbing ecstatically, vowing to forgive everyone and everything. Three days later, he leaves the monastery for good, obeying Zosima's order to "sojourn in the world"—an order I took to heart when I first read *The Brothers Karamazov*, as a graduate student.

The poet Joseph Brodsky suggests that Dostoevsky was a Protestant writer in spirit, despite his jailhouse embrace of Orthodoxy and distaste for things Western, because his artistic method— his relentless interrogation of the human psyche, his "dialogue of the spheres and the gutter"—demonstrates a profound distrust of hierarchical structures of belief. Too inquisitive for a creed that brooks no questions, the writer enacts on the page his own Last Judgment, refusing to forgive himself because he knows his own sins better than God or the Church does. He is content neither with the calculations that absolve believers of their faith, as in the parable of the Grand Inquisitor, nor with Alyosha's untested notions of belief; for in literature, Brodsky writes, "Grace doesn't count for much; that's why Dostoevsky's holy man stinks." Thus his novel balances, uneasily, the modern idea that in uncertainty lies our salvation with the ancient promise that the healing word of Christ will save us from the certainty of death.

Polyphony is the term that critic Mikhail Bakhtin used to describe the voices quarreling in Dostoevsky's work—a literary and philosophical strategy, invented by the novelist, to represent the battle between his own skepticism and faith. Unable to resolve the contradiction, he created a range of voices, each embodying an idea in conflict with other ideas, whose seeming freedom from authorial control lends a joyous, even carnival-like, sense of plenitude to the action. What the reader retains from these last novels is an impression of symphonic grandeur—a liturgical version of which I heard in the *katholikón* of St. Panteleimon, during vespers, in the choir's polyphonic chant, which sounded like the music of the spheres. It took a pair of monks to ring the czar's thirteen-ton bell that called us to the cavernous church. Square red posts decorated with gold scrollwork and portable icons supported eight onion-shaped domes; on the bright white walls were icons and frescoes inspired by Italian Renaissance painters — oversize realistic pictures, lavishly colored: garish testaments to the eighteenth-century Russian infatuation with the West, when the contagion of secular humanism spread through salons in St. Petersburg and Moscow, and chant in four-part harmony, another Western innovation, was introduced into the Russian Church. What came to the Russian monastic establishments on Athos was a taste for grandiosity tempered by a melding of diverse voices: a fair description of Dostoevsky's last novels. In the *katholikón* of St. Panteleimon the decor was gaudy, the chant divine.

Near me, a young monk with a wispy beard stood very straight, praying with the fervor of Alyosha Karamazov. In the next stall slept a visiting bishop. "We all live by the invisible energy of God," writes a former abbot of the Russikon. "Whatever man loves, whatever he turns to, this he finds. If he loves earthly things and they settle down in him, he will become earthly himself and will be bound up by those same things. On the other hand, if he will love heavenly things they will dwell in his heart and will make him fully alive. When man has God always in his mind, it means that the Kingdom of Heaven has come upon him." Evidently the bishop's love of earthly things had got the better of him. His snoring brought a smile to the face of another monk.

"Better to sleep inside the ark of the church than outside," he told me.

Into the nave (from the Latin *navis* and Greek *naus*, for "ship") of the *katholikón*, the ship with Christ at the helm, shuffled a thick-bearded pilgrim who had traveled for seven days by train from Vladivostok. Three times he fell to his knees before an icon, bowed his head to the ground, then rose to his feet, grandly crossing himself. At first I thought he was a Fool for Christ, but in fact he suffered from the same malady as the sleeping bishop.

"My mind is not right," he would tell me later. "I need Doctor Absolut." Not a healing vision of the Godhead, mind you, but the spirits distilled of fermenting potatoes.

It was time to cense the church. "Let my prayer arise in Thy sight as incense," the deacon chanted. The pilgrim and the young monk bowed gravely. The sleeping bishop did not stir.

THE RUSSIAN SOCIOLOGIST HAD MADE SEVEN PILGRIMAGES TO Athos since moving to Greece three years before—a providential decision, he said, born of his rediscovery of faith. He found solace in the religious customs of the Greeks, as well as a new subject for research: the resurgence of faith in his homeland. Yes, many religion teachers do not know the truth, he told me in the common room of the guest quarters, but children see through their falsehood, just as they saw through their lessons in communism. It was also providential that the bones of the last czar and his family had finally been laid to rest in St. Petersburg, in an elaborate church ceremony. Russia, the sociologist declared, is regaining its Orthodox heritage. Yet his own wife did not believe in God.

"After seventy years of teaching that there is no God, it is very hard," he said wearily.

Nor was it clear how he put bread on the table, since he was not attached to a university and his writings paid next to nothing. When I pressed him about his livelihood he replied, "If you believe in God, you don't have to worry about tomorrow."

His simple faith was more endearing than the bluster of an overweight hermit visiting from Quebec (he called himself a frequent-flying hermit) or the guestmaster's persistent salesmanship, which sent me scurrying to my room. Portable icons— St. Panteleimon, Gabriel and Michael, the Madonna and Child—hung from the white walls; the window opened onto the sea. My thoughts drifted back to a decisive encounter in graduate school with Joseph Brodsky. His fall seminar at Columbia—three hours of brilliant talk punctuated by an occasional question, the answers to which usually irritated him—left me reeling. He spoke aphoristically, in absolute terms: e.g., "The cornerstones of Western civilization are *The Iliad* and the Bible." His jesting had a moral purpose. When martial law was declared in Poland, he said, "The Russians have invented a new holiday: Tanksgiving." Even his tirades were instructive.

"You Americans have no sense of geography," he cried when a student made the mistake of asking him where Labrador was, "which means you have no sense of space. And you have no sense of history, which means you have no sense of time."

His own sense of time was acute: at forty, recovering from open-heart surgery, he seemed to savor everything, as if aware of his impending early death. Forbidden to smoke, at the sight of a student's cigarettes Brodsky would dive across the seminar table, begging, "Please, may I have one?" Then he would smoke in silence, inhaling deeply, preparing the next installment of his monologue. He favored the outlandish. In a lecture on the Greek poet Constantine Cavafy, for example, he promised to tell us the secret to becoming great poets. We leaned forward. "You must be gay," said the man who had just been named to *Cosmopolitan*'s list of the world's most eligible bachelors. He had a serious point to make: as a homosexual Cavafy viewed society from the privileged position of an outsider—the same privilege Brodsky must have felt in his involuntary exile from his homeland. The next week he advised us to go to law school, where we would learn a logic analogous to poetic logic and another language—this, from a high school dropout who was teaching himself to write poems and essays in English.

Needless to say, his commanding presence undermined my confidence as a writer. After class I would walk for hours, meditating on what he called a poet's "code of conscience," the formal, thematic, and linguistic choices that define an aesthetic sensibility, philosophy, and morality. Literature offers a sharper sense of how to live, and even though my writings lay lifeless on the page I was nevertheless forming a code of conscience under Brodsky's tutelage. For every week he required us to memorize a hundred lines by Auden or Hardy, to which I added poems by Hopkins and Donne, preparing the ground for my real work.

His most enduring lesson came later, in a commencement address he delivered at Williams College and then published in a book of essays. The form for such a speech is simple: to instruct graduates in their future conduct—a forgettable exercise for most speakers. Not Brodsky. His theme was evil: how to recognize it, how to combat it. He described a scene in a Soviet penal colony, where he had been sent for the crime of being a "social parasite" (read: poet and Jew). One day the guards challenged the prisoners to a woodcutting contest. The prisoners had no choice in the matter, but one man (no doubt Brodsky himself) rendered the challenge absurd by cutting wood through the morning break, lunch, the afternoon break, and dinner. The sardonic expressions on the faces of the guards and prisoners gave way to looks of bewilderment and then of terror. Not until long after dark did the man stagger into his cell and collapse on his bed. The guards never challenged the prisoners to another contest.

Brodsky credits the young man with remembering the Sermon on the Mount better than Tolstoy or Gandhi, the heroes of nonviolent resistance. Christ often spoke in triads, and while the advocates of passive resistance to evil frequently invoke the first verse of His saying—"whoever slaps you on your right cheek, turn the other to him also"—Brodsky reminds us that the Son of man continued without pause: "If anyone wants to sue you and take away your tunic, let him have your cloak also. And whoever compels you to go one mile, go with him two" (Matt. 5:39–41). Which is to say: turn evil on its head. Love your enemy to excess, until he recognizes the absurdity of his behavior—and your humanity. Otherwise, the poet concludes, "a line taken out of context will leave you crippled." It was his genius to restore the verse to its context, forging a link between poetry and faith: "In the beginning was the Word, and the Word was with God, and the Word was God" (John 1:1). As the sun set over the sea I reflected on his ecumenical spirit—he wrote dozens of poems about the Nativity, which he called "a universal point of departure"—and how the judge at his trial for social parasitism demanded to know who had made him a poet. God, Brodsky replied. No wonder he was packed off to Siberia.

KARYES, AGAIN. AFTER THE LITURGY AT THE RUSSIKON I HIKED back to the main road, where a laborer in a pickup gave me a ride to the capital. The sky this morning was overcast, the smoky wind strong off the sea. The laborer said the fires on the mainland had worsened. But the other news—that Serbian forces had destroyed hundreds of villages in Kosovo, sending tens of thousands of Albanians into flight; that Islamic terrorists had bombed two American embassies in East Africa, prompting the U.S. military to launch cruise missiles at their training camps in Afghanistan—took a backseat to the question of Bill Clinton's looming impeachment. I got out at the plaza, where an old fire truck was parked, its hose draped along the stone terrace, like a snake lying in the sun; and when I had secured an extension on my *diamonitirion* I visited the police station, intending to follow up on another news story: the recent disappearances of several pilgrims—victims, perhaps, of foul play. On the walls were signs for the missing men, most of whom were described as suffering from mental illness. But the policeman on duty refused to answer any questions about them, and then his superior emerged from his office to show me to the door.

It is no secret that the Holy Mountain attracts its share of troubled pilgrims—alcoholics, drug addicts, the addled and insane. One monastery even runs an informal substance abuse clinic, in which as many as twenty recovering addicts receive room and board in exchange for work and regular church attendance. The monk who described the program to me blamed the drug problem on the vacancy of materialistic society. We were drinking coffee in a room off the kitchen, seated at a table with a novice who was pressing linens on an antique roller iron, neatly stacking them beside the machine. The monk believed that in the industrialized world the connections between the soul, intellect, and body had been short-circuited. Repentance was our only hope. Otherwise, he said, we will soon be dancing on dead bodies. Just then the guestmaster entered with a young man in tears—a pale, bespectacled Greek in the throes of withdrawal from heroin; to salve his pain he had just polished off a bottle of whiskey. I'm crazy, he kept saying in English. Then, in Spanish, *sí, sí*. The guestmaster and monk agreed that the other addicts would watch over him until he had sobered up, and when the guestmaster led him away the monk shook his head: the drunken pilgrim was probably too young to be cured.

The monk waxed philosophical, wondering why modernity seemed to produce more drug addicts and depressives than what were once called the possessed. And while he traced a history of rebellion to contemporary society—from the sex, drugs, and rock-and-roll of his generation to the indifference (his word) of the next—I thought of the Austrian pilgrim who took me aside at St. Paul's to ask about my sneakers. It turned out he had been a professional long-distance runner—a shoe manufacturer had sponsored him—until he was trampled in a marathon. In the hospital he fell into a suicidal depression that persisted even after his broken bones had healed. Afraid to return to competition, unable to hold a job, he found no relief in analysis, counseling, or a regimen of psycho-pharmaceuticals. Not until he made a pilgrimage to St. Paul's did his spirits lift. He soon converted to Orthodoxy, and whenever his demons reappeared he would retire to the monastery to stay until he was well. The abbot even permitted him to run on the logging road above the monastery, out of sight of the monks. The pilgrim called his recovery a miracle. He hoped some day to be able to compete in a hundred-mile race through Death Valley.

Some Orthodox theologians believe that prayer and the counsel of the church fathers will cure any mental ailment, because it is sinfulness, the passions, that leads the mind astray. This is in keeping with Christ's ministry of healing the possessed— Legion, Mary Magdalene, the madman who lived in a cave. In the New Testament madness is the province of demons, and the language of demonic possession still fuels the writings of some theologians—sin is a disease, redemption is a remedy for the soul, the sacraments are spiritual medicines, the Church is a hospital, and so on. But when I put this to a monk with an advanced degree in psychology he warned against the dangers of adhering to a simplistic model. He said we must distinguish between spiritual illness, which is rooted in the passions, and mental illness, which results from a chemical imbalance, an injury to the brain, or other physical problems. Few monks, though, are trained to make such a distinction, which may well determine an individual's fate.

As for those who come to Athos and cannot be healed? Some fall or pitch themselves off cliffs or vanish, perhaps at the hands of the marauders said to prey on solitary pilgrims walking in the remoter parts of the peninsula. The rumors of foul play were still on my mind when I went from the police station to the Protaton, where the mason chipping away the saltpeter under an icon of the Harrowing of Hell was pleased to point out that in this version of the event Roman Catholic sinners rise while the Orthodox fall. There was no sign of the *prosmonarios*, the monk responsible for the *Axion Esti*, so I took a closer look at the miracle-working icon of the Virgin in its glass case. "Worthy it is to magnify Thee, Mother of God," the monks chant in the liturgy; on Good Friday they praise Christ in the same fashion: "Worthy it is to glorify Thee, Giver of Life"; and in the most popular modern Greek poem, *The Axion Esti*, Odysseas Elytis writes, "Worthy it is the song from afar," a song swelling with "the north winds and hazels of Athos." God works in mysterious ways: the Nobel laureate's spiritual autobiography, which adapts the liturgy to contemporary history, mixing hymns, psalms, and readings, was set to music in the 1960s; even as the Athonite monastic population was reaching its nadir, millions of Greeks were memorizing lines inspired by the most precious treasure on the Holy Mountain—an icon closed off to my view when the *prosmonarios* swept into the church and ushered me out.

On Holy Spirit Street a monk on a bulldozer stopped to let four of his brethren cross. Pilgrims drifted in and out of the shops and restaurant. The loudest voices in the crowd waiting for the bus to Daphne belonged to a pair of American monks. I yearned to speak with them—my mind was swirling with ideas—but they could not be distracted. So I set out for the northern monasteries (and the distant songs, the hazel trees), heading into a wind that tasted of smoke.

TO AVOID TEMPTATION, AN ATHONITE MONK WASHES ONLY HALF of his body at a time—the odor of stale sweat is an essential element of an encounter with a holy man—and pilgrims are advised to show similar restraint (a monk who entered a bathroom in the Russikon as I soaped my chest flared with anger at my indiscretion); short pants and swimming are forbidden. But after hiking for several hours in the heat I came to a deserted stretch of beach, beyond a pine grove north of the monastery of Docheiariou, and could not resist stripping off my clothes to wade into the sea. The water was warm, the sunlight blinding, and as I floated above the smooth rocks, washing my arms and legs, a memory surfaced from my childhood—the night my mother mistook my suntan for dirt and scrubbed my neck until my skin began to peel, which sent her into a fury.

We were visiting her parents in northern Maryland, in a split-level brick house known in the village as Mending Hill. My grandfather was a country doctor, my grandmother was the organist at St. James Episcopal, and when we stayed with them in the summer our lives revolved around his practice and the church. In the morning, while patients crowded into the basement office, my sisters and I attended vacation Bible school; in the afternoon I accompanied my grandfather on house calls to hill farms and ramshackle homesteads. At dinner, through the dining room window, I would watch the parking lot fill with cars and pickups for evening office hours, which lasted until it was nearly bedtime. Then my grandfather would climb the stairs and sit in the kitchen to drink a beer and eat a plate of cheese and crackers dipped in mustard. His grateful patients (he never took a vacation, he wrote off the debts of the uninsured) gave him so much cheese at Christmas that he had to buy a second freezer to store it all.

Of the church on top of the hill I remember very little: a white gravel driveway winding through the trees; a green stucco wall through which the rector put his fist one Sunday, during the sermon; a story of a drunken uncle making a scene at my parents' wedding. He was a businessman who hired a railway car to bring my father's family from New Jersey and drank so much on the trip that when the wedding party arrived at the church he stumbled into an open grave, dragging another woman down with him. The social chasm between Montclair and Mending Hill must have seemed unbridgeable. The tensions between the families never abated.

I barely registered this as a child. What I did know was that Mending Hill provided a safe haven for my sisters and me. My parents used the rod more sparingly than at home, and from my grandfather we learned lessons in the healing power of touch. Once he wrapped a handkerchief around a wart on my finger, promising it would vanish within a week—and it did. Another time he lanced a blister on the sole of my foot—I had just stepped on my father's discarded cigarette—and the relief I experienced as the watery matter poured out bordered on the miraculous.

Miraculous, too, was my grandfather's gift for water dowsing. One day he cut a divining rod from a hickory branch and walked with me across the backyard, between the martins' house fixed atop a flagpole and the small incinerator, until the wand curved downward toward the well. Nothing happened when I held the branch. But when he took it in his hands and let me hold his arms, which strained under the curving action of the wood, I felt the tug of the hidden water, like a calling—an intimation of the life of the spirit, a source I still seek in love, poetry, and prayer.

THE HERMIT HAD GONE TO KARYES FOR SUPPLIES. HIS LAY AT-
tendant, a short fat man whose mottled legs resembled sausages
spilling out of their skins, guarded the hermitage, a two-room hut
on a slope above the sea. The former naval commando had blue
eyes, a silver handlebar mustache, a drunkard's bulbous cheeks.
He was in bad shape, not because I had rousted him from a nap
to ask for water but because over the weekend he had polished off
his last two bottles of raki. Stavros, for that was his name, vowed
not to drink again until the weather turned cold, when he would
go to Vatopedi to cook wild boar for the laborers. Then he would
be drunk from morning until night for a whole month. All the
same he hoped the hermit would return with more wine and raki.

The privations of the ascetic life had taken their toll on
Stavros. There was no sugar for the coffee we drank at the picnic
table, no *loukoumi*, and nothing for the trio of cats that followed
him around the hut. Yet he had no wish to live on the mainland
again. "The outside world is too much problem," he said, and
then recited another grievance: how the hermit used a power saw
to carve crosses for the shops; when the diesel generator was running, Stavros headed for the hills to pick tea leaves, several bundles of which were drying over the sink, along with onions and
oregano; these he bagged and sold in Ouranoupolis.

The other problem was that after ten days of eating pasta and
beans he yearned for fish, which the hermit caught with a speargun, donning a snorkel and flippers and paddling far from shore;
on the table were more copies of a glossy spearfishing magazine
than holy books. Stavros himself was in no shape to fish today,
even from the rowboat.

A hermit with a speargun — I was trying to reconcile this image
with the writings of the church fathers when Stavros lit a cigarette
and extolled the virtues of a monk who laid mines around his garden and orchard to keep wild boars from trampling them — a vari-
ation on the local custom of fishermen hurling sticks of dynamite
into the water to stun fish before gathering them in. The trick is

timing: you have to light the fuse and let go of the dynamite just before it explodes, or else the water will extinguish it; hence the number of one-armed fishermen in Greece.

Bad timing had cut short Stavros's naval career as well, though he refused to discuss how he had shattered his leg, which left him with a limp. All he could think about was eating fish. In this he resembled the cats rubbing up against him. What to do? He tuned his radio to the church station broadcasting from the next peninsula and awaited the hermit's return.

THROUGH THE HEAT OF THE DAY I WALKED, SWEATING THROUGH one shirt after another, swilling water at every cistern. I was fasting—and felt full. I understood in a new light the Gospel story of Jesus feeding five thousand people with only five loaves of bread and two fishes (Mark 6:30–44). "Taking the five loaves and the two fish, he looked up to Heaven, and blessed and broke the loaves, and gave them to his disciples to set before the people; and he divided the two fish among them all." Take, bless, break, give: the four elements of the Eucharist are here in this story. What Jesus offered the hungry was the elements of faith, which during this pilgrimage I was beginning to experience in its dynamic dimension, as a process, not an accomplished fact. I was burning, I was walking at a brisk pace, I was learning to see. Prayer had become for me what Thomas Merton described as a "kind of hidden, secret, unknown stabilizer, and a compass too"—a compass that pointed to Athos, where I had entered into what a medieval theologian called "a dialogue and a union with God." And still I could not stop thinking about women.

AN ATHONITE FATHER SUGGESTS THAT "THE HUMBLE MONK IS always a painter—a 'zografos' in Greek, which means that he 'writes life' "—the life of Christ. And it was at the Bulgarian monastery of Zographou that I began to seriously consider how to inscribe His life into my own. I had embarked upon what early Christians called the Way, guided by prayer and reading, a journey that seemed as circuitous as my route to Zographou. Following Stavros's directions, I took the wrong trail from the sea to the ridge; my water bottle was dry and the shadows were lengthening when I entered the narrow courtyard of Kostamonitou, last in the hierarchy. Nor did I realize my mistake until a Greek monk hailed me. Begging his pardon, I hastened down the road to a trail that looked as if it cut across the wooded valley but which in fact ended beyond a pile of logs, in a tangle of brush. Exhausted, I returned to the coast, hiked to the next *arsanas*, and followed another dusty road for an hour until I came to Zographou, where vespers had just concluded.

An afternoon at a monastery in the mountains near Sofia had kindled my interest in the Bulgarian Church, the first Slavic national church. My host that day was a psychiatrist who had spent a summer in the monastery at the age of three. Parents were forbidden to visit their children in this Communist experiment in child-rearing, and the psychiatrist had a vivid memory of adults hiding in the woods to catch glimpses of their children. I am certain the experience left its imprint on me, he said dryly, refusing to follow the crowd of visitors into the church. I wondered if the resurgence of Orthodoxy would help his countrymen come to terms with the Communist legacy. He shook his head. A nun left off selling votive candles to shoo away a woman in a tank top and shorts, an argument ensued, the women screamed at each other until another nun intervened. The clerics are no help, the psychiatrist muttered. They're living in the Dark Ages.

It was true that after the fall of communism six Bulgarian bishops had publicly repented for conniving with the authorities. But the psychiatrist thought too much damage had been done to society for clerics untrained in counseling to address. Only skilled therapists can help, he said, his professional bias blinding him to the fact that the rite of confession provides the model for the talking cure. Just as the priest exhorts the penitent to tell all—"Take

care, then, lest having come to the physician's you depart un-
healed"—so the psychoanalyst leads the patient through memories, dreams, and desires to foster greater self-awareness. And the
clerics' lack of credibility was hardly confined to Orthodoxy. In
the midst of our marital crisis, for example, Lisa and I had never
considered turning to our Episcopal priest for counsel. Instead we
had embarked upon a course of therapy for couples, with uncertain results. It was one thing to recognize destructive habits of the
heart, quite another to escape their bonds: every prison has its attractions. And while divorce offered a possible escape route from
our problems, our love for our daughter kept coaxing us back to a
different vision of marriage. I have seeds in my belly, Hannah had
said on the eve of my departure. That's why I can walk. Her presence, her needs, her freshness of vision—these were helping us to
come to our senses. We had to make our marriage work.

In little ways—a word, a gesture—we might begin to repair
the damage we had inflicted on each other—a theme of individuals, couples, and nations alike, which I pursued at Zographou.
As it happened, my host was also a doctor, an internist who had
given up his practice in Sofia to become a monk, and after compline we took a walk through an olive grove lined with cypresses,
past a decrepit hospital once equipped to serve three thousand
monks (fifteen now lived at Zographou), to an abandoned school.
The monk unlocked the door and ushered me down a darkened
corridor of classrooms to a bench on a rusted balcony. In the twi-
light swallows swept around the trees as the monk described in
methodical English (his sixth language) a series of cures inspired
by prayers offered to Zographou's miracle-working icons; voices
warning one monk about pirates and commanding another to become a hermit; the vision granted to the monastery's tenth-
century founders. Three brothers from the ancient Bulgarian
capital of Ohrid, a town by the lake of the same name between
Macedonia and Albania, could not agree on the dedication of
their new monastery, so they prayed for guidance to help them
choose between the Virgin, St. Nicholas, and St. George. One

night a light shone down from Heaven onto the altar, where they had placed a blank panel of wood; by dawn this had turned into an icon of St. George.

"It was not made by man," said the monk. "It was divinely made." And when I raised an eyebrow he warned me about the invisible knife that cut off the finger of a skeptical bishop who poked the icon. The finger was still embedded in the icon, which I was not allowed to see.

Tradition holds that St. Luke was the first iconographer, painting Mary's likeness on her kitchen tabletop. The Gospels are sometimes called verbal icons of Christ, since they depict the Word of God revealed in the life of His Son. And *The Philokalia*, which in the words of its Russian translator "contains an interpretation of the secret life in our Lord Jesus Christ," also serves as an icon, a window onto eternity, revealing new vistas for the prayerful reader. Icons, Scripture, *The Philokalia*—these were my chief means of inscribing Christ's life in my own, of mending my marriage and my soul, all mediated through prayer, which now occupied a large part of my imagination. For iconography, artistic and verbal, is a form of prayer.

It was perhaps inevitable that a monk from Zographou, Dionysios of Fourna, wrote the authoritative text on iconography, *The Painter's Guide* (1853). He explains everything from the correct rendering of individual saints to the arrangement of iconographic cycles in a Byzantine church, in which elevation is the theme, with tiers of icons climbing from the visible world to the spiritual. On the lowest level are portraits of saints and ascetics, holy men and patrons. Then come scenes from the lives of Christ and the Theotokos; in the pendentives of the cupola are the four Evangelists, with Matthew and John placed in the east, toward the light, *Ex Orient lux*, to point up their descriptions of Christ's human and divine natures, respectively. In the apse beyond them rise the Theotokos, the Divine Liturgy, the apostles, and the church fathers, and then, near the cupola, the angels and prophets. Lastly, gazing down from within the cupola, the highest point in the church, is Christ Pantokrator, the omnipotent. In one hand He holds a book, a symbol of His presence in the liturgical assembly, and with the other He blesses the worshippers.

The role of religious imagery in worship troubled theologians from the early days of the Church. Some saw the legacy of pagan idolatry at work in the veneration of icons; others took to heart Jewish and Muslim criticism of the practice; all fed the controversy over Christ's nature: is He human? Divine? Both? In this version of the tension between the real and the imagined, which drives most human endeavors, including the first six ecumenical councils, the Church attempted to define the proper uses of the imagination. Broadly speaking, Western iconography veered toward the illustrative, Eastern iconography toward the liturgical: realistic biblical scenes versus images of the sacred. And this argument over the nature of representation, which continues down to the present (think of the debates between figurative painters and Abstract Expressionists), concerned the most intimate question of all: how can we know God? An icon is the Word of God ("written" in egg tempera, according to theologians, not painted), and if Christ is mysteriously present in the Eucharist, the Orthodox also believe that the veneration of icons makes His absence visible—an exercise of faith and the imagination, which always has its detractors.

They came to the fore in the eighth century, when the Ottoman threat in Asia Minor gave iconoclast bishops in Constantinople an excuse to blame the empire's weakness on the veneration of icons. In the name of reviving the faith, they convinced Emperor Constantine V to convene a synod, in 753, at which iconodules (image-worshippers) were condemned as heretics; monks were persecuted, icons destroyed. Orthodoxy's most violent theological debate left a long trail of blood across Byzantium, and it was not until the seventh, and last, ecumenical council, in 787, that the value of iconography was reaffirmed. Even so a second wave of iconoclasm washed over the empire in 815, during the reign of Leo V the Armenian. Once again icons were destroyed, church walls whitewashed, monks martyred. And the Triumph of Orthodoxy in 843 hardly vanquished the spirit of iconoclasm. Indeed Protestant Reformers burned icons, toppled statues of the Virgin, and whitewashed churches with the same zeal as the Turks and then the Communists. Distrust of the imagination runs deep, in religious, political, and cultural waters.

Not so in our emotional lives. The role of the imagination in affairs of the heart is the stuff of literature. In the first flush of love we invent details about our beloved, often later contradicted; navigating the distance between our imagined views of the beloved and their real presence is what determines whether a relationship sinks or sails. This I understood not only as a lover but as a poet praying to hear the call of either the divining or the recording angel. For in my pantheon of literary influences Kafka's fabulism was no less important than Dostoevsky's realism. And it was in *Another Republic*, an anthology of modern European and South American poets crucial to my apprenticeship, that the different workings of the imagination were first spelled out for me. The editors divided the writings into two categories: the mythological and the historical, poems that uncovered archetypal imagery to restore to the familiar world a sense of the miraculous, and poems that bore witness to political and social events. In a minor fashion I obeyed the same poetic impulses, now creating surrealist fables, now interpreting the contours of daily life. But as the monk on the balcony explained how icons can serve as prayers to lift us upward it became clear to me that the world brimmed with meaning, if only I had eyes to see. I realized my work as a poet was not to steer between the claims of the imagination and the imperatives of the real but to discover a route from the visible to the invisible, from witness to myth.

Such was the lesson of Georgia O'Keeffe's practice of painting several versions of the same landscape, abstracting it element by element until she caught its essence. If her first paintings of, say, a fold in the dry hills of northern New Mexico were highly realistic, in subsequent versions she would remove one detail after another, distilling the mysterious presence at the heart of the place: what the religious call God. Indeed O'Keeffe translated her spiritual ideas onto canvas; her images of flowers, bones, doors, ladders, mountains, rivers, and clouds became routes to the transcendent. And her resolution to intertwine her life and work in an artistic fashion, to fill space in a beautiful way, was akin to the Orthodox notion that beauty is the beginning of love, of prayer. An eye conditioned by beauty may come to see that everything is sacred.

I knew this from my courtship of Lisa, when the world around us seemed to shimmer—the Scotch broom blossoming on the bluff above Puget Sound, the purse seiners drawing in their nets, the snow gleaming on the distant peaks of the Olympic Mountains. She is a beautiful woman, which in the nature of things I sometimes forget. But from the very beginning of our courtship I loved her unadorned grace, her uncluttered sense of style, her restrained musicianship; the clean phrasing she favored on the violin corresponded to her preference for a natural look, which suited her features. Once, just before we were married, we got into an argument over a painting of Mount Rainier: the colors I praised as innovative she considered garish—an aesthetic vision I adopted over the course of our marriage. But now I had to learn to see her anew.

Marriage, like iconography, is a form of abstraction: ideally, we see through each other to the divine spark at the core of our separate selves—"each becomes for the other an icon," in the words of Philip Sherrard. But just as soot must be removed from icons, so we must cleanse our inward eye, the eye of the imagination, to really see the beloved. We think we know each other; avoid true intimacy; fall prey to temptation, seeking others or subscribing to debased forms of the imagination—the television ads for phone sex, for example, that kept me awake the night before my pilgrimage. Marriage can teach us how little we understand each other, how mysterious we remain even to ourselves—a lesson familiar to apophatic theologians.

Before my first pilgrimage I had blamed Lisa for most of our problems. No more. Prayer, Scripture, readings in patristic literature, sessions with a marriage counselor: my thinking, my sinfulness, was becoming clearer. An honest reckoning can foster the penitential spirit necessary for healing a rift, just as the sacrament of Confession, the prelude to Communion, is integral to receiving God's saving Word. This self-examination, this truth telling, is part of the process of purification recommended by the church fathers for ridding the soul of its destructive habits, its passions. On Athos I witnessed pilgrims confessing, not in a confessional as in Roman Catholic churches, but seated in a room by a monk who draped a vestment over his shoulder to administer the rite. If art is confession transformed into line and color, rhythm and rhyme, then for the sake of my marriage I needed to write with the confessor's words in mind: "Behold, my child, Christ stands here invisibly and receives your confession: therefore do not be ashamed or afraid, and hide nothing from me." But how many pages, in a lifetime of writing, possess that candor? A poet said he suffered from writer's block only when he did not tell the truth. This was precisely why poetry had deserted me — and why my marriage had fallen apart.

Just as I had to see Lisa afresh, so I had to train my eye to really appreciate icons. A monk said that iconography places the lives of Christ, the Theotokos, and the saints in a spiritual context, in images of grace as it exists timelessly in time: the future now. This accounts for the complex perspective and stylized appearance of the figures, which some Western critics mistake for a lack of artistic skill. Icons tell the story of the ineffable, said the monk, more in the geometry of a figure, the intersection of planes, and symbols than in themes and schools of style.

But many works of art map the journey from reality to the spiritual. There was, after all, a metaphysical dimension to the flowering of abstraction in modern art, as the color-field paintings of Mark Rothko testify. He wanted his viewers to experience before his abstractions the kind of religious awe they felt at the altar. But the retrospective exhibit of his career at the Guggenheim, which spiraled upward to the top of the museum as if in ascent to Heaven, concluded not with a vision of transcendence but with the late dark works that seemed to prefigure his suicide. In bright or muted colors Rothko's paintings point to the Beyond (one critic remarked that his work had the same "impassive authority of the authentic icon"), though when I saw this exhibit the darkness of his vision was what spoke to me. My college romance was on the verge of collapse, and I was closer in spirit to Rothko in his final days than to the church fathers he liked to read. That his search for transcendent meaning was doomed to failure I took as a given until I started reading patristic literature. Then I gained some insight into why an artistic enterprise may darken without the anchorage of tradition, which confers sacredness on even ordinary icons.

What Orthodoxy offers is light. Transfiguration, the last feast of the liturgical year, was in the offing, when monks and pilgrims would climb Mount Athos for a vigil in the Russian-built chapel known as Metamorphosis. What a change occurred in human thinking when Jesus took His disciples up a mountain and "was transfigured before them. His clothes became shining, exceeding white, like snow, such as no launderer on earth can whiten" (Mark 9:2–3). History itself was transformed when He said, "I am the light of the world" (John 8:12), a light that shines in the darkest recesses of the soul of every man, woman, and child. The candle lit before an icon calls us to that light, reminding us, in the words of a Russian theologian, that just as the vigil lamp cannot be lit without a match, so our virtues, which are combustible matter, require the holy fire of God's grace—the fire that touched Cosmas, for example, a saint from Zographou (d. 1323), who was saved by the Theotokos. The monk-physician said Cosmas was praying to an icon of her to save his soul when a voice instructed him to leave the monastery and go live in a cave. There it is, said the monk, pointing to a dark hill in the distance. You should visit it tomorrow.

ST. COSMAS'S CAVE WAS NOT EASY TO FIND IN DAYLIGHT. FROM Zographou I headed west on the dirt road to the sea, entered the woods at the half-hidden sign for Chilandari, and followed the trail to the top of the first hill. But something seemed amiss, so I returned to the road, which was more dust than dirt, walked back to the monastery, and started down the eastern slope of the peninsula, only to realize this too was wrong. And I had just regained the trail to the Serbian monastery when I met a Russian monk also in search of the cave. Up the stone walkway we hiked through the trees until we glimpsed the cave on the other side of a steep ravine. But how to get across? We descended to the road, doubted the wisdom of our decision, and doubled back to a trailhead marked by a large red cross pointing to the cave, two hundred meters away. This is how it is with the Way: the goal is right before our eyes. But few travel far enough to find it.

Spiritual progress depends upon prayer, penitence, purification—and, above all else, God's grace. The hermit knows better than most that the practice of the virtues is not enough. And a monk must pray ceaselessly for years, purging himself of every worldly attachment and devoting his energies to divine contemplation, before he can even consider becoming a hermit. The cellarer at Grigoriou thought our generation lacked the fortitude for such a difficult life. But the Russian monk seemed to yearn for it.

He was a figure out of *The Way of a Pilgrim*, the anonymous nineteenth-century Russian spiritual classic. In unadorned prose a nameless Christian recounts his journey through Russia and Siberia, visiting monasteries and holy shrines in search of instruction in the practice and meaning of unceasing interior prayer. From a *starets* he learns the Jesus Prayer, which he says thousands of times a day until it lodges in his heart, and discovers *The Philokalia*, which he reads several times through to fortify his prayer. He records decisive encounters with good and evil men and women. Thieves knock him senseless and steal his copy of *The Philokalia*, which he miraculously recovers three days later. A fellow sojourner shows him passages in the Gospels outlining a course of study in the art of prayer. A monk reads him essays on the power of prayer. The pilgrim begins to interpret everything through the prism of the Jesus Prayer, which he recites as he walks, eating only dried bread; at night he studies *The Philokalia*; his account is sprinkled with quotations from the church fathers. The prayer of the heart, he asserts, will cure the sick and heal the insane. As St. Gregory the Sinaite said, only prayer can drive away thoughts and purify the mind.

During his journey, which ends on the eve of his departure for Jerusalem (for the pilgrim is always on the Way), he experiences many strange and wonderful events. Walking through a forest one winter evening, for example, he is attacked by a wolf, which he fends off with the rosary he inherited from his starets. When he reaches the next village he tells his story to two men, the first of whom rejects it as the raving of a fool. But the other, a schoolmaster, argues that animals know when someone or something has holy power. He recalls how obediently the animals approached Adam in the Garden of Eden to receive their names; how they have experienced down through the ages the state of holy innocence lost by Adam and Eve and restored in the new covenant. "Now what is the meaning of sanctity?" the schoolmaster asks. "For the sinner it means nothing else than a return through effort and discipline to the state of the first man. When the soul is made holy the body becomes holy also." Thus the starets inoculated the rosary with "holy power—the power of the first man's innocence," which the wolf must have smelled.

Up two flights of narrow stone steps carved into the cliff the Russian monk and I climbed to the cave, gripping the rusted pipe that served as a guardrail. In the first chamber were three wooden chairs, an empty shelf covered with graffiti, and a pair of blue shutters that opened onto a shrine, before which the monk crossed himself and bowed. A blue door led to a smaller chamber in which the saint slept, following the custom of the desert fathers, who in turn built on the archaic tradition of seeking wisdom in a cave, the realm of the dead—in which pre-Socratic Greek philosophers, for example, mined their dreams for the truth. Cosmas's dreams were surely fed by the martyrdom, in his lifetime, of the twenty-six monks who locked themselves in the tower at Zographou, opposing the union of Rome and Constantinople, and were burned alive by the emperor's soldiers. Perhaps their example led Cosmas to implore the Virgin for guidance. For he shares his feast day with the martyrs, September 22, which also coincides with the autumn equinox, when the sun crosses the equator and everywhere day is the same length as night. Just so the monk and I sat in silence, former enemies worshipping together. Then he smiled.

"Prayer," he said. "God."

And that was all. We hiked back to the trailhead and went our separate ways. Through the woods I walked to a clearing of tall brown grass, in which were the remains of a campfire, then returned to the woods until I stumbled onto a road, one of several I would cross this day. Beyond was a plateau of heather and scrub pine baking in the sun. The road or the trail? St. Theophan the Recluse called *The Philokalia* "a spiritual forcing house," a useful metaphor for my approach to my pilgrimage: in my backpack was this guidebook to the Way instead of a map of Athos. For too long I had sought wisdom exclusively in books; if my spiritual life had begun to blossom thanks to my patristic readings, I knew that salvation demanded more. I said a prayer, chose the trail into the woods, favoring the shade, and eventually followed a dry stream to Chilandari.

The fellow feeling the Russian monk and I shared did not exist at the Serbian monastery. The soft-spoken guestmaster who had worked there at Great Lent was gone; his replacement, a surly young man in a gym suit, did not disguise his contempt for me. With Kosovo in flames and talk of NATO intervention against the Serbian military machine, I expected the worst.

"You like racquetball?" he said.

I nodded.

"Yugoslavia just won the world championship," he sneered.

"Russia second, USA third." When he went off to meet a busload of Serbian pilgrims, I made my escape.

Under the cypresses I walked down the road to a new wooden shrine and turned right toward the monastery of Esphigmenou. Shocks of cut hay lay in the fields; olive seedlings filled a draw lined by beehives. The black bee on the sign by the beekeeper's house brought to mind the desert father's saying: "Just as a bee, wherever she goes, makes honey, so a monk, wherever he goes, if he goes to do the will of God, can always produce the spiritual sweetness of good works." This was what I felt from the Russian monk at St. Cosmas's cave. To my surprise, I felt it as well from the guestmaster at Esphigmenou.

I had not planned to stop at the "Tight-belted" monastery, remembering my unpleasant reception there at Great Lent. The black banner reading ORTHODOXY OR DEATH still flew above the walls, the monks still believed that Jews spiked Coca-Cola with the blood of Christian children. But the sight of a boat bobbing in the harbor gave me the idea of trying to hitch a ride down the coast. Alas, by the time I arrived at the pier, where two monks were fishing, the wind had picked up and the surf was too rough for the boat to dock. So I went inside to ask for a guest tray. The guestmaster offered lunch, which I took with a Greek American chef from Cleveland.

He was a world traveler, and over bread, olives, and bean soup he gazed out the window at the brown hills and cerulean sky, wearily listing the places he had visited: "Africa, Afghanistan, Iran, Sri Lanka, Indonesia, South America." But with tourists overrunning even the most remote spots on the planet, Athos had become his favorite destination.

Anthropologists have long noted similarities between ancient religious pilgrimages and modern secular travel (holiday derives from "holy day"), without accounting for the increasingly religious nature of modern travel plans. The chef, for example, appreciated the chance to hike in Greece, at the height of the tourist season, in solitude. But he also attended services at each monastery; with the approach of middle age the religious dimension of his pilgrimages took on new importance. "Man instinctively regards himself as a wanderer and wayfarer," Thomas Merton writes, "and it is second nature for him to go on pilgrimage in search of a privileged and holy place, a center and source of indefectible life. This hope is built into his psychology, and whether he acts it out or simply dreams it, his heart seeks to return to a mythical source, a place of 'origin,' the 'home' where the ancestors came from, the mountain where the ancient fathers were in direct communication with heaven, the place of the creation of the world, paradise itself, with its sacred tree of life." Athos was one of the last places of origin.

"You can just disappear into these woods," the chef said in a faraway voice, as if talking to himself. "You don't have to go back to the outside world."

THERE WAS NOT ANOTHER SOUL ON MY HIKE FROM ESPHIGMENOU to Vatopedi. Up hills and down valleys I walked in blazing sunlight, among clumps of heather and mountain tea, ferns and gorse, the calm sea far below. In the shade of a rock walkway, nailed to a tree, was a handbill displaying a bar code with the numbers 666 highlighted and a woman placing her hand inside a machine—designed by the Antichrist, said the caption, to identify her in the last days. I recalled a conversation with a monk who took *The Protocols of the Elders of Zion* at face value. He said the evidence of the Jewish conspiracy was everywhere—in the number of oil companies operating in the Middle East; in the political alliance formed between Israel and Turkey; in the way that bar codes add up to 666.

"The Jews are really on a roll," he said bitterly.

From the woods I followed a set of tire tracks through a savanna of dry grass bordered by a chestnut grove. I was examining the charred embers of a recent campfire when a helicopter lifted off somewhere in the distance, in the direction of Vatopedi. I wondered who was on board. A politician? A war criminal? Along the cliff I hiked down to the bay, my imagination racing. But the Australian monk who greeted me in the courtyard of the monastery at the start of vespers feigned surprise when I asked about the helicopter. Not until months later did I learn the identity of the mysterious guest: Prince Charles had spent the afternoon at Vatopedi.

The British royal must have appreciated the silence here, after all the hoopla attending the death of his estranged wife, Princess Diana. Indeed her funeral might have furnished my daughter with her first memory of a public event, as my first such memory was of the funeral of John F. Kennedy—my family huddled around the black-and-white television set; the drums and riderless horse; the overcast sky when I stood outside on the hill by our house. Hannah was born during a media spectacle—the conclusion of the O. J. Simpson murder trial—and before long she would realize the currency of fame in our culture. The guestmaster's refusal to let on about the prince, a counter to our fascination with celebrities, was a function of his monastic vows to praise God, not temporal matters. "Getting and spending," Wordsworth wrote, "we lay waste our powers." But even the poet could not imagine the degree to which money and the media would coarsen our culture. How sobering it was to enter a community devoted to prayer.

What do you *do* on Mount Athos? a friend asked.

Walk and pray, I said.

Lest we think such activities have no bearing on society, the authors of *The Message and the Kingdom,* an archaeological and social history of the genesis of Christianity, note that in the ancient world the Greek word *leitourgia* (the root of "liturgy") was "an active demonstration of political power." Prayer and the Gospels upended the Roman imperial order; and if the new global order seemed impregnable, an order predicated on money, the media, and fame, I knew that the Pax Romana once looked equally strong. Against this I set the lessons of Orthodox monasticism, in which I was discovering an answer not only to the problem of mortality but also to the aesthetic project of shoring up the ruins of modern culture: hope—eternal hope.

The fragmentation of society was fairly complete by the time I read *The Waste Land*. And my college professor's prediction that T. S. Eliot would lose his standing in academia was sadly accurate. That Eliot foresaw the consequences of the breakdown of a lettered society makes the denigration of his witness all the more ironic; in academic circles his despair over the erosion of the religious imagination is generally considered reactionary, like his embrace of Anglicanism; his anti-Semitism did not help matters. Yet he articulated a crisis of meaning now lost on much of the intelligentsia. The range of reference and subjects of dinner-table discussions among my friends, for example, had shifted from books and literary gossip to films and political or celebrity scandals, and so I was brought up short by Gregory of Nyssa's description of Constantinople during the second general council, at which it was determined that the Holy Spirit is fully God:

> The whole city is full of it, the squares, the market places, the cross-roads, the alleyways; old-clothes men, money changers, food sellers: they are all busy arguing. If you ask someone to give you change, he philosophizes about the Begotten and the Unbegotten; if you inquire about the price of a loaf, you are told by way of reply that the Father is greater and the Son inferior; if you ask "Is my bath ready?" the attendant answers that the Son was made out of nothing.

This is, of course, another species of political argument, the stuff of conversation down through the ages, but it is worth noting the decline in quality of what fills our thinking, a logical outcome of the erosion of the religious imagination. The arts are said to have replaced God as the arbiter of meaning in the nineteenth century, only to be supplanted by the media in our time—a diminution, by any calculation. Which is why Czeslaw Milosz felt compelled to write about theological matters, as he explains in a prose poem entitled "Why Religion?":

> I lived at a time when a huge change in the contents of the human imagination was occurring. In my lifetime Heaven and Hell disappeared, the belief in life after death was considerably weakened, the borderline between man and animals, once so clear, ceased to be obvious under the impact of the theory of evolution, the notion of absolute truth lost its supreme position, history directed by Providence started to look like a battle between blind forces. After two thousand years in which a huge edifice of creeds and dogmas has been erected, from Origen and Saint Augustine to Thomas Aquinas and Cardinal Newman, when every work of the human mind and of human hands was created within a system of reference, the age of homelessness has dawned. How could I not think of this? And is it not surprising that my preoccupation was a rare case?

If Eliot announced the arrival of the age of homelessness, Milosz was its scribe. And it seemed to me the link forged between them in the fires of World War II, recorded in Milosz's autobiography, *Native Realm: A Search for Self-Definition*, might inspire a new poetics. Milosz describes a scene on the verge of the Warsaw Uprising. One afternoon he and his wife cross a potato field on the outskirts of the city, enjoying the sunshine on their way to visit a friend, when suddenly they are pinned down by machine gun fire. Not until dawn can they make their escape, and through the night the poet clutches his copy of Eliot's *Collected Poems*—he hoped to discuss a new translation with his friend—because, as he writes, he needs it. (*The Waste Land*, he notes, "made for somewhat weird reading as the glow from the burning ghetto illuminated the city skyline.") If I had once interpreted this incident as a testament to the power of poetry now I recognized its theological import. For what unites Eliot and Milosz is their identification of the dangers inherent in the erosion of the religious imagination. And just as I had come to prefer the liturgical bent of Eliot's *Four Quartets* to *The Waste Land*, so I read Milosz's work, including the poems of wartime witness on which his reputation rests, in the light of his religious concerns. He had indeed translated not only Eliot and Shakespeare during the Nazi occupation but also Simone Weil and the French theologian Jacques Maritain. And like Eliot, Milosz was acutely aware of his sinfulness: the place from which great works of the spirit originate.

Unfortunately, my spiritual homelessness acquired a physical dimension at Vatopedi, when I could not convince the guestmaster to overlook my failure to reserve a place for the night. The next monastery, Pantokratoros, was several kilometers away, and when I left—with no guarantee of finding lodging there—my legs were cramping, my neck throbbed. A laborer offered me a ride to the top of the first hill, but from there I had to trudge through the dust to a grove of holm oaks, then through ferns and gorse and elderberries to a cliff above a watchtower and a *kellí*. It was nearly dusk before I saw, on a headland by the sea, Pantokratoros. This was the last idiorrhythmic monastery to revert to cenobitism, and the monks were zealously preparing to celebrate both Dormition and Pantokratoros's feast day of Transfiguration. I thanked God when the guestmaster gave me a room overlooking the water. In no time I was fast asleep.

FROM DOORWAY TO DOORWAY, WORLD TO WORLD—THIS WAS THE visual effect of watching the liturgy from the glazed narthex of the *katholikón*. Outside, the sun rose red over the sea, lighting the paved courtyard sloping away from the church, the orange trees in white planters filled with herbs, a pilgrim pacing under an arch, a cat curled up on the stairs. Inside, the icons were covered with so much soot I could make out only those of Christ Pantokrator and the Virgin Gerondissa (the Elder), one of the Holy Mountain's three protecting icons—which, it is said, once ordered a priest to hurry through a service so that the abbot might receive communion before he died.

"Most reckless things are beautiful in some way," writes the poet John Ashbery, "and recklessness is what makes experimental art beautiful, just as religions are beautiful because of the strong possibility that they are founded on nothing." Sometimes I think it hardly matters whether Christ was the Son of God, given the number of artistic, literary, and musical masterpieces His story has inspired, some of which I saw after the liturgy (a creative wonder in itself), when the librarian showed me Pantokratoros's treasures: vestments, medallions, coins, icons under restoration. In a glass case was a ninth-century Psalter, with a Byzantine cross holding open a page on which three miniature paintings bordered the Psalms—Judas kissing Jesus; Jesus rebuking Peter for cutting off the ear of a Roman guard; the guards leading Jesus away. This codex, which contains nearly a hundred illustrations of the Old and New Testaments, scenes from the life of Christ, portraits of the Virgin and saints, and church history, dates from the period between the last ecumenical council, in 787, where it was affirmed that icons should be venerated in the same manner as the cross and the Gospels, and the second wave of iconoclasm inaugurated by Leo V the Armenian, in 815—created, that is, in a time of uncertainty not unlike our own; perhaps its radiance owed something to the anxiety the artists must have labored under. It was as if they painted with ash, in the shadow of destruction; they could not have imagined their work surviving for a millennium or more, not with the Triumph of Orthodoxy still in the offing.

Two theologians figured prominently in the defense of icons, St. John of Damascus (c. 675–749) and St. Theodore the Studite (759–826), who is also remembered for reforming cenobitic monasticism. John thought the iconoclasts had revived the clash of visions embodied in the Old and New Testaments, in the Law handed down to Moses and the Love of Christ Jesus, by resurrecting the Jewish prohibition against worshipping graven images (which coincidentally dovetailed with the practice of the approaching Islamic forces). He explained that since God was never seen in the Old Testament (except in the form of the burning bush), only heard, His voice could not be represented in pictorial terms until He offered a new covenant. And His Incarnation obliges artists to "paint and make visible to everyone Him who desired to become visible"; the relationship between God and mankind, and between God and creation, changed when the "Word became flesh and dwelt among us" (John 1:14); icons portray this intersection of the unknowable and the known, God and mankind, eternity and history. The rejection of sacred images was thus tantamount to denying the Incarnation and the decisions taken in the first six ecumenical councils. But for John and other iconodules an icon is a witness to the Incarnation and an emblem of the ways in which contemplation of the things of this world can lead to the spiritual realm—and perhaps to the restoration of harmony between the body and the soul. The route to the transcendent is always through the physical: an icon, the other, nature.

St. Theodore the Studite developed John's argument about the relationship between Christ, who was both fully human and fully divine, and an icon, a material image which may nevertheless participate in the holiness of the figure represented. Theodore, the poet-abbot of a monastery in Asia Minor, led a turbulent life. He was exiled for criticizing Constantine VI's adulterous marriage; when the emperor was deposed by his mother, Theodore was allowed to return to his monastery, which now lay in the sights of the Ottoman army. So he moved with his brethren to Studion, an estate in a suburb of Constantinople, to build the most vibrant monastery in Byzantium (where St. Athanasios, Great Lavra's founder, would experience the rigors of cenobitic monasticism). But the second battle over icons was under way, the iconoclasts having gained the favor of Nikephoros I, and it was not long before Theodore's arguments supporting the union of divinity and humanity in Christ drew the emperor's ire. He was exiled again in 809, recalled in 811, and exiled for a third time by Leo V, whose reign of terror began in 813. Lashed and flogged by the emperor's men, Theodore continued to write to his followers (the monastic rules he outlined in one letter guided the creation of the cenobitic system on Athos), exhorting them not to lose heart, though he himself would never return to his monastery. Not until 843, at a council in Constantinople (attended by a delegation of Athonite monks), was the veneration of icons vindicated. The defeat of iconoclasm, the Triumph of Orthodoxy, ensured that prostrating before an icon, like taking communion or saying the name of Jesus, has a sacramental function, initiating the faithful into the divine mysteries.

The writings of St. John of Damascus and St. Theodore the Studite reinforced the findings of the last ecumenical council and enhanced the Church's Christological understanding. It is thus fitting that the divines of Eastern and Western Christendom never took another binding conciliar decision, since the miracle of Christ is the central tenet of the faith. In a note about the history of the Church, Czeslaw Milosz writes: "For two thousand years I have been trying to understand what It was." The ecumenical councils, church fathers, poets—all tried to answer that question, which continues to trouble the religious minded. "For you died," Paul wrote to the faithful of Colossae to bolster their resolve against the heretics of their time, "and your life is hidden with Christ in God" (Col. 3:3). What is discovered in the deepest recesses of faith is what remains most mysterious—and most sacred: the icon of Christ Jesus.

Iconoclasm was in the end an argument over the proper uses of the imagination, like most clashes of religions, cultures, and individuals. How will you write your life? To what will you accord the truth? Iconoclasm arose in the face of Islamic claims to a purer form of faith. Similar forces were at work today. The Serbian paramilitaries in Kosovo loathed Albanian Muslims in the same fashion as their ancestors who lived under the Turkish yoke. The mullahs who hated the images generated by the Western media had their counterparts in Christian fundamentalists—and among the monks on Athos. The quarrel between images and ideas is as old as mankind.

The sunlight through the windows of the treasury cast an amber glow over the ceremonial vestments displayed in the glass cases. Two icons prepared for restoration were propped on easels. On another page of the Psalter, said the librarian, there was an un-forgettable juxtaposition of images: on one side of the text were two soldiers torturing Christ on the cross, on the other an icono-clast whitewashing a mural of the Savior. In their red tunics the soldiers and the iconoclast looked alike; they used similar staffs to commit what the librarian called crimes of the same order. Just then three French peacekeepers came in to have a look around. On their way to deployment in Macedonia they were making a pilgrimage first to Athos and then to the grave of a French officer killed in the first Balkan Wars. In Belgrade and Pristina, Wash-ington and Paris, you could hear the drums of war beating again. The soldiers grimly studied the Psalter.

WHEN ASKED WHAT HE WOULD SAVE FROM A BURNING HOUSE, Jean Cocteau replied, the fire. And it was the purifying fire of grace I sought on the eve of Dormition, notwithstanding the Or-thodox belief that I would not find this without heeding St. John the Baptist's prophesy of Christ—"He will baptize you with the Holy Spirit and fire. His winnowing fork is in his hand, to clear his threshing floor and to gather the wheat into his granary; but the chaff he will burn with unquenchable fire" (Luke 3:16–18)—and acting accordingly. Worn out from my hike the day before, I felt a bit like chaff when I took the monks' taxi service from Pantokra-toros to Karyes; in the crowded van, which spun around the cor-ners and drifted in the dust, a wave of nausea came over me. But my spirits lifted once I started walking out of town. It was bright and warm, the wind was high, the road to Daphne was empty. At the top of the hill above Karyes I found a woodland path heading south, which soon disappeared in a maze of logging roads. The road to the summit looked promising—I hoped to hike along the ridge before descending to the monastery of Grigoriou—until a log truck thundered past, coating me with dust. The wind howled in the trees.

At the next trailhead I turned westward, arriving eventually at a vista of cliffs and the sea. From an outcropping south of Daphne I spotted a large *kellí* wedged into a ravine. Down a steep slope of thorn bushes I slid and stumbled to a series of stone terraces that brought me to a vineyard and a garden fed by a drip-irrigation system. The wind had leveled rows of tomato plants staked crosswise. No one answered at the *kellí*. From a new cistern I refilled my water bottle, then climbed along the side of the mountain. Around a bend was a *kellí* under construction, with three laborers pounding nails into the roof. It was not long before I gained the road to Simonopetra.

The wind died, and in the heat of the afternoon I was circling a ravine, lost in thought, when I heard the howl of a wolf—a long, eerie call that set my nerves on fire. I scanned the hillside before me. Nothing. But the landscape had sprung to life: the rocks and brush and scrub oaks; the clouds scudding toward the summit. Wolves rarely howl in daylight. And I was of a mind to read this as more than an aberration of nature. The monks do not dismiss natural portents, which bear God's word, like the whole of Creation. Nor would I. And what better way to glimpse divinity than to encounter a wild animal. I remembered walking one winter morning in Connecticut with Hannah in a backpack, when a red fox darted out of the woods to nip at our dog's tail, as if to play with her—a flash of red that made the landscape quiver with meaning. Had wolves returned to the Holy Mountain? Had this wolf called to me? I did not doubt it.

What energy I had for my hike to Simonopetra! I stopped for a guest tray, then hurried down the switchback to the *arsanas*, stripped off my clothes, and waded into the sea. Dust was caked to my skin, and when I lay down in the water to scrub myself clean a line from Thomas Traherne's *Centuries* drifted through my mind: "You never enjoy the world aright till the sea itself floweth in your veins, till you are clothed with the heavens and crowned with the stars." I had the sea in me for the last leg of my journey to Grigoriou, uphill and down, arriving just in time for dinner, where an Italian pilgrim's baptism was being celebrated.

Baptism on the Holy Mountain requires immersion in the sea. Three times in the topsy-turvy reasoning of faith the catechumen is plunged into the element closest to the amniotic sea in which we journey from conception to birth, in order to be reborn in Christ. A Pharisee called Nicodemos came to Jesus under cover of night and asked Him to explain why a second birth was necessary for salvation. "Jesus answered, 'Most assuredly, I say to you, unless one is born of water and the Spirit, he cannot enter the kingdom of God" (John 3:5). To which Paul adds: "Or did you not know that all of us who have been baptized into Christ Jesus were baptized into His death? Therefore we have been buried with him by baptism into death so that, just as Christ was raised from the dead by the glory of the Father, so we too might walk in newness of life" (Rom. 6:3–4). The pilgrim at Grigoriou wore the traditional white robe, and in the cool of the evening I watched (with some envy) as the abbot took him by the arm to walk under the grape arbor—a gesture that brought to mind a passage from an essay by Odysseas Elytis, in which he recounted the last time he saw Angelos Sikelianos, then the elder statesman of Greek poetry. The young poet stopped by Sikelianos's house one summer day, unannounced, to deliver some books on surrealist theory. He found the front door open:

> I called a couple of times and, when no one answered, entered in my light cloth shoes that made no sound. Then an unforgettable image: Sikelianos, barefoot in a long white nightgown draped like an ancient tunic, eating a stem of grapes! Every so often, he'd raise one to the open window and admire it in the light. It was he. An authentic Greek

poet who did not deny sensation, but pushed it instead until
it fell and he could read in it its secret signs.

Sikelianos was neither displeased nor embarrassed when he noticed Elytis. He cut a stem of grapes for him and launched into a
discourse on some apocryphal texts. The future Nobel laureate
also wished to read the secret signs of sensation, and in Sikelianos's fusion of spirit and matter he recognized the need to con-
secrate the whole of existence—an Orthodox notion. "Naked the
soul prays to You," Sikelianos writes to his beloved, to God: "grant
me deliverance,

> *to feel again the uncreated Eros*
>   *filling my breast,*
> *and to be to all, to things near and far away,*
>   *as the wind's sound and breath.*

A lifelong devotion to poetry and prayer can make one a vessel for
the secret signs of Creation. Thus the elder takes the aspirant by
the arm and leads him into the arbor of eternity.

THE OLD MONK REMEMBERED WORKING IN THE FOREST WHEN A
wolf attacked a mule, tearing a chunk of flesh out of its hindquar-
ters. That night the other mules formed a circle around the injured animal to protect it from another attack, and the mule
recovered. Nor was the monk surprised to hear that wolves had returned to the Holy Mountain. Resurrection was his theme, after
all. And he had another story of a miraculous healing. A wealthy
businessman from Thessaloníki fell from a ladder and broke his
elbow. He was rushed to the hospital, where six doctors attended
to him, and while being wheeled into the operating room he
prayed to the saints. A local anesthetic was administered. Nothing
happened. Then a bolt of energy surged through his arm, healing

the break. The doctors were about to give him more anesthetic when he told them he was fine. They did not believe him, not even after he banged his elbow on the table to prove his point. You'll be back in three days begging for surgery, said the chief resident, and I won't operate. But the businessman *was* healed. And instead of returning to work he asked his wife for permission to enter a monastery on Athos, which she granted. She was a pious woman, said the monk. At her memorial service a dove flew into the church and circled her casket three times.

PSALM 91, ORTHODOXY'S FUNERAL PSALM, IS READ AT COMPLINE, which means "complete." At the end of the day, at the end of life, the deacon promises that God "will deliver you from the snare of the fowler and from the deadly pestilence; he will cover you with his pinions, and under his wings you will find refuge; his faithfulness is a shield and buckler" (Ps. 91:3–4). I have just begun to understand what it means to make the Lord my refuge, but the promise of salvation leads me now to read James' Epistle in a new light: "See how great a forest a little fire kindles! And the tongue is a fire, a world of iniquity" (James 3:5–6). This pilgrimage has set fire to my spirit.

After compline I accompany the cellarer up the hill behind the monastery to visit an aging hermit who lives in a *kathisma*, a small dwelling with a chapel next door. Figs are ripening on his tree; in his garden the tomatoes are ready to pick; tufts of basil spill over the EU cartons on his thatched veranda. The cellarer brings him melons and news of the monastery. The hermit will say extra prayers for the monks who have business in the world. We drink raki and watch the sun dip toward the sea. The hermit tells a story about the nineteenth-century Russian designs on Athos: how thousands of Russian monks marched from Karyes to Daphne for a showdown; how a Greek abbot ordered monks from the other monasteries to line the route with ample supplies of wine and raki; how the would-be conquerors got too drunk to harm anyone.

We say good night to the hermit and hike up to the founder's cave. A candle burns in the shrine to St. Gregory of Sinai (c. 1265–1346), hesychasm's first systematic teacher. His name is often linked with that of St. Gregory Palamas, hesychasm's defender, and while they lived on the Holy Mountain at the same time it is unclear if they knew each other. There were nonetheless several points of convergence between them. Like Palamas, Gregory of Sinai was born in Asia Minor, traveled widely, and endured captivity at the hands of the Turks. Tonsured at Mount Sinai, where he steeped himself in the writings of St. John Climacus, on a pilgrimage to Crete he learned the Jesus Prayer, then came to Athos, settling in a *skete* near Philotheou, where monks were avid for his counsel. "Prayer is God," he wrote, describing the transition from the active to the contemplative life: first the hesychast prays to God, then God prays in him, unceasingly. And this process of emptying the mind of images and ideas in order to pray alone with God, this spiritual poverty in the service of listening to God, is the work of a lifetime, as the Sinaite knew. He could not bear to be parted from contemplation, but because his teachings kept drawing monks to him he had to move to ever more remote settings in search of more solitude. One of his disciples, St. Gregory the Younger, decided to build a monastery here to protect the hermits from Turkish raids, which had caused the Sinaite to flee to the mountains in Thrace—where he did not find much solitude. But the monks who gathered around him, under the protection of the Bulgarian czar, spread hesychasm to the Slavic lands, inspiring the fifteenth-century *startzi* movement, the monastic counterweight to the political machinations of the Third Rome.

What wisdom he possessed! "As the physical eye looks at written letters and receives knowledge from them through the senses," he tells us, "so the mind, when it becomes purified and returns to its original state, looks up to God and receives Divine knowledge from Him.

> Instead of a book it has the Spirit, instead of a pen, thought and tongue ("my tongue is the pen" says the Ps. [xlv. 1]);

instead of ink—light. Plunging thought into light, so that thought itself becomes light, the mind, guided by the Spirit, traces words in the pure hearts of those who listen. Then it understands the words: "and they shall be all taught of God" (John vi. 45), and "he that teacheth man knowledge" (Ps. xciv. 10).

My second pilgrimage is ending where my first one began: in a meditation on pure prayer, the hesychast heart of Athos. But I am a different person from the writer who kept falling asleep during the vigil at Iveron for St. Gregory Palamas. Now I am a pilgrim praying for light instead of ink, mindful of the desert father's saying about a believer who practices the virtues and yet refuses to be transformed. An abbot visits an elder and says he keeps his little rule and little fast, his prayer and contemplative silence. He tries to cleanse his heart of thoughts. What more can he do? "The elder rose up in reply and stretched out his hands to heaven, and his fingers became like ten lamps of fire. He said: Why not be changed totally into fire?" Why not indeed?

Our last stop is the chapel of the Holy Mother, which is attached to a two-story *kellí*, where an older monk is grilling fish for a visiting novice. The sun has set, and I am thinking of Paul's mission to Thessaloníki: how only a few Greeks and Jews were persuaded by his argument that it was necessary for the Messiah to suffer and then to rise from the dead—that Christ is the Messiah (Acts 17:1–15). When a ruckus was raised in the city, the faithful had to send Paul and his companion, Silas, to Beroea, where they found a better reception. The secret of poetry, of faith, of love, is openness, and in the novice's eyes I see the hunger for wisdom that my writing teachers might have noticed in me; that Lisa must once have glimpsed—and perhaps still did. Now the elder takes his seat at the table on the bluff and offers instruction to the young man: a timeless scene. Nor am I bereft of counsel. Before entering the chapel, the cellarer recalls a saint's description of the spiritual journey: when a shepherdess falls in love with a shepherd on the next hill, nothing will keep her from running to him. Such is the soul in pursuit of God.

"We accept everyone as we find them, not as we would like them to be," says the monk. "We know they have weaknesses, just as we do. We can only hope to turn them toward God."

I feel such a turning in my life, which will force me to reconsider every relationship in its light—with my family, my writing, my position at Holy Cross. Call it a conversion, or a deepening sense of faith: with the Dormition of the Theotokos, which I am marking in a chapel cut into a steep hillside, my soul is waking from forty years of sleep. The chapel has a special fragrance, says the monk, and indeed there is a sweet smell, distinct from incense, which the fathers liken to the fragrance of holy relics, brimming with eternal life. When the archangel Michael told Mary she would be taken to Heaven, the monk continues, she prayed for the apostles to return from their evangelical missions, and they flew to Jerusalem on clouds. She was buried in Gethsemane, the site of her Son's agony, and from her tomb rose mysterious voices praising Christ—and a divine perfume; after three days, when the voices went silent, the apostles opened the tomb, which was empty. The monk makes the sign of the cross. Then he lights a candle in a lamp and venerates the icon of our Lady. "Stand in awe, and sin not," sings the Psalmist. And again: "Be still and know that I am God" (Pss. 4:4, 46:10). I stand beside the monk, and even if I am unable to empty my mind of every thought, sinful and otherwise, I am, at long last, still.

part three

PRAYER

K YRIE, ELEISON, THE DEACON CHANTS FOR the third time. Lord, have mercy. In Simonopetra's crowded nave, on either side of a table draped in an embroidered sash, two priests in gold and green vestments cense a silver replica of the church. Three times each they fling smoke from their censers, then change positions to repeat the ritual until they have circled the table. Sunlight streams through a window near the ceiling. Monks and pilgrims hold long candles, spellbound.

I have arrived on Christmas Eve in time for vespers. After a night of hard rain and thick morning clouds, a cold north wind cleared the sky during my hike from Daphne. Waterfalls tumbled down ravines which in summer were dry as bone; russet leaves clung to the branches of scrub oaks marching up the hills; a brown mongrel with one white leg followed me until three mules blocked the muddy road. I picked my way through the mules, climbing steadily, and immediately upon reaching the monastery set on the rocks high above the sea I left my backpack outside the door to the church, and accompanied an elderly British translator into the service.

In his blue blazer and fuchsia tie, with a flowered handkerchief in his lapel, John Leatham cuts a regal figure among the more casually dressed Greeks. Athens has been his home, on and off, since World War II; and his involvement with Mount Athos— he translated a book on its paper icons; he is writing a text to accompany the photographs he took during his first pilgrimage more than forty years ago; he climbed the mountain twice the summer he turned seventy—has led him to a momentous decision: at Easter this lifelong Roman Catholic will be baptized here in the sea. Athos is the gauge by which he measures the decline of the West.

"Uniformity will be the end of civilization," he told me yesterday during a tour of Ouranoupolis. The sky was overcast; a handful of fishing boats plied the sea. As dusk fell, John marched toward the Athonian border, waving his walking stick like a cudgel at the new hotels under construction, the sight of which left him in a "peckish" mood. He remembered when Ouranoupolis was little more than a collection of huts put up to house refugees from Asia Minor, before it succumbed to what he called the three scourges of modern Greece—tourists, cement, and bulldozers. The way of the world. And nowhere was the drive toward sameness more apparent than in his homeland. England, he said, was breeding out all of its eccentrics.

"A nation cannot survive without its eccentrics," he insisted. "They give it flavor."

The pavement ending, we followed a muddy road past field gardens, a boatyard, a homestead named Paradise. Old women in a meadow gathered buckets of dandelions for salad. A peasant with a shotgun slung over his shoulder said he was hunting for woodcocks; gunshots echoed in the hills. At the top of a rise, between an olive grove and a neglected orchard, was an archaeological excavation of a church and tower erected by the Franks—legacies of the Latin occupation. Two pickups were parked by the stream flowing along the border into the sea. Barbed wire was strung atop a cement wall, beyond which lay a complex of ramshackle monastic buildings, a pair of rebuilt cottages used by the police, and through the trees a narrow road winding up toward the ridge.

Our conversation turned to a more recent crusade—the one against communism—in which John had played a part. He and his cousin went into the shipping business after the war, carrying freight around the Mediterranean. Then, in 1949, British intelligence recruited them to ferry armed Albanian dissidents back to their homeland: the West's first covert action against the Soviet bloc. Supplied with a powerful engine for their boat, the young men made runs up and down the Albanian coast, landing freedom fighters to provoke an uprising against Enver Hoxha, the Stalinist dictator. One night, caught in a storm, they had to put in close to shore, and at daybreak their boat was peppered with rifle fire. They managed to escape, but the Albanians in their charge were not so fortunate. The operation was doomed from the start: the notorious British double agent Kim Philby had betrayed their plans to Moscow. John and his cousin unwittingly delivered hundreds of Albanians to certain death.

From a vineyard at the north end of Athos a white minibus wended down the road along the ridge, parked at the gate, and unloaded some laborers, who piled into a pickup and drove off. Rain was imminent, so we caught a ride in the other pickup with the vintner who leased the land from the Russian monastery; and when he let us out in town John described him as one of the richest men in Greece. In our hotel lobby was one of the poorest, a gaunt, wild-eyed hermit from the desert. He sat in front of the Christmas tree, his beard flecked with foam from a cup of cappuccino cradled in his hands, a rare luxury for a "sheaver"—one who lives in a cave or hut accessible only by rope pulley. He had left his hermitage to sell his rosaries in Thessaloníki. John supposed he did not even know what day it was.

Why is it so hot in the church?

All at once I am dripping sweat. The sweet smell of incense and beeswax is cloying. Monks, candles, icons—everything is spinning. I have to sit for fear of fainting. John looks at me, alarmed. My chances of surviving a heart attack, if that is what this is, are slim: the nearest hospital is hours away. Rising abruptly, I wade through the pilgrims to the narthex, where the monks in their wooden stands form a semicircle, and find a seat among them. Voices swirl around me, and I am falling, falling into darkness. Melting wax burns my hand as the candle slips through my fingers. Flushed, disoriented, I stumble out to the balcony, slump to the plank floor under the bell, and strip down to my sweat-soaked T-shirt. In the gusting wind I gaze at the cliff and the white-capped sea, taking deep breaths until I begin to feel better.

I wonder what triggered this fainting spell—the onset of illness? Standing in one position? Ironically, in the West this is the feast day of Symeon the Stylite, the fifth-century Antiochan saint who stood on a pillar for thirty-seven years, in wind and rain, in hot sun and freezing weather. This illiterate monk, dismissed from his monastery for "excessive asceticism," climbed a pillar ten feet high (he later moved to one six times higher) to preach against the decadence of his society. Renowned for the force of his moral outrage and for his healing powers (his specialty was curing infertility), Symeon inaugurated the stylitic tradition, which persisted until the tenth century. At one time every peak near Antioch had its own stylite (those struck by lightning were judged to be secret heretics), and of an afternoon rich women would visit the pillar saints for instruction and healing. "The Byzantines looked on these stylites as intermediaries," William Dalrymple writes in *From the Holy Mountain: A Journey Among the Christians of the Middle East,* "go-betweens who could transmit their deepest fears and aspirations to the distant court of Heaven, ordinary men from ordinary backgrounds who had, by dint of their heroic asceticism, gained the ear of Christ." And the extremes of their devotion seem absurd only under what Dalrymple calls "the harsh distorting microscope of skeptical Western rationality." Byzantines credited the stylites' access to the divine, their powers of discernment and prophesy to their exertions. Thus Symeon would prostrate himself 1,244 times a day; chained to a stake, he would stand for the first two weeks of Lent. Whereas I have blacked out after only an hour in church.

It is true that a cloud hangs over my life. I have come from a family vacation in London, where my father-in-law, a silent, elegant man, tested our patience, shuffling from one museum to the next, until it dawned on us that he was gravely ill—which deepened Lisa's depression. For hours in bed one night she recited a list of my failings. I lay in the dark without replying. After a while, though, I had a perverse desire to count up her separate charges to see when she would repeat herself. The answer was fifty-two, which of course I was mean enough to tell her, only to suffer a redoubling of her fury. Days passed before we were on speaking terms again. And when I left for Greece I did not know what to expect upon my return.

The wind is invigorating, the sea a blur of grey and white. My lightheadedness passes, but I am very weak. I take comfort listening to the lines of chant floating out of the church. The annual sacrament of anointing is about to start, in which the faithful renew their baptismal rite, their calling to a life in Christ. I think of the calling that sanctified Romanos the Melodist (d. 530), a tone-deaf monk who underwent a miraculous transformation. In his monastery he was a kind of Rudolph the Red-Nosed Reindeer, ridiculed by the other monks for his inability to sing. Then one Christmas Eve he dreamed that the Theotokos gave him a scroll of music to eat, and in the morning he spontaneously sang the first of a thousand hymns attributed to him, "The Virgin brings forth today the Omnipotent," the main hymn of the Feast of the Nativity.

What does it mean to be called? Monks say the monastic life is the highest calling, yet we are all called—if not to belief, love, and a vocation, then certainly to death. In Dino Buzzati's short story "The Scriveners," a scribe writes what he describes as idle tales to please his Lord and Master, uncertain whether He even reads them. One day, though, a red light flashes on his typewriter: the sign that he has been called to spend the rest of his days tethered to his desk. What writer does not dream of continuous inspiration? But the scribe's neighbor, a historian on the verge of retirement, ignores the summons he receives at the last moment—a decision anyone might make. Liturgy, lovemaking, artistic inspiration, fever, psychedelic drugs, death watches— these take us out of ourselves, reorienting our relationship to the world. But who can bear it for very long? Called to the things of this earth, it seemed to me that each step I took in the spiritual life was matched by a slide into debauchery; often the only progress I could detect was the growing certainty of my helplessness. More than ever I realized that a calling to belief could organize my inner resources, my will, against the fragmentation of modern life—and my own demons.

What God offers is transfiguration. No one knows how He will seek to use us, but perhaps our enthusiasms reveal paths to divine union. Mine is for literary work, and in my apprenticeship the urge to duplicate the perfect freedom I sometimes felt in composing a poem or fashioning a sentence in a short story became my Holy Grail. I ransacked artists' biographies, hoping to discover some permanent means of invoking that form of grace. Haydn's description of his working methods stayed with me:

> I get up early, and as soon as I have dressed I go down on my knees and pray God and the Blessed Virgin that I may have another successful day. Then when I've made some breakfast I sit down at the clavier and begin my search. If I hit on an idea quickly, it goes ahead easily and without much trouble. But if I can't get on, I know that I must have forfeited God's grace by some fault of mine, and then I pray once more for grace till I feel I'm forgiven.

And when Haydn was stuck, according to his biographer, "he would walk up and down, rosary in hand, and after a few 'Hail Mary's' the ideas would begin to flow again."

Writing poetry is predicated on a similar sort of supplication. I suspect that writer's block consists of not knowing what you should write on any given day—that is, of ignoring or misunderstanding the dictates of the Muse, the unconscious, the other voice, the language. What is the surrealist discipline of automatic writing but a petition to forces larger and more mysterious than reason? Courting inspiration is one way to monitor what happens in the deepest recesses of the heart. Prayer is another. As the poet W. S. Merwin writes in his elegy for John Berryman:

> *he suggested I pray to the Muse*
> *get down on my knees and pray*

right there in the corner and he
said he meant it literally

I fashioned a poetics from lines like these, searching for ways to quicken my spirit, though it took a grave illness for me to understand that supplication is necessary in every artistic and spiritual endeavor. In his Nobel lecture Saul Bellow suggested that "there is another reality, the genuine one, which we always lose sight of. This other reality is always sending us hints, which, without art, we can't receive." But art is not the only intermediary between us and the divine. My pilgrimages to Athos, my encounters with holy men, my readings of Scripture and patristic literature—these have convinced me that prayer is a more direct route to the other reality, which is why Gregory of Nyssa called prayer "the leader in the choir of virtues." Christ says, "whatever things you ask when you pray, believe that you receive them, and you will have them" (Mark 11:24). I pray to experience His loving-kindness, which I imagine to be akin to the radical overturning of everything we know when we fall in love and glimpse the divine union offered to us by the Redeemer. Transformation is all.

THE READING IN THE REFECTORY IS FROM THE PASSION—TO remind us of Christ's destiny, John Leatham explains under his breath. The journey from His birth to His death and resurrection will preoccupy the monks through the winter and spring. My life is likewise bound to this seasonal celebration in a way I could not have foreseen before my first pilgrimage. I am still shaky, though, when we return to church for the display of the relics—Athonite saints, martyrs, a piece of the True Cross. Nor have I fully recovered when John takes me to the pilgrim greeting area to talk with Father Ieronymos, Simonopetra's secretary. I am happy all the same. For once I sat in this very place, estranged from a group of pilgrims receiving counsel from this elderly, bespectacled monk, and now I am engaged in a lively discussion with him.

"Orthodoxy never blackmails consciences," he is saying. "We are not like soldiers under fire. Just watch the monks during the services. They come over to talk or tell jokes, they are open. They know that each of us must decide our own course of action. If God has given us free will, how can we impose our will on others?"

John has brought sweetmeats for the monk, whose gifts for us include compact discs of the monks chanting hymns to the Virgin. Our conversation turns to an Anglican priest who has lately published a bitter account of his pilgrimage to the Holy Mountain. It seems he was put off by the monks' otherworldliness: their hospitality he deemed spurious, their safekeeping of their churches and treasures he disdained. He got into arguments with several monks, dismissing their vision of Christianity. Father Ieronymos shakes his head. Christ does not demand that others follow Him, he says, only that they open their hearts to His message.

"A man who comes to Athos with a hard heart will never return," he says softly.

Openhearted John's work on Simonopetra's behalf has earned him a separate suite, where a bed has been reserved for me. Bidding good night to Father Ieronymos, we retire to these quarters to find a plate of honey-and-walnut biscuits laid out for us. John brews a pot of linden tea, which we drink in a sitting area refurbished in the style of a grand hotel. Blue is the theme: there are blue glass bottles on a trunk, and on the table are blue candles, blue candlesticks, and a glass dish of blue beads. The drawing of the monastery hanging above the radiator is by Robert Curzon, an Englishman who memorialized his grand tour with the publication, in 1849, of *Visits to Monasteries in the Levant,* a jaunty account of his efforts to collect valuable manuscripts from unsuspecting monks. In this he was very successful. On Athos, for example, a knife-wielding monk at Karakallou cut an inch of leaves from an eleventh-century manuscript and gave them to him, believing he would use them to cover jam pots. "I ought, perhaps, to have slain the *tomecide* for his dreadful act of profanation," Curzon reflected, "but his generosity reconciled me to his guilt, so I pocketed the Apocalypse, and asked him if he would sell me any of the other books, as he did not appear to set any particular value upon them." The monk replied that since he needed money for renovations he would be happy to sell him the lot. From Simonopetra Curzon made off with two manuscripts—an eleventh-century biography of St. John Climacus and an ancient folio containing the Acts and the Epistles; a third quarto, of the Gospels, would have been his if not for a monk's "unlucky" discovery, on its last page, of the donor's anathema against anyone who tried to sell it. Curzon's plunder now resides in the British Museum.

As it happens, the next Englishman to write about the Holy Mountain was John Leatham's ancestor Athelstan Riley, who recounted a different kind of pilgrimage in *Athos or The Mountain of the Monks* (1887). Riley, an Oxford don and emissary of the archbishop of Canterbury, had an ecumenical spirit. Charged with reporting on the state of Orthodoxy and its monasteries, he found points of convergence everywhere on his journey. Sailing out of Constantinople, he met an Anglican prelate who quoted from a letter sent by high ecclesiastical figures in the Bulgarian Church, which was then in schism from the patriarchal see. They hoped the prelate would use his influence "to get them admitted into the Anglican communion; 'for,' said they, 'you have so many sects in your Church—Presbyterians, and Lutherans, and Calvinists, and many others—that it cannot do you any harm to have one more; so please take the Bulgarians as well.' " Riley's sense of humor forged more links on Athos. When a monk objected to the Church of England's nineteenth article of faith (which states that Orthodoxy and Roman Catholicism have erred), Riley was quick to reply, " 'perhaps we are wrong; only one Church is infallible.' This of course produced a general laugh and a chorus of '*Polycala* [Very good]'. 'When in doubt play a trump' is an old whist rule: Rome is the trump card here."

Anglicans have played that card often since 1534, when King Henry VIII established the Church of England, formalizing the break with Rome. If Constantine united Christians for political reasons, which did not survive the schism, then love completed the splintering of Christendom. It was a woman, Anne Boleyn, who touched off the English Reformation, which led to the creation of a national church, a national identity, and nationalism—"a style of thought," in one scholar's words, which became modernity's sine qua non. And this welter of passion and politics inspired as well the twin ideals of individual rights and democracy, all because Henry wanted a male heir—and Anne Boleyn, famously loved by the poet Thomas Wyatt. After he lost her to the king Wyatt wrote in despair: "I leave off therefore / Since in a net I seek to hold the wind," echoing the anonymous author of *The Cloud of Unknowing*, who said of God: "He may well be loved, but not thought. By love can He be caught and held, but by thinking never." Love, earthly or divine, is fueled not by reason but by desire. Henry wanted a new wife. The rest, as they say, is history.

From the reign of Elizabeth I, who sealed England's Protestant destiny, some Anglicans have yearned to belong to an undivided church, which relies on the authority of the church fathers and the ecumenical councils. An Orthodox theologian told me that because Anglicans possess a keen sense of the patristic spirit (that ritual is a language, and so on) they are not really Protestants. Of course Anglicans and Orthodox have much to agree on, from the unity of Scripture to the belief that only God is infallible. And if Henry VIII's defiance of the pope was by Orthodox lights belated recognition of the truth, still it furnished theologians from both sides with a starting point for a dialogue. In the twentieth century Anglican-Orthodox conferences were held in London, Bucharest, and Moscow, the prelude to the 1984 Dublin Agreed Statement, in which high-ranking ecclesiastics explored the mystery of the Church, the Holy Trinity, the *filioque*, and matters of prayer, worship, and tradition, discovering enough common ground for the authors to declare that the points of disagreement between the churches are not insoluble: "Anglicans and Orthodox alike, we are called to 'reach out towards that which lies ahead, pressing forward to win the prize which is God's call to the life above, in Christ Jesus' (Philippians 3:13–14)."

It is perhaps appropriate, given the history of the Church of England, that the chief stumbling block between the visible union of the Anglican and Orthodox communities is the Anglican practice of ordaining women. Nor have the recent Anglican debates over whether to bless same-sex unions and ordain homosexuals allayed the Orthodox suspicion of the Anglicans' "elastic" understanding of tradition. Nowhere is this more apparent than on the Holy Mountain, where you would be hard pressed to find support for an Anglican-Orthodox union, to say nothing of the larger ecumenical movement. (The two enemies of Orthodoxy, a monk once told me, are ecumenicalism and ethnicity. But that's a contradiction, I said. Exactly, he smiled.) In two weeks, between the feasts celebrating the conversions of Peter and Paul, churches around the globe would pray for Christian unity—a week of communion, inaugurated ninety years ago, in the service of a vision that, if the monks of Athos have their way, will only be realized when the rest of Christendom returns to the right worship, the right praise, of Orthodoxy.

"The union of the Churches," suggests the Protestant theologian Karl Barth, "is not made, but we discover it." And John Leatham is searching for that lost homeland of Christian unity. This Roman Catholic descendant of an Anglican emissary, soon to convert to Orthodoxy, is building bridges in his translations between the Holy Mountain and the English-speaking world. "East or West, God is best," said an old hairless monk at Simonopetra—an attitude congenial to John's work, which carries on his ancestor's mission to Athos. Riley's good-natured account of his pilgrimage not only delighted readers but also helped to foster the Anglican-Orthodox dialogue. He must have made quite an impression at Simonopetra, where one day on the balcony he picked up the speaking-trumpet used to communicate between the monastery and the *arsanas* and cried, "God save the Queen!"—to the monks' amusement and the astonishment of some pilgrims at the port. Riley's only regret about Simonopetra was the garish repainting of the frescoes in its *katholikón*, which in any event burned down within the decade. The walls of the rebuilt *katholikón* are as bare as those of any Protestant church.

"In my father's house are many mansions," Jesus said (John 14:2), as two thousand years of church history reveals. The Venerable Bede (c. 673–735), for example, whose *Ecclesiastical History of the English People* was the first English literary masterpiece, celebrates Christianity's triumph refracted through the medium of Anglo-Saxon culture—one of many versions of Christ's message. I am thinking about what the Anglican tradition can offer to Orthodoxy: the poems of Donne and Herbert and Eliot; the meditations of Thomas Traherne and C. S. Lewis; the hymns of Ralph Vaughan Williams—and, yes, the practice of ordaining women, which has enriched the Anglican communion. Some day my Church, recognizing that the light of Christ "enlightens everyone born into the world" (John 1:9), may take the decision to ordain homosexuals and bless same-sex marriages, perhaps leading our Orthodox brethren to a deeper understanding of Scripture. Meantime we must pray for Christian unity. Before turning out the light John Leatham quotes Bishop Ware: "We have everything to gain from continuing to talk to each other."

BECAUSE OF CALENDAR DIFFERENCES, CHRISTMAS IN THE EASTern Church coincides with Epiphany in the Western. Thus when I rise a little before three in the morning on Christmas Eve I have the chance both to celebrate the Nativity anew and to ponder the meaning of Twelfth Night. I like this double vision, which suits the season. Advent is the time of waiting not only for the birth of our Lord but also for His Second Coming or *Parousia*. The Prophet said, "The Lord himself will give you a sign. Behold, a young woman shall conceive and bear a son, and shall call his name Immanuel" (Isa. 7:14)—the Messiah, who promised to return to judge the living and the dead: "And this is the will of Him who sent Me, that everyone who sees the Son and believes in Him may have everlasting life; and I will raise him up at the last day" (John 6:40).

The blue walls of the *katholikón*, dedicated to the Nativity, are fresh as an unwritten soul. The uncluttered look appeals to the Puritan in me. And John Leatham's fortitude is a thing of wonder: despite his age, a lingering cold, and recent heart surgery, he stands in the nave for the duration of the service, which runs until one in the afternoon, with a two-hour break for a nap. Slumped in the stall beside him, I gaze uncomprehendingly at a gaudy portable icon of four modern Greek saints, hung from one of the wooden portals supporting the dome, and listen to the choir, the best on Athos. The leading chanter carries lines from one side of the nave to the other, the two laymen chanting with the choir do not miss a beat, and before long the sun is shining through the windows. The service concludes with a dazzling sight: seven priests in red and green and gold vestments, bearing crosses or silver boxes inlaid with precious jewels, stand beneath the corona, which a monk sets in motion with a kind of pruning hook, the outside ring spinning back and forth in quarter-turns, the inside ring, lined with candles, revolving counterclockwise. Faster and faster whirl the rings, signaling the arrival of the Holy Spirit, with the sound of shaking metal. And then we follow the chanting monks into the refectory.

"There was not a pause, a hesitation, a misplaced book," John exclaims. "Everything was choreographed to perfection. What ordered souls these monks have!"

Every table is full—a dramatic change from the early 1970s, when only seven monks lived here, six over the age of seventy. That was when monks from a cliff-dwelling monastery in Meteora, in central Greece, tiring of tourists, took over Simonopetra, swept up the debris, and in short order created one of the most vibrant monasteries on the Holy Mountain. After the feast the librarian, a Meteoran monk whose grey beard reaches to his waist, takes us down a long flight of stairs in the original tower, which until recently was filled with rubble. Now one rock wall houses a panel of gauges for a computer-driven power system, which uses four kinds of fuel—solar panels, wood, diesel, and hydroelectric power from the water coursing down the mountain. The jovial monk who designed the system greets us in perfect English. It turns out that we once lived in New York at the same time, where he worked as an engineer, making plans to become a monk. "That's where I know you from," he jokes. The librarian has another joke: a man falling from a skyscraper cries, "St. John, save me!" At once a hand reaches out to grab him. "Thank you," says the man. "But which St. John are you?" "Which one did you want?" asks the voice. "The Baptist," replies the man. "I'm the Theologian," says the voice, and the hand lets go of him.

Across from the panel of gauges is a raised map of Simonopetra's property, some 3,500 acres, two thirds of which burned in the fire of 1990, a century after the razing of the monastery and the library. After the fire the librarian hiked up the ravine between Simonopetra and Grigoriou to inspect the pair of caves depicted on the map. To his surprise he discovered twelve more caves, one of which had a view only of the rising sun.

"That's why monks are called blind mice," he explains.

He leads us down another flight of stairs to the cistern, which has been converted into a library, with handsome oak vaults and shelves. The windows open onto a view of the sea; on the librarian's desk, next to his computer and a printer, are copies of *Studies in Byzantine History*, a hymnography, and Joseph Campbell's *Myths to Live By*. On the floor below are twenty thousand books on rolling bookshelves from Denmark; two floors down is the room in which Albanian stonemasons mix mortar to reinforce the foundation. The wall of one office is a bulging rock.

"We are never without the rock." The librarian smiles.

He has altogether different feelings about his collection, which he has meticulously rebuilt, from those of the monks who let Robert Curzon plunder their libraries. He has acquired three thousand Slavonic manuscripts and texts, many from cash-strapped monasteries in the former Communist bloc, and I detect in him a keen sense of both the spiritual and the monetary value of what he chooses to show us—first editions of the Greek and Russian versions of *The Philokalia*. Then he moves on to priceless items—a medieval manuscript of Simonopetra's *typikon*, and Plutarch's *Life of Isocrates*, in a Roman edition dating from 1513, which sparks John's memory: his grandfather was reading Plutarch when he died. John is eager to see the librarian's latest find—a trio of photographs taken by Athelstan Riley—as well as a manuscript of demotic hymns he hopes to translate. But first the librarian removes from a display case a handwritten life of Hadje-Georghis the Athonite, a nineteenth-century ascetic who lived in the desert. Fasting was his specialty. He was so rigorous, according to his spiritual son, Neophotos, a hesychast calligrapher from Cappadocia, that he painted potatoes to look like Easter eggs. Neophotos composed this biography in Turkish, using Greek letters. The sight of his childlike script is oddly affecting.

"If there is any good reason for Athos to exist," says the librarian, "it's to hide hesychast enthusiasts like Hadje-Georghis and Neophotos."

Riley's photographs and the hymns will remain hidden until I open another gift—a reprint of a photographic itinerary of Athos made in 1935. Leafing through the sepia-tinted pages, I see how little has changed over the years: the *phiale* at Great Lavra; the *katholikón* at Grigoriou; the view from the balcony of Simonopetra. Two monks stand by the sea. Another strikes the *sémantron*. A third rests by a fountain. Here are photographs of crosses and cloisters; of illuminated manuscripts; of monks reading, painting icons, baking bread. Here is a monk gazing out the window in the belfry of Iveron. Here is the monk ringing the bells.

SALVATION SEEMS SIMPLE, AT LEAST ON THE HOLY MOUNTAIN: to love God; to study Scripture and the writings of the church fathers; to pray without ceasing. I have long been in the habit of carrying a book of poems everywhere, in case I find myself with a free minute and nothing to do—in line at the bank, say, or stuck in traffic: anything to avoid peering into the abyss that lies beyond the edge of every thought. But the regular practice of reciting the Jesus Prayer has lessened my anxiety, and some day it may even dwell in my heart, governing my thoughts. "Prayer will arrange everything and teach you," says a monk in *The Way of a Pilgrim*. What I have learned on Athos is that prayer is the secret we carry on this journey to judgment—and the Promised Land.

HALFWAY BETWEEN SIMONOPETRA AND ITS ARSANAS IS A COVERED shrine, where John Leatham and I say farewell late in the afternoon. We have walked down the cobbled mule path that switchbacks across the steep slope, and when he takes a seat on the stone bench I continue to Grigoriou, following the narrow footpath behind the shrine, a twisting root- and rock-strewn descent to the shore, where I must leap from boulder to boulder to ford the stream feeding into the sea. The sun is bright, the sea is calm, and I am grateful to my friend for the instruction I have received in his company in Orthodoxy, which St. Gregory of Sinai defined as "true knowledge of things visible and invisible: visible—that is, sensory; invisible—that is, of thought, intellect, spirit and God." This definition appears in the first English version of *The Philokalia*—a book continuously in print since 1951, when T. S. Eliot overruled the editorial board at Faber and Faber in London and insisted on its publication, even if, as seemed likely, it would lose money. The irony is that it turned a profit. More irony: it was an Anglican poet who made available to an English readership Orthodoxy's most important theological work, building a bridge between the confessions.

I thread my way through more rocks, pass a *kellí*, and climb the trail along the cliff. Eliot's dirge for the loss of a common culture in *The Waste Land* acquired a Christian cast in his later work; his farewell to poetry, *Four Quartets* (1943), is a kind of modern liturgy—the poem, he believed, upon which he stood or fell, both in terms of his literary reputation and of his hopes for salvation. The decline of Christianity he traced to the cultural impoverishment resulting from the Reformation, even as his work was informed by the seventeenth-century English scholar-clerics, Donne and Herbert in particular, whose writings reinvigorated the poetic language and culture. A descendant of Congregational ministers, at thirty-seven he converted to Anglo-Catholicism, the denomination closest in his mind to the ancient Church.

An Anglican priest once said to me that no one ever knows which part of the liturgy—the lessons, psalms, hymns, plainchant—will open his or her heart to God's loving-kindness—an insight reflected in Eliot's mixture of forms and cadences in *Four Quartets*. "Theology has no frontiers," he wrote, and in this poem he explored the unmarked expanses of the spirit, loosening his meters nearly to the point of prose, in an effort to catch the Word—the divine spark integral to religious poetry. His biographer, Lyndall Gordon, suggests that in the Bible's repetitions and alternation of prose and poetry Eliot discovered a model for writing a long poem—and his spiritual testament. Any line may open the careful reader's heart.

This is Eliot's most autobiographical poem, written in the most arduous circumstances: during the Nazi blitz of London, where he served as a fire warden. He devoted his two free days a week to poetry, and it is in "Dry Salvages," the third or American quartet, named for a group of rocks, with a beacon, off the coast of Massachusetts, where he summered as a boy, that his poetic and theological ideas merge. The quartet opens with him drifting back through his memory to his childhood home in St. Louis—and the ubiquitous presence of the Mississippi River:

> . . . *a strong brown God—sullen, untamed and intractable,*
> *Patient to some degree, at first recognized as a frontier;*
> *Useful, untrustworthy, as a conveyor of commerce;*
> *Then only a problem confronting the builder of bridges.*

It was there that Eliot first glimpsed the sacred underpinnings of the quotidian. The river is a force like unto that of a divinity: powerful, difficult to comprehend.

But the river is a minor deity, and so the poet turns his attention to the sea—specifically, a stretch of the Atlantic near Gloucester, where he used to sail around the Dry Salvages, a shelf of rocks on which countless ships foundered. The first section thus neatly divides between the river and the sea, between the element over which industrialized man has some control and that which surrounds us. He hears the tolling of the bell, which "Measures time not our time," and then rings his own variations on the theme of time—the nightlong imaginings of the anxious wives of sailors, "the ground swell, that is and was from the beginning." What he seeks is the silence he heard between the waves as he sailed into the fog, a silence rich with religious meaning.

"To pray means to stand before God with the mind," wrote a seventeenth-century saint of the Russian Church, Dimitri of Rostov, "mentally to gaze unswervingly at Him and to converse with Him in reverent fear and hope." Which is what Eliot did as a child, unconsciously storing up memories of the sacred: the rank ailanthus, the smell of grapes, the halo around the winter gaslight. These primal images may not seem like the stuff of divine revelation, but they are precisely the sensations upon which to build an edifice of belief. Indeed the visions vouchsafed to prophets and saints are exceedingly rare. "For most of us," Eliot argues, "there is only the unattended / Moment, the moment in and out of time." And he instructs the reader in the meaning of those "unattended moments" that everyone experiences, when time and the timeless intersect: the Incarnation. Our lives revolve upon such moments, whether we know it or not:

> The moments of happiness—not the sense of well-being,
> Fruition, fulfilment, security or affection,
> Or even a very good dinner, but the sudden illumination—
> We had the experience but missed the meaning,

And approach to the meaning restores the experience
In a different form, beyond any meaning
We can assign to happiness.

We might call this quartet a study in approaches to the meaning of the Incarnation, when God assumed human form and time merged with the timeless. Hence the childhood memories, which the poet attempts to read in the light of revelation. For just as the river flows into the sea, so our experiences wash into the vast of undifferentiated time, unless we pay attention to those "sudden illuminations" granted to all—hints that most of us ignore. Fortunately, the ones that Eliot received—"a shaft of sunlight, / The wild thyme unseen, or the winter lightning / Or the waterfall"—were followed up by guesses as to their meaning, and then the forging of a life rooted in the Incarnation, a life of prayer and observance (he caught the 6:30 bus each morning to attend mass), out of which arose the miracle of this poem. Discipline and preparation are necessary for the recognition of the sacred, which is always near at hand, even in the darkest times—in a bomb shelter, or on the roof of a city in flames. The American novelist Mary Lee Settle, who served in London during the war, wrote of the publication of *Four Quartets* that Eliot "had somehow refined what he had to tell us, beyond the banality of disappointment and hopelessness, into a promise like steel." What he promised was nothing less than eternity—which, as he reminds us, is available at every moment. Is this not what is promised by the Incarnation?

Once on a transoceanic flight, sick with a stomach virus and unable to eat or sleep, I read and reread *Four Quartets*. Seeking relief late in the night, I put on the headphones and heard a composition for violin and piano by Arvo Pärt, titled *Spiegel im Spiegel*, which is translated as "Mirror in Mirror." Like Eliot, Pärt returned to his Christian origins for spiritual and artistic inspiration. Pärt's work derives from Byzantine chant, and his hauntingly beautiful lines were for me nothing less than what Eliot described as "music heard so deeply / That it is not heard at all, but you are the music, / While the music lasts." I wished it would not end. But in the silence that followed the performance I realized that for whatever reasons—sickness, my reading of Eliot, the disorientation of travel—a crack had opened in the armor I customarily wear against the world, and the music freed me to experience a moment in and out of time.

I quicken my pace near the top of the hill, where the narrowing path winds in and around the bushes, and when I descend to see Grigoriou on its outcropping above the glittering water I recognize an incident from my first pilgrimage, when I stopped here to gaze at the monastery, for what it was: an unattended moment. Now I know, as Eliot wrote, that the rest is indeed "prayer, observance, discipline, thought and action." I hurry toward the gate.

"I WAS BORN BEFORE MY TIME," NICCOLÒ TUCCI WRITES IN A novel. "When my time came, the place was occupied by someone else; all the good things of life for which I was now fit had suddenly become unfit. It was always too early or too late"—a sentiment close to my own. I was not among those who grew rich at the end of the millennium. Indeed when my peers were making their first fortunes Lisa and I were the caretakers of an estate in Santa Fe, my academic career having come to nothing. In the high desert I gardened, chopped wood, translated surrealist poetry; Lisa played in the New Mexico Symphony; our combined annual income was less than ten thousand dollars. And when our college friends were making their next fortunes we were freelancing in Portland, Oregon, accumulating credit card debts. Of Tucci an astute reader said, "He lived in the aftermath of belonging, and that is where he belonged." This is a working definition of the Holy Mountain, a place for those, like me, in search of solace, in the aftermath of belonging.

Which I find at Grigoriou on the eve of the Christmas vigil. The monk who befriended me in the summer has a gift for me: a leather-bound copy of my last book of poems, with a tiny cross engraved on the cover, courtesy of a visiting bookbinder from Athens.

"I am not a very good Christian," says the bookbinder. "That's why I am here. I wanted to come to the roots of Christianity."

The monk is experiencing his own spiritual crisis, I later learn over a cup of tea with him. He has locked the door to a small room off the kitchen so that we will not be disturbed.

"I don't feel the same joy I did a year or two ago," he begins. "It's not a problem of faith or vocation. I wouldn't have come here if that weren't sure. It's just the sense that I may have to live with this for some time, and I'm prepared to do that. Unlike the outside world, where you have so many distractions, here we have nothing but ourselves to come to terms with."

His reading of Revelation has darkened his outlook. He believes the next Messiah will be the Prince of Darkness, that world war may be imminent. The warming climate is a sign of things to come. There used to be snow in the courtyard at Christmas; now the peninsula has been hit with torrential rains. Last week a monk hiking to Dionysiou for the liturgy lost his footing, fell into a flooding stream, and was swept out to sea on a surging wave; his body has not been recovered.

The silence deepens in the room. I feel the weight of the monastic vocation. "If Christ is not raised, your faith is futile and you are still in your sins," Paul said. "Then those also who have fallen asleep in Christ have perished. If for this life only we have hoped in Christ, we are of all people most to be pitied" (1 Cor. 15:17–19). What if all our hope is for naught? The fear that afflicts every Christian at some point must weigh continually on the monastic. What if a life of prayer, fasting, and vigil does not lead to the Kingdom of God? What if this devotion ends in nothingness? "Lord Jesus Christ, Son of God, have mercy on me, a sinner." Prayer is the weapon of choice in the unseen warfare of the doubting heart. The monk is smiling. He has more gifts for me: an icon of St. Nicholas and a reading list. Heaven, he tells me fervently, is another dimension, in which everything will be revealed. He says my spiritual journey may save my marriage.

"What have you learned from your pilgrimages to the Holy Mountain?" he asks.

"I'm more conscious of my sinfulness," I reply.

The monk smiles. "You're making progress."

PAUL PREDICTS THAT CHRIST WILL COME "AS A THIEF IN THE night" (1 Thess. 5:2). The delusional pilgrim in the guest room, however, seems more dangerous than redemptive. I have returned from the vigil to rest, but when I stretch out in my clothes I cannot take my eyes off the bearded man across the aisle. He sits on the edge of his bed, with his shirt unbuttoned and his head in his hands, moaning as if in terrible pain. I should be in church, but I am tired. So I tell the pilgrim the vigil is under way, hoping he will leave. But he speaks no English, his Greek is garbled, and when I close my eyes he begins to make strange clicking noises with his tongue. Better to sleep in the ark of the church, I figure, rising in frustration, than to provoke a crazy man.

In the *katholikón*, though, I feel renewed. An old lame monk shuffles around the narthex, reverently kissing the icons. The candles lit by the pilgrims to commemorate the dead are burning down, and the care with which a monk tends the candleholder, dipping the wicks in a bucket of water and then rearranging the remaining candles in the sand, reveals the prayer at the heart of his every action. The deacon's rich baritone fills the church. The choir answers. The door opens on the north side. The entering pilgrim, my mad roommate, prostrates himself on the floor. What was I thinking? He is a Fool for Christ. My shame knows no bounds.

THE HAIRS RISE ON THE BACK OF MY NECK. HAS A JACKAL CAUGHT my scent? A wolf? I have been hiking toward Eremos since early morning, through canyons deep in shadow, in the hope of glimpsing what ascetics in the remotest hermitages learn in devoting their lives to prayer. "Let your hearts' resolve be to climb," John Climacus writes in *The Ladder of Divine Ascent*. So I climb through scrub oak and madrona, mountain tea and the red globes of ripening arbutus.

The hour of sleep I caught after the feast did not promote clear thinking: in my haste to be on the trail I foolishly left Grigoriou without filling my water bottle, expecting to find some water along the way. The streams were running hard in the canyons, spray from a waterfall hung in the air, and the trail was quite slippery. But the taps outside the monasteries of Dionysiou and St. Paul were turned off for the winter. Likewise the cisterns near Nea Skete, below the snowbound peak. As the sun emerged I removed my wool cap, gloves, and down vest. But it was not long before I sweated through my shirt, and I was just about to change into another when I realized someone or something was watching me from the top of the next rise—a white-bearded hermit, as it happens. He is clutching a plastic bag of wooden stamps bearing likenesses of the Madonna and Child, carved in the primitive tradition of the renowned hesychast elder Joseph, who said that highly detailed work might distract him from the constant remembrance of God. Christ equated a wandering mind with drunkenness and debauchery, and Joseph was afraid of losing his soul, despite his asceticism and spiritual gifts. The hermit wants me to buy all of his stamps. How can I refuse? Yet I am running short on funds, and when I try to explain my predicament he presses them on me for half price. What to do? Haggling with a hermit is unforgivable. I take the bag of stamps and climb the eastern slope of the mountain with a heavy heart.

It is noon before I reach Eremos. The sun is high, the sea calm. Silence everywhere. Parched, famished, I stumble down a hillside to the settlement of St. Basil, a clutch of *kalyvae* overlooking the sea, some of them protected by barbed wire. After ringing the bell in vain at several places, I head westward. A sea eagle soars above the cliff. Archimandrite Ilian said, "The ascetic is truly renewed as an eagle." Exhausted, I trudge toward the settlement of Katounákia and the hermitages of Karoúlia, where ascetics devote themselves to prayer.

Katounákia: huts and caves scattered across the mountain's southwestern slope, a sight that makes me break out in gooseflesh. Here is an original vision of Christianity—of monks retreating to the desert to meditate on the Incarnation, preserving the tradition of martyrdom, of bearing witness to the truth. The Church's establishment as a state religion did not slow the need for some to test their faith. On the contrary. The blood and sacrifice of the first martyrs gave way to the arduous forms of penance practiced by the desert fathers. And what I see in this voluntary exile by the sea, this white martyrdom, is the indescribable power of faith.

The conjunction of Orthodox Christmas and Epiphany in the West is fortuitous for my journey into faith. For even as the Eastern Church celebrates the Nativity, and Roman Catholics and Protestants recall the revelation—the showing forth—of Christ to the Magi, I am having my own epiphany: that the mystery of the Incarnation endures in my life. Leaving the trail, I climb down a set of stone steps to an abandoned hermitage, a stone hut with a slate roof and two small rooms with white walls. No telling how long it has lain empty. A large earthenware jug is propped against one wall, and through the window I gaze at the sea, toward the Holy Land, where a child born two thousand years ago promised to redeem mankind.

"What child is this?" we sing on Christmas Eve. The answers are revealing. If Matthew's genealogy for the Son of man descends from Abraham through David and the captivity in Babylon, forty-two generations in all, Luke reverses course, tracing His heritage back seventy-five generations to Adam, to include everyone in His doctrine of salvation. John the Baptist invoked a prophesy of Isaiah to herald Christ's arrival: "A voice cries: 'in the wilderness prepare the way of the Lord, make straight in the desert a highway for our God' " (Isa. 40:3). Asked if he was the Messiah, John replied, "I baptize you with water; but one who is more powerful than I is coming; I am not worthy to untie the thong of his sandals." Thus in the waters of Jordan he baptized Jesus, whose name means helper, deliverer, and savior, and His true identity was revealed: "the Holy Spirit descended upon him in bodily form, as a dove, and a voice came from heaven, 'Thou art my beloved Son; with whom I am well pleased' " (Luke 3:16, 22).

A shiver runs up my spine. What a glorious calling is monasticism! But how to live in such austerity? Still I am moved to think I have been granted insight into the mystery of faith, and perhaps even a measure of grace, the meaning of which I may spend the rest of my life examining. I leave the hut and head for the center of Katounákia, a dependency of Great Lavra, established by a hermit named Daniel. Originally a *hesychasterion*, Katounákia has always attracted iconographers, and in the sitting room of a new *kalyve* a painter-monk serves me water, raki, and cookies. The tables and chairs arranged on the patio remind me of a taverna, with red geraniums in planter boxes and a panoramic view of the sea. How I would love to spend the afternoon here, reading and writing, or talking, perhaps, with the monk. But he has other matters to attend to, and I cannot stay, not if I hope to make my flight home. I climb to the notch between the mountain's southern and western slopes and stop at a shrine to rest, leaning back against a rock to read the Gospel (literally, "the good news") of Luke: "The coming of the kingdom of God cannot be observed, and no one will announce, 'Look, here it is!' or, 'There it is!' For, behold, the kingdom of God is within you" (Luke 17:20–21). What a radical idea: with these words the cosmic drama moves into the individual soul, unfolding on a private stage. The revolutionary implications of this interiority, to say nothing of the linguistic ramifications, continue down to the present. Milosz argues that "Only one language can do justice to the highest claim of the human imagination—that of Holy Writ." But so few of us are fluent in this language now that the highest claims on our imagination go unexpressed, despite the proliferation of therapists, self-help manuals, and creative writing programs. We no longer possess what might be called a scriptured mind, a soul lettered in Holy Writ—the one Christmas present I never received.

For so long I have loathed the holiday season and the ruthlessness with which the spirit of commerce drowns out the Spirit of God. What place does the Nativity hold in our celebrations? The exchange of gifts has replaced the workings of faith, hope, and love. Yet two millennia ago, when God incarnated Himself in man, there was a miraculous birth in Galilee, the meaning of which continues to elude me. How strange that I have lived through a reckless youth, sickness, and war, only to discover how much I want to hear His message. I turn to the passage in which a disciple asks the Lord for instructions on prayer. Jesus offers the Lord's Prayer, which I have recited thousands of times while drifting off to sleep, or taxiing in an airplane, or huddling in the basement of a building under shellfire. But to really say it, I realize, I will have to turn my life toward God and meditate on the singular presence of His Son, Jesus Christ, as revealed in the Holy Writ. An osprey takes flight from the cliff below me. Out at sea a monk in a motorboat is fishing. I begin to pray: *Our Father, who art in Heaven, hallowed be thy name.*

——

A YEAR PASSED. POPE JOHN PAUL II TRAVELED TO BUCHAREST IN May to meet with Romanian Patriarch Teoctist, the first papal visit to an Orthodox country since 1054—a conciliatory gesture undone, in October, by his decision to beatify Cardinal Alojzije Stepinac, the archbishop of Zagreb during the murderous Ustaša regime. And the turbulence on the world stage—Bill Clinton's impeachment, the NATO campaign against Yugoslavia to reverse its ethnic cleansing of Kosovo, the Russian invasion of Chechnya— had echoes in my own life, as sickness took its toll among my loved ones: a severe regimen of chemotherapy and radiation treatments left my father-in-law an invalid; my father was hospitalized three times with an incurable form of pneumonia; my best friend was diagnosed with inoperable brain cancer; one of Lisa's closest friends was dying of colon cancer.

At the same time my marriage seemed to be on the mend. Something changed between Lisa and me after our terrible row in London. It was as if a dam had broken inside her, and in the flood of her emotions some of her bitterness washed away. She welcomed me home from Greece in a spirit of reconciliation, insisting that we make a fresh start. Nor did she pick another fight for weeks; and when we did argue now the level of invective was often lower, the route to making up more direct. I thanked God for her change of heart, which I did not pretend to understand, and for the peace reigning in my household—which, for my part at least, seemed connected to my journey into faith. At Advent I returned to the Holy Mountain full of prayers.

The afternoon of the Christmas vigil was pleasant enough for a monk and a former classics professor from South Africa to hike with me from Grigoriou to the waterfall marking the boundary with Dionysiou. The monk was eager to discuss a recent visit by a delegation of Serbian monks who claimed to have dug up mass graves of Serbs; their catalog of Albanian crimes in Kosovo—desecrated and destroyed churches and monasteries, attacks against Serbs—testified to the failure of the peacekeeping mission. But this monk would not hear of the apartheid-like conditions under which Kosovar Albanians had lived for the last decade, or of their losses during the war—hundreds of villages laid waste, thousands killed or missing, hundreds of thousands sent into flight: crimes against humanity for which Slobodan Milošević and his cohorts had been indicted by the International War Crimes Tribunal at The Hague. Nor did the monk wish to be reminded that after the NATO campaign Serbian Patriarch Pavle had traveled to Kosovo to denounce his countrymen's atrocities. "If the only way to create a greater Serbia is by crime," the patriarch had said, "then I do not accept that, and let Serbia disappear."

The Afrikaner wisely changed the subject. He was pursuing graduate studies at an Orthodox seminary in America—"Once you've tasted patristic theology," he explained, "it is difficult to go back to the cerebral pleasures of classical philosophy: the fathers strike much deeper, through the heart"—and his reading of romantic accounts of life on the Holy Mountain had convinced him to stay at Grigoriou until he discerned whether he had a monastic vocation.

"I wanted to see if I could live with the . . . deprivations," he said judiciously.

Thin and greying at the temples, he sashayed up the trail and over boulders with his hands in his pockets, preoccupied with the changing order in his homeland. The fluid conditions of post-apartheid rule left his people searching for direction, he said, and he hoped some day to help fulfill the dream of an Afrikaner poet: "I long to see white chapels in every field."

We came to the waterfall, where the monk kissed me good-bye on both cheeks.

"Our people need to learn to bless their fields, their animals, their wells," the Afrikaner said softly. "They know how to bless their meals, yes, but they must bless every element of life."

PAUL WAS IN PRISON WHEN HE WROTE, "LET THE SAME MIND BE in you that was in Christ Jesus, who, though he was in the form of God, did not regard equality with God as something to be exploited, but emptied himself, taking the form of a slave, being born in human likeness" (Phil. 2:5–7). A radical form of freedom is what the saint, quoting a Christian hymn, envisions for the Son of man and mankind. In these verses he invents the doctrine of *kenosis*, of self-emptying, from which developed the Jesus Prayer: invoking His name, we empty ourselves of sin, glimpse the freedom of eternity through the bonds of our earthly sentence, and clear a space for the inflowing of God's loving-kindness. Humility is the key. Simone Weil blamed the imagination for sealing the fissures through which grace might pass, just as a poet knows the distractions—the passions—that inhibit the making of verses. For a poet must listen to the language as intently as a penitent prays to God. Indeed the openness fostered by prayer resembles the emptiness preceding artistic creation, although the stakes are higher for the faithful. The poet wishes to be read down through the ages, the faithful to be read by God eternally. Which is why Paul suggests that because Christ "humbled himself and became obedient to the point of death—even death on the cross" (Phil. 2:8), we must drop to our knees at the sound of His name and confess His glory. "Lord Jesus Christ, Son of God," I say, negotiating the cliff between the monasteries of Dionysiou and St. Paul, "have mercy on me, a sinner." What I feel opening in my heart at the sight of the sea I cannot say.

DUSK. THE MONKS ARE RESTING UP FOR THE VIGIL WHEN I arrive at St. Paul. In the empty waiting room I sit for hours by the cold radiator, shivering in my sweaty clothes. A light bulb flickers above the tea table on which the guest register is propped open, and when a group of pilgrims shuffles in a brawny Greek sits at the table and scans the names. Then he launches a harangue against America and NATO, only parts of which I understand, though his malice toward me is unmistakable. The other pilgrims nod in agreement, casting angry looks in my direction.

To encounter such hostility on Christmas Eve is unpleasant, even if it brings home the fact that conflict is woven into the Christian message of love, beginning with the account of Jesus's birth in the Gospel of Matthew. An angel appears to Joseph in a dream, instructing him to flee with his family to Egypt, for Herod, king of Judaea, fearing the birth of a rival, plans to kill Him. Every male child in Bethlehem under the age of two will be put to death—the Holy Innocents revered in Orthodoxy as saints and martyrs. And the flight into Egypt, a grand theme of Western art, is much on my mind after the latest Balkan War, in which Serbian forces sent eight hundred thousand Kosovar Albanians fleeing for their lives. Every refugee reenacts the plight of the Holy Family on the run, Pieter Brueghel the Elder suggests in his painting of Joseph leading Mary and Jesus on a donkey through a mountainous landscape that might pass for the Balkans. It was no accident that Jesus entered Jerusalem on a donkey, reinforcing the meaning of His self-*kenosis*: the Son of man was born into poverty and died in abject humiliation. And there is no excuse for Orthodox Christians sending Muslims into flight, even if the Ottomans treated their ancestors as second-class citizens. Christ teaches forgiveness—an insight lost on the pilgrims glaring at me.

All at once jackals are howling outside the monastery walls. It takes some minutes for a pilgrim to call the haranguer's attention to their eerie song. He listens for only a moment before resuming his diatribe. I am grateful when the guestmaster finally arrives to show me to a room, which to my dismay I will share with the haranguer and his two friends.

Fortunately, the vigil is about to begin. In a cold rain I stand outside the cast-iron door to the *katholikón*, warned off by the sign, in English, forbidding the entrance of non-Orthodox, until an old monk, taking pity, escorts me into the nave. A priest in gold vestments, bearing on his shoulder a silver replica of the church, is censing the icons, monks, and pilgrims. Strange to think the gifts of the wise men—gold for a king, frankincense for God, and myrrh for the man destined to suffer and die—brought to Jesus in Bethlehem and later presented to the monastery by Sultana Maria, are stored in this sanctuary. And stranger still to realize that a monk's consideration for my well-being has again trumped the rules, allowing me to participate in the vigil.

My fear of the rain triggering a flood or avalanche above the monastery is tempered by the glory of the ceremony, the hierarchic splendor of the church—"an icon of the universe according to the Christian pattern," writes Philip Sherrard. Hence the figure of Christ the Pantokrator gazing down from the dome on the marble walls and columns, the monks and pilgrims. The chanting in His honor sustains me through a night of prayer, and the holy hush of faith is what I carry into the refectory at daybreak. I sit with a hermit at a separate table for the feast, which concludes with a monk distributing (to everyone but me) the rest of the leavened bread used for the Eucharist. Out we file then through two long lines of bowing and blessing monks, who chant through the ringing of the bells. My roommates catch the ferry to Daphne. I take a nap.

IT IS COLD AND CLEAR WHEN I LEAVE FOR EREMOS, EXCEPT around the mountaintop, where storm clouds are gathering. The snow line ends just above the monastery, yet I am sweating before I reach the first rise in the trail, awash in snowmelt. If I knew that the monk tending his orange grove in Nea Skete would be the last person I would see for hours I would surely hail him. But he is working in such a prayerful manner that I walk by without disturbing him. Nor can I find anyone at the *skete* of St. Anne. It is just as quiet in the neighboring *skete* of Little St. Anne. Under an old telephone line I scramble up the mountainside to Katounákia, which once presented itself to me as a vision of the original desert monasticism. This day, though, every *kalyve* is deserted.

The sky is clouding over as I head toward the settlement of St. Basil, and the footpath along the mountain's southern slope turns to snow, which deepens with each step, obscuring the trail markers and seeping through my jeans. Following a set of footprints eventually brings me to a large *kalyve* with a fine view of the sea, but when I ring the bell at the locked gate I raise only a mule foraging in the courtyard, which eyes me with incomprehension. And no one answers at the next place, where the footprints disappear. Then the trail vanishes in a snow squall. My jeans and turtleneck are icing up, my waterproofed boots leak.

I stop to change my shirt and collect my wits, then make a rash decision: to climb through the snow to the high trail and take it back to St. Anne. It is another hour before I gain the point where the trail goes off in five different directions, including the mountaintop, which is lost to sight. Unaccountably, another set of footprints convinces me not to return to St. Anne but to follow them eastward to Kerásia. In knee-deep snow my spirits suddenly soar, and at the fork in the trail, instead of descending to Kerásia, I stay in the snow for the sheer pleasure of tracking the footprints, which to my chagrin end at the dwelling of Paliópyrgos. No one is home. What to do? This late in the day I have little choice but to break trail down the mountain to the seaside *skete* of Kavsokalívia, the remotest settlement on Athos.

The snow, I am happy to discover, is light enough to glissade down the steepest sections of the trail, which drops seven hundred meters in altitude in less than two kilometers. I am counting my blessings—that my boots are sturdier than sneakers; that the wind has died—even before the sun emerges from behind the clouds. The sea glitters below. The snow gives way to mud, rocks, and stands of madrona; carved into the bark of one tree trunk is a pair of crosses. The trail merges with a stone walkway, and soon I hear a voice rising through the air—the commands of a laborer leading a mule up the steps, *clip-clop, clip-clop*. Atop the mule is a sleepy-eyed monk bound for Paliópyrgos. He asks about the conditions farther up the trail and about my profession, which I cannot make him understand until I show him my copy of Donne's poems.

"Ah, poet," he says with a smile. "Very good."

After hours of walking in silence I am hoping for more substantial conversation, but with the sun low in the sky the laborer goads the mule up the steps. I go to Kavsokalívia, which means "burned huts," commemorating the practice of Maximos, a fourteenth-century saint who burned down his grass hut whenever another hermit took up residence near him. A light surrounded Maximos in prayer, and he was said to possess the gifts of levitation—he used to fly to the mountaintop to talk to the Virgin—and prophecy, which, alas, caught the emperor's attention. And that is why this lover of solitude ended his days dispensing wisdom in Constantinople.

A paddock holding six mules stands at the entrance to Kavsokalívia, an idiorrhythmic *skete* renowned for its iconographers. The muck is deep; the stench of manure carries into the communal kitchen, a dark hovel in which a grey-bearded monk is heating a pot of leftover fish stew on a propane stove. Two pilgrims from Thessaloníki invite me to join them at a roughhewn table to drink coffee, water, and raki. The monk says that in the last century the population of the *skete* has declined from 150 to 35; most of its 40 *kalyvae* are empty. He turns to a brighter subject: the intricate paper icon of the Holy Mountain, tacked to the wall behind us, over which he labored for thirty years. Even in the dim light I can make out his marvelous draftsmanship. A half-circle of prophetic scrolls and opened copies of the Gospels and the Revelation curves around the peninsula, almost every inch of which is taken up with churches and monastic buildings. Here are detailed renderings of biblical stories; portraits of saints and of the condemned. A ladder reaches into the clouds where the Queen of Heaven in a golden halo stands in a blue robe and red cape, her arms outstretched in a dark sky of angels, stars, and a silver sun; beyond the firmament are hand-lettered texts containing hundreds of saints' lives—thousands of words of praise.

"Thirty years," I exclaim.

The monk smiles.

Some monks join us for dinner, and by 6:30 the pilgrims and I have retired to a barren room lit by a bulb, the size of a Christmas tree ornament, hanging above a wood-burning stove. The pilgrims, a plump waiter and an unemployed baggage handler, spent the previous night at Great Lavra, lodged in a room with a broken window. This is even colder, the waiter sighs. A strong wind off the sea blows through the cracks in the wall; the stove gives out almost no heat, and our supply of wood is gone within an hour. It was wishful thinking on my part to spread my pants and boots to dry on the cement floor by the stove. The baggage handler has a better idea. He goes to the kitchen to beg for extra raki—to stay warm, he tells the obliging monk.

Under a mound of blankets I lie in the dark, taking stock.

There is no phone, a boat is not due for three days, the nearest monastery is hours away by foot. Yet I am warm enough to join the Greeks in making light of our situation. What has Athos taught you? they ask. Not to waste my life, I reply. They are serious young men—the baggage handler has a spiritual father—but after a while they prefer to trade jokes in Greek until they fall asleep.

This will be for me a sleepless night, "a night of watching" (Exod. 12:42). Not that I am anxious. Far from it. Tucking the blankets up to my chin, I listen to the wind and waves, grateful to be alive, alert to everything. "I sleep, but my heart waketh," Solomon tells his beloved (Song of Sol. 5:2). Too worked up to sleep, I feel my heart waking just the same. I picture Lisa chasing Hannah across the lawn, laughing. How often I have failed them. To the sound of the storm-tossed sea I make resolutions: to love my family better; to paint a true portrait of the Holy Mountain; to use whatever time I have left to serve God. What joy I feel!

CZESLAW MILOSZ CONCLUDES HIS POEM *FROM THE RISING OF THE Sun* with this assertion:

> *Yet I belong to those who believe in* apokatastasis.
> *That word promises reverse movement,*
> *Not the one that was set in* katastasis,
> *And appears in the Acts* 3, 21.

> *It means: restoration. So believed: St. Gregory of Nyssa,*
> *Johannes Scotus Erigena, Ruysbroeck, and William Blake.*

> *For me, therefore, everything has a double existence.*
> *Both in time and when time shall be no more.*

A verse from Psalm 113—"From the rising of the sun to its going down let the Name of the Lord be praised"—furnished the title for Milosz's book-length poem, which is by turns an eschato-logical meditation, a hymn of praise to the natural world, and an exploration of his poetic roots, a vanished world evoked in a variety of forms. In one section he mixes prose and poetry to resurrect his homeland in a part of Lithuania that once belonged to Poland and then passed into the Soviet sphere of influence, a place he must have assumed he would never see again at the time of the poem's composition, in 1973. This is the kind of bitter knowledge that spurs both the artistic and the religious imagination. For exile informs Milosz's poetics no less than faith: his work is filled with wonder at his lost childhood, that other paradise. Perhaps God grants us what Wordsworth described as "intimations of immortality"—the freedom of childhood, ecstasies of love, moments of clairvoyance—in order to instruct us about the next world, just as that which is lost or taken away—innocence, love, health—can draw us closer to Him.

Poetry and prayer are complementary routes to restoration, as *From the Rising of the Sun* illustrates. And the authorities invoked by Milosz for his belief in *apokatastasis*, which *The Oxford Dictionary of World Religions* defines as "the restoration of the created order to a condition either of its intended perfection, or to its source (e.g. God as creator)," present an alternate history of the Christian imagination. Aligning himself with a Cappadocian father, a medieval Irish interpreter of Pseudo-Dionysios the Areopagite and St. Maximos the Confessor, a Flemish mystic known as the Ecstatic Doctor, and a visionary English poet who set himself against rational religion, Milosz reminds us that there are other ways to approach God than what we hear in Western churches. "In Blake," he writes in *The Land of Ulro*, an essay on the split in the West between thinking and feeling, "religion and poetry merge, art becomes prophesy, just as religion, before it became debased, was once prophesy—the writings of the prophets of the Old Testament and the Gospels stood for him as perfect models of inspired speech." If the "inspired speech" of poet-prophets helped lead me to the Holy Mountain in the first place, I have returned because of my acute sense of what Milosz calls the "double existence" of everything.

His verses are running through my mind when the *sémantron* calls me to the liturgy. I pull on my damp boots and pants and go outside. There is no light in the outhouse, so I urinate into the muck of the paddock. An ominous cloud spreads from the sea to the mountaintop, covering the stars. It is not long before my anxiety has returned. If only I could flee from here!

A dozen monks enter the *kyriakon*. Ordinarily I would have to remain outside but in this freezing weather the iconographer who served dinner last night does not hesitate to invite me in. The chanting calms my nerves. Soon I realize there is no place I would rather be than here. "And the light shines in the darkness," said the Evangelist, "and the darkness did not comprehend it" (John 1:5). And I have attended enough services to recognize and respond to the different parts of the liturgy—the antiphons and readings, entrances and processions, hymns and litanies, prayers and petitions—which will transform this community of monks and pilgrims into the Body of Christ, sanctifying them through the sacrament of Holy Communion. This is the corporate life of the Church, in which bread and wine are mystically changed into the Body and Blood of the Savior, and the faithful—judged, forgiven, and granted new life—become Christ-bearers.

The liturgy is divided into two parts, the preparatory and the sacramental, the Liturgy of the Word and the Liturgy of the Faithful, which correspond to the movement from the Old Testament to the New, from Law to Love. In the first part, which begins with the priest entering the sanctuary, through the central door—the beautiful gate—of the iconostasis, to bless the altar and the Gospel, and concludes with the Creed, Christ's life is celebrated—His birth, teachings, death, resurrection, and ascension into Heaven—as preparation for the Eucharist. This divine mystery is an example of what some commentators call the double experience of the Church, which married Jewish custom to Hellenistic thought:

Jerusalem and Athens. Building on the feasts of love the apostles held after the Crucifixion, the Liturgy of the Word adopts the Jewish practice of readings in the synagogue, illustrating through the Gospels the Savior's public ministry; in the Liturgy of the Faithful, the Eucharist, the Word becomes the Word Incarnate: a marriage of Heaven and earth, the future and the present. An eschatological community is created.

The original meaning of *liturgy* is public service—that is, for the common good. Octavio Paz called poetry the freest activity of the spirit, since it is generally composed without concern for material gain. The same holds for the liturgy, the work of the people—a continuous song, a priest writes. And this morning I think I am listening to the most wonderful poem of all.

Time out of time: this is what the faithful experience in the liturgy, celebrating the eternal mystery of the Church: "the cross, the tomb, the resurrection on the third day, the ascension into heaven, the enthronement at the right hand of the Father, and the second glorious coming." And so the liturgy concludes with another verse from Psalm 113: "Blessed be the name of the Lord from this time forth and forevermore!" Blessed indeed.

THE LOWER TRAIL FROM KAVSOKALÍVIA TO GREAT LAVRA FOLlows the cliff, which in some places drops off sharply into the sea. This morning a purse seiner lies near the coast, drawing in its nets. Another storm is gathering on the mountaintop, but I am hiking in sunlight, on reasonably dry ground, and my legs feel strong as I enter the gorge above the Bay of the Standing Ship, in which the ship carrying Peter the Athonite stalled more than a thousand years ago—in a favoring wind. It was here that the Holy Mountain's first ascetic pleaded to be left on shore, releasing the ship from its strange spell and inaugurating an ascetic tradition that still feeds the imagination. Across the chasm, near the top of a rocky precipice, behind a small chapel cut into a ledge several hundred meters above the sea, lies the cave of St. Nílos the Myroblyte. Fasting and spiritual exercises are just the first steps toward divinization in such *asceteria*. On some bluffs a hardy ascetic will tie a rope to a tree trunk, loop it around his chest, and spend his life leaning over the abyss, praising God: "Be my strong rock, a castle to keep me safe; you are my crag and my stronghold" (Ps. 71:3). And sometimes the fruit of his devotions takes a tangible form. For example, it is said that when St. Nílos lived here in the seventeenth century so much myrobalan poured from his cave that ships would sail into the bay to collect the dye as it spilled into the sea. I circle the gorge, climbing toward the settlement of St. Nílos, my eyes fixed on the cave.

The sky has clouded over by the time I arrive at St. Nílos. Two mules are feeding in the courtyard by the chapel; herbs are drying under the eaves. When no one answers the door to the largest building, I walk through an olive grove and gingerly descend a long staircase to the saint's cave, dizzy with fear. The chapel inside the cave is all but decomposed, and the fall to the sea is five times greater than the jump from the Golden Gate Bridge. I do not trust myself at this height and climb back up the steps, chagrined to discover once again that I am no athlete of God.

From Nílos the trail cuts across a steep scree field more than a kilometer wide. An hour's hike in worsening weather, exposed among the rocks then sheltered in the woods, brings me to a series of switchbacks. I am climbing toward the pass between the mountain's southern and eastern slopes when birdsong stops me in my tracks. "Look at the birds of the air," Jesus tells His disciples, "for they neither sow nor reap nor gather into barns; yet your heavenly father feeds them. Are you not of more value than they? Which of you by worrying can add one cubit to his stature?" But my shirt is soaked with sweat, and the temperature is falling. "So why do you worry about clothing?" Jesus continues. "Consider the lilies of the field, how they grow: they neither toil nor spin; and yet I say to you that even Solomon in all his glory was not arrayed like one of these. Now if God so clothes the grasses of the field, which today is, and tomorrow is thrown into the oven, will he not much more clothe you, O you of little faith?" (Matt. 6:26–30). His questions plague me until I reach the pass, marked by the ruins of a stone hut and a cross propped in a cairn. But my anxiety dissolves at the sight of the Romanian *skete* in the distance. Then I notice a hermitage tucked in the bluff at the tip of the peninsula, across from a *kellí* that doubles as a radar station, and my heart quickens. I may never escape the pull of the life apart.

This is the theme of Elizabeth Bishop's late poem "The End of March." In cold, windy weather she joins two friends for a walk on a Massachusetts beach. The details she registers from the natural world, the ebb tide and straggling seabirds and dark sky ("*withdrawn* is the key word," the poet James Merrill notes: " 'Everything was withdrawn as far as possible, / indrawn' "), point to a kind of spiritual emptiness, borne out by the facts of her biography. Bishop's last years were difficult: she lost her partner to suicide; she suffered from depression and alcoholism; and in this poem she hopes to get as far as her "proto-dream-house, [her] crypto-dream-house, that crooked box / set up on a pilings," where she can retire "and do *nothing,*

or nothing much, forever, in two bare rooms:
look through binoculars, read boring books,
old, long, long books, and write down useless notes,
talk to myself, and, foggy days,
watch the droplets slipping, heavy with light.

Who has not dreamed of finding such a haven? If my first pilgrimage was prompted by despair at the way my life had turned out, I have learned that world weariness has little to do with the monastic vocation as conceived in the desert. Unceasing prayer, fasts, and vigils are not the same as the *grog à l'américaine* the poet imagines drinking at night in her dream house; the monk guards his heart differently from embittered refugees from life, who close themselves off to all affection. Monastic vigilance is designed to open oneself to the possibility of grace.

The storm is holding off, and the sun comes out before I reach Timiou Prodrómou, where the fathers are asleep, the guestmaster is nowhere to be found, and the laborers hired to build a dormitory by the sea have gone home for the holiday. Beyond the tilled garden, off the dirt road to the coast guard station, an electrical line draped across the brush leads to the bluff, in which lies the cave of St. Athanasios, the founder of Great Lavra. Against a cistern someone has laid a broom with a cross worked into its bristles; a mechanical crane hangs above the abyss. Down more than two hundred stone steps I descend to a gate, which opens onto a view of a bay, nearly two hundred meters below. A low rock wall runs along the ledge, shielding a narrow kitchen plot into which water trickles from a hose. Wedged into the cliff is a new L-shaped wood-and-stucco *kalyve*, with a bed in one room—the only piece of furniture—and icons on the walls; a set of steps behind the building leads into the cave, where the pews, iconostasis, and an icon of the Madonna and Child are veiled in darkness. I sit on a step in the sun and gaze at the sea. This is a perfect setting to contemplate the goodness of Creation. But who will occupy this hermitage?

Bishop's reverie about solitude in "The End of March" is interrupted by her realization that it is too cold to walk to her dream house, which in any event is boarded up. On her way back the sun emerges briefly to transform the drab, damp stones along the beach into rainbow-colored jewels, which cast shadows as if to tease "the lion sun," a godlike figure "who perhaps had batted a kite out of the sky to play with." Bishop's fantasy of withdrawing from daily life seems hopelessly small in the light of the sun god. And while I would not presume to call her a religious poet (although George Herbert was her favorite poet), "The End of March" can be read in a theological context. No god supplanted by another ever entirely disappears, *pace* Christianity's solar orientation: Christ is the Light of the World. His Nativity at Christmas was first celebrated in Rome in 336—the date of His birth is uncertain—to oppose the feast of the "birthday of the unconquered sun" on the winter solstice. Bishop's epiphany takes on added significance when we recall that it occurs at or just after the vernal equinox, when day and night are of equal length, for this is ultimately a poem about maintaining a balance between despair and delight.

I climb the steps and wander over to the next bluff, where another new *kalyve* stands on an even more precarious ledge. Peering over the edge at the tin roof, I try to imagine the faith required to stay here, even as images from my own life flood my mind—Lisa playing her violin, Hannah skating. I cannot live in solitude, though I may yet learn, in the words of Bishop Ware, to be "a hermit of the heart," cultivating a silent space in which to hear God's voice. My destiny is elsewhere. Called to marriage, fatherhood, and literary work, in the same way that an anchorite will be called to this hut, I must take up the cross in the midst of a busy life. It is said that marriage is hard work. In fact it is sacramental work, another kind of martyrdom, which demands joyful acceptance of the limitations it imposes on our lives. Just as poets know that traditional forms can either imprison or free the imagination, so marriage, and indeed any calling, can either liberate or confine—or, as often happens, both liberate and confine. The line blurs between rigid formalism and beauty of the sort that Dostoevsky thought could save the world. Our task is to discover how to maintain a fresh perspective on the forms in which we must work out our destiny, rediscovering their intrinsic beauty at every stage of our lives. The desert fathers tell us this perspective is rooted in humility—the land, said Abbot Alonios, "where God wants us to go and offer sacrifice." And perhaps one consequence of the modern revolution in politics, culture, and aesthetics—the rise and fall of ideologies; the decline of organized religion; the wealth of artistic and literary experimentation—will be to foster humility, reawaken the instinct for wonder, and remind us of the glories of certain forms: blank verse, marriage, liturgy.

It is instructive that Elizabeth Bishop dedicated "The End of March" to the two friends who walked with her on the beach. "No man is an island," John Donne said near the end of his life, a maxim which applied even to St. Athanasios, whose days and nights in this cave must have been filled with God's presence. But just as Bishop chose the company of others over solitude, so the saint left his hermitage in order to build a monastery—a decision I echo when I rise to my feet and depart for Great Lavra, which, I remember, means brotherhood.

———

THE ADDER SLITHERS INTO THE UNDERBRUSH JUST BEFORE I step on it. Ten meters farther on, where the path between Grigoriou and Dionysiou is so narrow the vegetation scrapes my trousers, a second Balkan adder—the first one's mate?—slides by. At once I am alert to every nuance of this warm spring day—the smell of nectar, the distant rumble of a fishing boat, the sun high overhead. "You see a snake?" said an eighteenth-century monk. "Do not run away—it will not attack you. You see your terrible enemy, the devil? Do not be troubled: show him your Cross . . . It is the hour for prayer." And I am praying, stepping gingerly around a clump of prickly pears. Adders will kill you, a monk once told me, in such a peaceful manner that I grew ashamed of my fear. Death is the only thing we have to prepare for, the monk continued. Everything else is ephemera.

A common Athonite sentiment. An American monk, newly arrived on the Holy Mountain, who told me that if he fell seriously ill he would catch the first flight home, stood apart from his brethren. But the American's way of thinking was familiar to me. A foreign journalist, a veteran of the siege of Sarajevo and the NATO campaign in Kosovo, had lately asked me to account for what she called the unhealthy American relationship to death. It was the Day of the Dead in Montenegro, where I was on assignment; the cemeteries in the capital of Podgorica were filled with mourners and flowers; there was a kind of fatalistic joy in the air, which countered the dread I carried from my interview with a

Serbian paramilitary who had raped and murdered his way across Kosovo. At my insistence the paramilitary had met me in the café of the Grand Hotel, where there would be enough people, I hoped, to discourage any violence. He was armed and agitated, high on cocaine. He wore a black prayer rope around his wrist. Once he winked at me. His cold-blooded description of his killing sprees left me sleepless.

Genesis blames the serpent for mankind's expulsion from the Garden of Eden. And if in the Old Testament we learn that the cycle of birth and death is the punishment we must endure for our knowledge of good and evil, then the Gospels offer redemption through Christ's incarnation, death, and resurrection. "The sting of death is sin," said Paul (1 Cor. 15:56), which Christ destroyed—a tenet of faith that my encounter with the paramilitary has shaken. Which is why I am hiking, on Good Friday, in the Virgin's Garden, the new Eden, through a riot of color—daisies and anemones, lupines and clumps of thorny broom scattered across the hillsides. The Judas tree is in blossom, and the mimosa. The air is flush with songbirds, butterflies, bumblebees. This is the season of transformation. A blue-throated lizard, turning from green to brown, darts in and out of the rocks. Clouds cover the mountaintop and sail on. "You must change your life," Rilke wrote. "Follow me," Christ said (Mark 1:17). Remembering the monk's warning about the viciousness of adders during the mating season, I watch my step as I continue down the trail. Christ said: "Whoever would save his life will lose it; and whoever loses his life for my sake will save it" (Luke 9:24). But I have a good reason to stay alive: Lisa is pregnant.

THE SPIRITUAL CHILDREN OF ELDER JOSEPH THE HESYCHAST (d. 1959) were responsible for the revival of several Athonite monasteries, including Dionysiou, where I arrived in time for vespers. And now, after a light meal in the refectory, I sit with pilgrims on a stone wall stretching southward from the gate. The sea is calm, but clouds are gathering above the mountain that rises in folds and ravines behind the monastery set on a cliff eighty meters above the water. One pilgrim is advising a monk on the proper way to prune a grapevine. Another smokes and flicks his prayer beads. Swallows skim over the slate roof of the laborers' quarters across from us. Above the cistern, in the shade of a yellow rose, a laborer hammers a silver plate for an icon of the Virgin. Birdsong mixes with clanging metal, murmuring pilgrims, and the rumbling of the diesel generator—a sound that Father Joseph was spared. Indeed the silence he cultivated living in a cave (he was known as the Cave Dweller), on a ridge above the *skete* of St. Anne, was integral to the instruction he dispensed to the men who brought new life to the Holy Mountain.

His was a stern regimen of fasts, vigils, and unceasing prayer. An acolyte reports that his punishment for saying even two or three words while on an errand away from the hermitage was two hundred prostrations; that sometimes after prayer the elder's body was bathed in light; that in his cell the fragrance of prayer surrounded him. What attracted the religious to Father Joseph was his purity, which may be ascribed to the purifying grace (his phrase) that made him a vessel for divine revelations. He "saw" monks lined up to fight demons on a plain; a splendid palace in which Mary carried the infant Jesus; three identical children blessing him in his cell. In a vision from the Theotokos he learned that he would die on her Dormition. And so it happened.

Father Joseph called himself illiterate, and if he had little formal education his letters on spiritual matters, collected after his death and published in a book entitled *Monastic Wisdom*, reveal a sophisticated theological sensibility, rooted in his close readings of Scripture, patristic literature, and the lives of the saints. He told his followers to read with the same attention so that "the soul may increase and grow. Thus the 'old man' fades away and dies, whereas the new man is renewed and overflows with the love of Christ." When Father Joseph's health broke down from living in such austerity, he moved to Nea Skete, and for the new men who followed him in the Way he said he wished to write three books proclaiming first that man is nothing, then that God is everything, and finally that we must be patient in everything until death. His own patience was rewarded: even as pilgrims to Mount Athos despaired of its seemingly inevitable decline he was planting the seeds of renewal, which grew imperceptibly, like the fruits of prayer.

This chimes with Christ's teaching: "But you, when you pray, go into your room, and when you have shut your door, pray to your Father who is in the secret place; and your Father who sees in secret will reward you" (Matt. 6:6). The central phrase can also be translated as, "Pray to your Father, who is hidden and whose ways are unknown to you"—that is, who knows what riches may be discovered in the hidden heart of Christianity? Father Joseph counseled his followers always to seek God, and so they passed weeks in silent prayer, communicating only by signs. In the stillness of hesychasm they become aware of God's presence, aligning their wills with His—which, it seems, ordained the resurrection of Athonite monasticism.

"It is a matter not of finding what to say," writes another divine associated with the Holy Mountain's revival, Archimandrite Vasileios of Stavronikita, "but of how to be silent, how to hear the Spirit speaking in our silence or our speech: the question is, how can we become instruments of the Spirit?" Like Father Joseph, Vasileios obeyed God within the solitude of a hermitage until, in 1968, he was called to become the abbot of Stavronikita, which had been deserted. He imposed the cenobitic rule on the monastery and, with a small band of monks, restored it to its former glory, setting the standard for the renewal of other monasteries on Athos.

He also became a spokesman for the Holy Community against the ecumenical movement. In *Hymn of Entry*, an essay on the liturgical life of Orthodoxy, he argues that "To give the cup of life to non-Orthodox, without unity of faith and the communion of the Holy Spirit, is a merely mechanical action, an act of magic."

Salvation begins with the recognition of Orthodoxy's truth, which is expressed anew each day in the liturgy. And if, as he writes, "The mystery of communion with and participation in God is accomplished as a gradual internal change," I can readily believe that the spiritual transformation I have undergone on Athos is incomplete.

But Christ may also love the Anglican tradition of allowing every baptized Christian to take communion. "Because there is one bread," Paul wrote, "we who are many are one body, for we all partake of one bread" (1 Cor. 10:17). For everyone is invited to the messianic feast, saints and sinners alike: this was the promise of the Last Supper, where Jesus celebrated the first Eucharist (which means "thanksgiving") with His disciples, including Judas Iscariot. Then He went with Peter, James, and John into the garden at Gethsemane to pray. Three times His disciples fell asleep while Jesus prayed in sorrow for what He was about to suffer. "Stay with me, remain here with me," was the refrain of the communion hymn we sang in my parish during Lent: "Watch and pray." The Savior's words to His disciples at Gethsemane are crucial to those embarked upon the Way. For just as He was bolstered by His prayers, so we may find strength in His plea: "Watch and pray." I held my daughter's hand and sang. My eyes brimmed with tears.

THE MOUNTAIN IS SHROUDED IN CLOUDS WHEN I SET OFF FOR the summit on Holy Saturday morning. I am climbing a muddy path, exhausted from the vigil at Dionysiou, the climax of which occurred an hour before dawn, with a candlelit procession around the courtyard. *Kyrie, eleison*, we chanted in the warm air. Rain showers had punctuated the service, but now the clouds were stalled over the mountaintop and the sea was still. The pilgrims circled the *katholikón* in a silent, orderly fashion, in contrast to the mob scene they had created the day before at the pilgrims' bureau in Ouranoupolis. At first light I breakfasted on olives, bread, and tea, then started hiking.

This is the most fearful day on the Christian calendar. Jesus's death on the cross was marked by a solar eclipse (fulfilling an Old Testament prophecy) and a powerful earthquake—"Then the sun was darkened, and the veil of the temple was torn in two" (Luke 23:45)—that opened the graves and raised the bodies of the saints. A centurion was the first in the crowd to proclaim Jesus a righteous man. Then Joseph, a council member, risked his own life by asking Pontius Pilate for the body of Jesus (a display of courage noteworthy in the face of Peter's denials of Jesus on the night of His arrest), which he wrapped in linen and laid in a tomb hewn from a rock. The miracles of Christ's resurrection—His appearances to Mary Magdalene and the other Mary, then to two perplexed believers, and finally to His disciples, who are commanded to "make disciples of all the nations" (Matt. 28:19); His commissioning of Peter to lead the Church; His ascension into Heaven—belong to the future. On Holy Saturday the entire history of the Church, beginning with the Acts of the Apostles, hangs in the balance, while Jesus lies in a tomb on the Jewish Sabbath, in a silence that extends into eternity.

Psalm 119, the longest psalm, is prayed this day at matins—176 verses dedicated to the law of the Lord, in evenly divided sections named for the letters of the Hebrew alphabet. The psalm thus alphabetizes the world, spelling out the glories of obeying God's Word. Christ alone perfectly prays this psalm, which is Orthodoxy's funeral psalm (along with Psalm 91), because in His perfect obedience to God He was crucified. But climbing toward the pass above the *skete* of St. Anne I am guided by the memory of the choir radiantly chanting the psalm over the imagined tomb of Christ: "Your word is a lamp to my feet and a light to my path" (Ps. 119:105).

At the trailhead to the summit are four Austrian pilgrims debating the wisdom of climbing on. The midday sun is bright over the sea, the sky dark above the mountain. The weather is as hard to discern as God's will. And the Austrians are still arguing when I start up the steep, winding path strewn with rocks. Prickly pears give way to withered bushes and islands of grass; near the tree line, where a pack of mules grazes, an empty birds' nest hangs in a shriveled pine. Higher yet is Panagia, a squat stone *kalyve* the same shade of white that reaches to the summit, 1,500 meters away. Inside is a chapel; the walls of the sleeping area are covered with graffiti. Through a small window I gaze at the clouds surrounding the mountaintop.

Panagia, the all-holy epithet of the Theotokos, also refers to the grace said after a major feast, when a triangle cut from the Eucharist loaf is raised for the community to share. A footnote in the Byzantine Book of Hours suggests that the tradition dates from the apostles' practice at mealtime of leaving a piece of bread on an empty cushion for Christ; after eating they would raise up the bread and praise Him, a practice they followed until the Dormition of the Theotokos, when clouds carried them to Jerusalem for her burial. Three days later, when they lifted the bread named for Christ, Mary appeared, bearing greetings from her Son. The apostles hurried to her empty tomb, and so began the tradition that she too was raised from the dead.

Odysseas Elytis concludes his poetic masterpiece, *The Axion Esti*, with a Gloria to the Virgin, who in his imagination may also take the form of the Muse or the Girl of Poetry. As he said in his Nobel address: "Whether it is Apollo or Aphrodite, whether Jesus or the Virgin who embodies and personifies the necessity for us to see in material form what in certain moments we intuited, is not important. What is important is the breath of immortality that they permit us. Poetry, in my humble opinion, is obliged to permit this breath from beyond specific dogma." My journeys to the Holy Mountain have brought me to a different understanding of my literary vocation, and here in sight of the summit I glimpse in the work of the Greek poet ways to proceed. In *The Axion Esti* he married surrealist imagery, historical incidents, and liturgical forms to his love of the land, in the service of honoring his language: "My only care my language with the very first Glory Be to Thee!" This is indeed a poem about language, which seeks to letter the world in the same fashion as Psalm 119, with "the breath of immortality." And it seems to me that in the age of homelessness it is the poet's task to revitalize the language of the spirit—to discover a place in the heart in which the truth may reside.

"Poetry is a means of redemption," wrote Wallace Stevens, seeking a supreme fiction by which to live in the absence of God. He believed the loss of faith was a form of growth, yet a priest reports that on his deathbed Stevens converted to Roman Catholicism, saying it was time "to get in the fold." I treasure this story, which complicates our picture of a poet who once said that "God is a symbol for something that can as well take other forms as, for example, the form of high poetry." But Stevens often visited churches, and I suspect that in his last days he discovered the limits of the poetic imagination. As a friend said, "He wasn't taking any chances." Nor am I.

But my immediate goal, the chapel of Metamorphosis, lies somewhere in the clouds. And I am so weary, my life is changing enough as it is. Not only is another child due but I have been offered a job which will require me to put into practice some of the lessons I have learned on Athos about repair and renovation, leaving the comfort of what has become a permanent chair at Holy Cross to rebuild a writing program in the Midwest—a politically charged assignment that will test my resolve to pray without ceasing. At the same time my marriage is healing—invisibly, it seems—perhaps because I keep St. John Chrysostom's admonition in mind: "You are very mistaken if you think that one thing is expected of lay people and something else from a monastic. The difference between them is that one enters into marriage and the other does not; in everything else they have the same responsibilities." Marriage is a discipline, which I am just learning to follow—a vast terrain, much of which is inaccessible: so much left unsaid. And what remains hidden is what we use to negotiate difficult passages: faith, hope, and love.

This Holy Week I am aware of the relentless march to Pascha. In Orthodox iconography the Last Supper is called the Mystical Supper to reinforce its perpetual nature, just as prayer teaches us to stand always before God. Indeed the sacraments, the divine mysteries, remind us of Christ's constant presence. His death and resurrection are the tokens of what we experience in countless ways, large and small, on our journey to the Kingdom of God — the endless deaths and resurrections of hope, love, and faith: my marriage, for example, which has, against all odds, been blessed with new life. I have already celebrated Easter in my parish, and now I am not so much partaking of a second holiday as recognizing Pascha as a constant feature of my life.

Even so I feel the full force of the conflict between celebrating the Eucharist here and there. I am not in communion with the Orthodox, who believe that my salvation depends upon my taking a step I am not prepared to take, in the same way that the Lenten fast and vigil have left me too weak to summit the mountain. A storm is rolling in, and I am thinking about the nature of the Godhead. In his *Life of Moses* St. Gregory of Nyssa distinguishes between the prophet's two encounters with God, suggesting that his ascent of Mount Sinai, in darkness and confusion, was more meaningful than the burning bush. "Then Moses saw God in light," writes Vladimir Lossky; "now he enters the darkness, leaving behind him all that can be seen or known; there remains to him only the invisible and unknowable, but in this darkness is God. For God makes His dwelling there where our understanding and our concepts can gain no admittance. Our spiritual ascent does but reveal to us, ever more and more clearly, the absolute incomprehensibility of the divine nature." All we can do is pray that our actions are aligned with God's will. What I know is that in my state of exhaustion an attempt on the peak might very well cost me my life. I hike down through the loose rock, stopping frequently to rest. I have never been so tired. Nor will I sleep tonight: the Easter vigil is the most magnificent of all. I cannot take my eyes off the sea.

THE *SKETE* OF ST. ANNE IS A HIVE OF ACTIVITY WHEN I ARRIVE late in the afternoon. At a picnic table in the courtyard an old monk slices onions for the feast. Some pilgrims sort greens or chop herbs, others drag firewood into the kitchen, where fish stew simmers in large tin canisters. A novice washes the Byzantine and Greek flags before raising them from the stone wall, above the yellow streamer draped across the courtyard. Monks from the *skete* of Little St. Anne and hermits from Katounákia arrive. Excitement builds, as if before a show. By dusk the faithful milling outside the church are impatient to enter. What drama is about to unfold.

In the half-lit nave a long reading is the prelude to chanting and censing, to prostrations and more readings. The deacon and hieromonks wear vestments of white and gold and green. Palm fronds cover the floor, in the center of which is a portable icon of Christ, bordered with red and white carnations. The candles we light toward midnight are extinguished for the climax of the Passion story, read in several languages—to emphasize the universality of the Church and to look forward to Pentecost, seven Sundays hence, when the apostolic gift of tongues will be celebrated. Then we stand in darkness and silence until the chanting resumes—the signal to relight our candles for a procession, behind the icon of Christ, through the church and around the courtyard. The *sémantron* sounds, bells ring, fireworks light up the sky. The icon is set under the banner, and we shake hands, as if it is the New Year. But it is new life we celebrate: "Come, take light from the light that is never overtaken by night," the deacon chants. "Come, glorify Christ, risen from the dead." St. Gregory Palamas said that after resurrection "man, being himself light; if he regards himself, he sees the light, and if he regards the object of his vision, he finds the light there again, and the means that he employs for seeing is the light; and it is in this that union consists, for all this is but one." This is the light we praise when we walk through a double line of censers and back into the church for the rest of the vigil, which lasts until dawn.

Upstairs in the refectory, where a feast is laid out (bread, hard-boiled eggs dyed red, and a piece of whitefish garnished with herbs, in honor of the broiled fish the risen Messiah ate in the presence of His disciples, Luke 24:42–43), Athonite saints stare at us from the murals. The lector reads from the life of a modern saint. There is a story about a hieromonk from St. Anne who lived in a room near the ossuary, praying unceasingly. One day, hearing a noise in the ossuary, he opened the door to find a group of handsome young men. Some were carrying away the bones of the fathers, others were bringing bones from elsewhere to place in the ossuary. The monk gazed in wonder until one of the men explained that they were angels sent by the Theotokos. The bones they were transferring here belonged to those whose minds were always on Athos, even though they ended their days in the world; this is where they will be resurrected at the Second Coming of Christ. The bones the angels took away were to be placed in the world.

"These are the relics of monks who were here only in body," said the angel. "Their minds were with the world. They wanted to be in contact with their relatives and other worldly people, so on Judgment Day they won't be resurrected on the Holy Mountain but in the world."

The monk who translated this story for me, describing himself as a little piece of broken glass at the bottom of the hill that reflects the light from the top of the hill, signed his note, "Least Among Monks." He said he thought this story was meant for me.

Christos anesti! Alithos anesti! Christ is risen! Risen indeed.

THE SUN IS STILL BEHIND THE MOUNTAIN WHEN I FOLLOW SOME monks and hermits south along the rocky path toward Eremos. They are returning from the Easter vigil at St. Anne, leather satchels slung over their shoulders, swinging kerosene lamps like censers. Two ride mules sidesaddle, bells tinkling in the stillness. One takes an elder's hand to help him up the trail to the *skete* of

Little St. Anne, where the monks bid us farewell. We have just gained the ridge above the *skete* when we hear the monks chanting psalms in the courtyard of their chapel—a practice dating from the earliest years of Christian history, when worshippers would sing hymns and litanies on their way to church. The hermits chant in response. Back and forth they sing, and the air is alive with their voices, even after the monks have entered their chapel and we have walked on.

Christos anesti! Alithos anesti! Christ is risen! Risen indeed!

I have no destination in mind, no plan. I have to be in Athens by the next night to catch a plane home, yet I am happy to follow the hermits to the distant reaches of the peninsula, vaguely imagining I will figure out a course of action. Presently the trail forks, and when the hermits climb to Katounákia I hike down into the "vertical desert" of Karoúlia. The path winds in and out of a ravine, skirting clumps of thorny broom and prickly pears, and brings me to a chapel attached to a hermitage, which resembles a small inn. The gardens are freshly turned. The grape arbor has been cleared of its dead wood. But there is no other sign of life, so I pick my way to a cement staircase descending several hundred meters to the sea. At one switchback, halfway down, I obey an impish desire to set out across a scree field to the east, toward Byzantium, joyfully hopping from boulder to boulder. Blue water is on my right, and wedged in the cliff overhead, above a tumbledown hut, is a white two-story *kalyve*, which looks deserted. In a clearing between two boulders I discover the remains of a campfire, a pile of rusted food tins and empty beer cans, a canvas bag of men's clothing. I am puzzling over these marks of habitation when I hear voices rising from the *arsanas* and the rumble of an engine—I have forgotten about the ferry to Daphne. Without another thought I hurry back to the stairs and run down to the water's edge.

The sea is calm when I board the ferry. From the deck some pilgrims are gazing up at the dwellings on the ragged cliffs and in the steep ravines. The sun emerges from behind the mountain, and despite my lack of sleep I feel exhilarated when the ferry departs. What a thrill it is to sail this close to the *asceteria* and *hesy-chasteria*, the caves and stone huts with conical roofs that cling to the cliffs, like eagles' nests. These are the starkest living conditions. One pair of huts, perched on a narrow ledge fifty meters above the water, can be reached only by clambering along a sheer rock wall, then climbing down a long, rickety ladder; for provisions the hesy-chasts depend upon passing fishermen to leave them rusks of bread in baskets lowered to the sea by pulleys. (*Karoúlia* means "the Place of Pulleys.") Some *asceteria* are located so far up a cliff that baskets of food must be lowered from above to the anchorites, the hardiest spiritual athletes, who praise God and keep vigil day and night, without regard for their physical well-being.

Theoria is the vision, vouchsafed by the Holy Spirit, by which hesychasts are initiated into spiritual knowledge—a revelation of God's mysteries, of His uncreated light. Like the desert fathers who wanted "to pull the world to safety after them," in the words of Thomas Merton, the ascetics of Karoúlia, awaiting the Second Coming, pray for our salvation. And I take comfort in the knowl-edge that they are praying for me, even though I cannot see them.

The ferry sails by a promontory on which a cross has been raised, and soon we pull into the *arsanas* of St. Anne, pick up some pilgrims, and depart again. My mind drifts back to the film shown on my transatlantic flight, *Man on the Moon*, Miloš For-man's portrait of Andy Kaufman, the comedian whose radical humor often alienated his audiences. But this much misunder-stood performer revolutionized comedy, and it occurred to me that the filmmaker's loving view of him was of a piece with early Christian efforts to spread the good news of Jesus Christ. Not to equate the comedian with the Messiah, but to note how Kauf-man's genius, which survives in film clips and in the work of other comedians, can reshape our sensibilities, if we are open to the ways in which he upsets our expectations. My travels to Athos, my experiences of God's loving-kindness, have likewise turned my world upside down. And this is the week to celebrate that overturning. Thus later in the afternoon, after walking from

Daphne to Simonopetra for the sheer pleasure of feeling the sun on my body, I am surprised to see, from the balcony of the monastery, six pilgrims practicing on the *sémantron*. They are allowed to do this only during Bright Week, which begins today. It is hilarious to watch middle-aged Greeks march around the garden taking turns banging on the wooden oar. *To-tá-lan-ton, to-tá-lan-ton*—this is the rhythm the pilgrims are attempting to learn: what have you done with the talents the Lord has given you?

What a racket they make, says one monk.

A joyful racket, says another, echoing the psalm recited this week: "Make a joyful shout to God, all the earth! Sing out the honor of His name; make His praise glorious" (Ps. 66:1).

Do you think about becoming Orthodox? the first monk asks me.

It's difficult in America, I reply.

If it is God's will, he says.

Christos anesti! Alithos anesti! Christ is risen! Risen indeed!

HE WAS KNOWN AS "THE SILVER PHANTOM" FOR THE COLOR OF his hair and his reluctance to hold office hours. But David Wagoner's poetry workshop at the University of Washington, in the winter of 1982, was a revelation to me. He encouraged his students to give themselves over to the language, writing wildly in the hope of discovering an image or a phrase with which to start a poem, then to employ every element of craft to shape these materials into a finished work. He urged us to re-create the music of nature—birdsong, the movement of a river; our poems must bring things to life, he insisted, sounding out awkward passages until we grasped their rhythmic problems. To make a point he would recite one of the hundreds of poems he knew by heart, introducing us to a wide range of works in English—a strategy that bored some of my classmates. I was thrilled.

True, he was often distracted. Our morning class conflicted

with his writing schedule—he said he had not taught at this hour for more than twenty years—and some days he would stare out the window, as if he were working on his own poems. He had plenty of material. His wife, who had left him for another man, was dying of cancer. In the meantime he had fallen in love with a younger woman. What a welter of conflicting emotions he must have felt.

I understood none of this, of course, preoccupied as I was with my own writing and medical problems. The weeks I lived with the knowledge that the tumor in my neck could spell my end I remember for the clarity of vision I gained—and the freedom with which I began to write. Every book I read, every conversation I had, every encounter seemed to open new doors of consciousness; the rooms I entered—of poetry and desire and mortality—were at once terrifying and exhilarating, more so after surgery revealed that my tumor was benign. From the hospital a family friend drove me home through the arboretum, where the azaleas were in bloom—a sight that brought tears to my eyes: "O taste and see that the Lord is good" (Ps. 34:8).

My recovery was mercifully short. My friend, who lived at the edge of the woods, cared for me during my convalescence. And the happiness I felt doing ordinary things—drinking tea at daybreak; reading poems; gazing at the red camellia blossoms by the door—persisted for weeks. One day I let the Siberian husky puppy out to run on the lawn. Two coyote pups emerged from the trees and played with the dog for twenty minutes, watched over by a grown coyote on the other side of the fence: a vision of primordial harmony. My brush with death had opened my eyes to Blake's insight: "Every thing that lives is Holy." It was only a matter of time before I fell in love with the woman who would become my wife.

Not long after I returned to school Wagoner unintentionally delivered a vital lesson about the art of poetry. Indeed he had seemed even more remote than usual that morning until he recited George Herbert's "The Flower," which opens with a cele-

bration of God's gifts—"How fresh, O Lord, how sweet and clean /
Are thy returns! ev'n as the flowers in spring"—then asks:

> *Who would have thought my shrivel'd heart*
> *Could have recover'd greennesse? It was gone*
> *Quite under ground; as flowers depart*
> *To see their mother-root, when they have blown;*
> *Where they together*
> *All the hard weather,*
> *Dead to the world, keep house unknown.*

"The drama of Herbert's life was largely inward," the poet Anthony Hecht writes. Herbert was born of Welsh parents in 1593—his
mother was a friend of John Donne's—and after graduating from
Cambridge he was elected orator at the university, a customary first
step in the career of a public man. But his political hopes were
dashed when his patrons died; he entered the Church, and instead
of aspiring to high ecclesiastical office he married and became a
parish priest. Another well-connected man in such a position would
have farmed out his pastoral duties. Not Herbert. He used his own
money to rebuild the church in which he preached. He visited the
poor, prayed with the sick, attended the dying. A lutanist and composer who may have set some of his intricate stanzas to music, he
possessed a liturgical imagination, and in three years of service to
his church, during which he wrote his only book, *The Temple*, he
impressed his parishioners as "a learned, godly, and painful divine."
He died of consumption in 1633, secure in God's love:

> *These are thy wonders, Lord of power,*
> *Killing and quickning, bringing down to hell*
> *And up to heaven in an houre;*
> *Making a chiming of a passing-bell.*
> *We say amisse,*
> *This or that is:*
> *Thy word is all, if we could spell.*

And the gift of tears spurs this acute psychological portrait of the proud soul humbled by God. It was when Wagoner began to recite the penultimate stanza—

> And now in age I bud again,
> After so many deaths I live and write;
> I once more smell the dew and rain,
> And relish versing: O my onely light,
> It cannot be
> That I am he
> On whom thy tempests fell all night

—that he broke down and cried. In the classroom there was a stunned silence. It was as if a veil had been lifted, and we saw into the soul of a very private man. This poem of resurrection—of flowers, of love, of poetic inspiration, of the Lord—breathed new life into our teacher's heart—and mine. It was a sacred moment, in a secular place. "I should know better than to attempt those lines," Wagoner said softly when he had regained his composure to finish the recitation.

He turned to a student's poem, apologizing for his loss of control. But "The Flower" had taken root in my imagination. Weeks passed, the rains of winter gave way to a lush spring, I read and reread the poem. Indeed I was pondering the connections forged by Herbert between poetry and nature, faith and the mysterious currents of the heart, when Lisa dropped by one morning to invite me to a performance of Mahler's *Symphony of a Thousand*—the euphoric beginning of our courtship. Poetry and love were thus intertwined in my soul. That I had lately felt stirrings of new work was perhaps another sign that Lisa and I had come through. And one day, reciting "The Flower" in my own poetry workshop at Holy Cross, my voice caught in the same place that Wagoner's had all those years ago: "And now in age I bud again, / After so many deaths I live and write . . ."

"THE LADDER THAT LEADS TO THE KINGDOM IS HIDDEN WITHIN your soul," wrote St. Isaac of Syria. "Flee from sin, dive into yourself, and in your soul you will discover the stairs by which to ascend." This is what I have learned from my journeys to the Holy Mountain. Yet in the evening when I enter the *katholikón* at Grigoriou for a special Easter vespers service, I have but the dimmest understanding of what this knowledge will mean in my life. It is as if I am grasping rungs in the darkness, praying the ladder will hold. Still I am bolstered by the candles lit for the departed; the icons linking the visible and the invisible, the senses and the spirit; the readings from Matthew, chanted in seven languages, about Christ's appearances to the apostles and to Thomas: the mystery on which hangs all my hope and fear. From a topaz-and-silver Bible the deacon, a husky baritone in white vestments, chants the same passages in Greek, his voice echoing around the church. Then we follow the choir into the refectory for a simple dinner, which I devour.

At dusk I hike up to the monastic vineyard with the monk who befriended me on my second pilgrimage. The *kellí* overlooking the vines is empty—the monks who live and work here will spend the week in the monastery; even the mules wandering in the orchard are on vacation—and after serving me coffee on the balcony the monk launches into salvation stories, which border on the miraculous: 1) A mule carrying a basket of sulfur up to the vineyard lost its footing, the sulfur struck a rock, the basket ignited; if not for the quick-witted muleteer, who pulled out his knife and sliced the reins, the mule would have burned up. 2) Two monks were resting on a rock by the sea when a monk seal weighing three hundred pounds or more rose up out of the water to sprawl on the same rock, twisting away at the last moment. And 3) before he came to Athos he was crossing a bridge when a gang attacked him. The monk calls it a miracle, not that he survived a stabbing just above the heart, but that he thought he had only been head-butted in the chest; if he had seen the knife, he might have pitched the thug into the river and either lost his life or gone to prison. Instead he is here on a warm spring evening, working out his fate.

Our conversation drifts from prophesies of the end time to Orthodox views on raising children to his fear that our generation lacks the fortitude of the ancient hesychasts. As the sun sets over the sea I am thinking that after searching for so long for symbolic meanings in poetry and fiction I have found a place in which everything resonates with spiritual force—an insight I must somehow carry back into the world, where I am all too easily distracted. But now we must return to the monastery before the gate closes for the night.

Although it is dark when we arrive, the bald monk who manages the bookstore asks me which is shinier, his head or the sun? Your head, I say, shielding my eyes. His laughter fills me with joy. It is good to laugh on Easter, he says, and laughs his way through a story about a senile monk who called his sister twice today to wish her Merry Christmas! Which he thinks makes a crazy kind of sense: the Bible was presented twice during vespers, once at the beginning of the service to symbolize the birth of our Lord, once at the end to commemorate His Resurrection. And when I buy a book about Grigoriou's icons the monk cries, "Merry Christmas!"

LITANIA, THE BLESSING OF THE HOLY WATERS, FOLLOWS THE liturgy on Easter Monday morning at the monastery of Grigoriou. The service begins in the courtyard with bells ringing, then a pilgrim hammers the *sémantron*, and then a procession, led by a pilgrim bearing the Greek flag, winds toward the gardens on the ridge above the monastery. Two monks with silver lamps escort a monk with a silver cross, followed by a second pair of monks clutching silver heralds, embossed on one side with the figure of Christ and on the other with the Madonna and Child. Then come the deacon and priests in white vestments bearing the monastery's relics, and monks with icons from the *katholikón*, and pilgrims with icons brought from home or newly purchased on the Holy Mountain. Everyone holds a candle, shielding it from the wind. A gust blows an old monk's stole into my face, momentarily blinding me; and when I untangle the fabric the monk's broad smile summons me to attend to the procession, at each stop of which—before the fresco of St. Nicholas under the archway, by the grape arbor, on either side of the main gate, in front of the flower garden, at the overlook surrounded by cypresses, at the switchbacks on the trail behind the monastery—the deacon leads us through a litany of supplications, always ending with us singing back to him *Kyrie, eleison. Kyrie, eleison. Kyrie, eleison.*

"The whole of creation is Christ's sacrament," Philip Sherrard writes. And *Litania* marks how the mystery and miracle of the Incarnation inform nature itself. The procession halts at the edge of a garden of cucumber and melon seedlings growing in cold frames, and from atop a stone wall I watch the service. Under a grape arbor which is just leafing out, in red vestments held up by a novice, the abbot waits, having taken the elevator on account of his bad knees and ample girth. On the table before him lies a chalice of rosewater around which the priests place the relics. If man has fallen, so too has every creature, and this rite celebrates Christ's redemption of nature, which has lately sent such strong winds to the Holy Mountain that panels were torn off the roof of Grigoriou's *katholikón.* Now the abbot makes the sign of the cross, first with a small silver cross, then with a clump of basil (in a bed of which, according to tradition, the True Cross was discovered) dipped in water, which he sprinkles over the bowed heads of the deacon and the priests. "Athonite life is fundamentally a Mystery," the abbot has written, "a Mystery which defies any description. Our eyes must be opened if we are to behold the Mystery.

> We must be initiated into the Mystery. Initiation does not spring from rational understanding alone; it is a question of spiritual ascent. As Man ascends and God descends, it is at

the point where they meet that the Mystery is celebrated. It is this Mystery which makes Athos not merely a mountain, but a Holy Mountain.

This is such a celebration, as are all things on Athos, according to the abbot—the prayers and rituals, architecture and icons, nature and hospitality, all of which express the Mystery. I cannot describe what I have experienced of the Mystery here, but I know It has changed me.

The abbot leaves, and a new procession begins with the deacon blessing the monks and the pilgrims. Then they bring their icons to be kissed by the priests lined up before the table, each of whom offers in turn a relic for the faithful to kiss. It is a glorious sight, and the wind is only partly to blame for the tears in my eyes. Strange to think of the mysterious currents in my life that have led me to this garden by the sea. How else to imagine these journeys to the Holy Mountain, these promptings of the spirit, than as manifestations of God's will?

I have a ferry to catch. The monk from the bookstore accompanies me to the monastery, saying not to worry, the Holy Mother is guarding my steps. But I waste no time in collecting my things—the book about icons leaves no room in my backpack for my coat, which I stuff under the bed for another pilgrim to use—and departing. The courtyard is empty, the sun is blinding, the pair of clocks on the wall of the *katholikón* show different times when I hurry by. The affable monk is waiting for me at the overlook, pacing anxiously under the cypresses.

When will you return? he asks, brightening.

Soon, I assure him, adjusting my backpack.

But I have not even reached the boathouse before my mind is taken up with worldly concerns. Past the guest quarters and stands of prickly pears I set a brisk pace, lost in thought about our new baby, my new job, deadlines. My forty days on the Holy Mountain are over, the temptation to stay resisted; and I am climbing the stone path above the harbor, near the spot where I once gazed at Grigoriou in a spasm of grief about what I had missed during my Lenten pilgrimage, when the knocking of the *sémantron* calls me to attention. The *Litania* procession is coming full circle. I turn around in time to glimpse the white vestments of the priests disappearing through the monastery gate, and then the bells begin to ring.

.

GLOSSARY

Arsanas: port

Asceterion: a single dwelling for an ascetic

Avaton: a Byzantine edict prohibiting women from entering Athos

Axion Esti: a famous miracle-working icon of the Virgin Mary

Cenobitic: a communal form of monasticism

Chrysobul: an imperial edict with a gold seal

Corona: a large brass candelabra suspended in the nave of the church

Deification: the doctrine by which mankind shares in the divine nature —
    "God became human that we might become divine," according to Byzantine theology

Diamonitirion: the permit required for entrance to Athos

Docheiaris: the monk in charge of provisions

Epistasia: the governing body of the Holy Community on Athos

Evergetinos: the sayings of the desert fathers

Filioque: the doctrine stating that the Holy Spirit proceeds from the Father *and* the Son

Hesychasm: the tradition of contemplative prayer practiced on Athos

Hesychasterion: a remote hermitage

Hieromonk: priest-monk

Iconostasis: the stand, separating the altar from the nave, on which icons are displayed

Idiorrhythmic: a self-regulating form of monasticism

Kalyve: a cottage-sized monastic dwelling containing a small chapel and no land

Kathisma: a cell with a chapel next door, close to the parent monastery

Katholikón: the main church of a monastery

Kellí: a monastic dwelling about the size of a farmhouse, which contains a small chapel and enough land for three or more monks to farm

Kenosis: the emptying of the self to let God work through one

Konaki: the house maintained by each monastery for its representative to the Holy Assembly

Kopanos: a wooden blade hung from a pair of chains or an omega-shaped piece of iron, struck with a mallet to call the faithful to services

Kyriakon: the common church of a *skete*

Lavra: an assembly of anchorites

Loukoumi: Turkish delight, served to pilgrims on a guest tray, along with coffee, water, and either raki or ouzo

Metanoia: to repent; to turn toward God; to make the sign of the cross and bow or prostrate

Orthros: matins

Panagia: immaculate or all-holy, an adjective used to describe the Virgin Mary

Parousia: the Second Coming of Christ

Phiale: a basin for holy water

Prosmonarios: the monk responsible for the icon of the *Axion Esti*

Schema: the monastic habit

Sémantron: a kind of double-bladed oar struck with a mallet to call the faithful to services

Skete: one of twelve monastery-like settlements on Athos

Starets: a Russian holy man

Stasidia: the wooden chairs lining the walls of the church

Stylite: an ascetic who lives atop a pillar

Theoria: the vision by which hesychasts are initiated into spiritual knowledge

Theosis: deification, the mystical union between God and man

Theotokos: Mother of God

Typikon: the charter spelling out the rule of a monastery

Vematoris: the monk in charge of a sanctuary

What are you reading? a poet (and Orthodox convert) asked upon learning of my interest in the Holy Mountain. An unexpected pleasure of researching this book was reading so many works of the highest imaginative order—beginning, of course, with Scripture. I count it a blessing that the poetry of the King James Version impressed itself on my ear as a child; hence the biblical passages I cite come from this translation, or from the New King James Version contained in *The Orthodox Study Bible* (Nashville, Tenn.: Thomas Nelson Publishers, 1993). I have also consulted *The Blackwell Dictionary of Eastern Christianity* (Oxford: Blackwell Publishers, 1999) and *The Oxford Dictionary of World Religions* (Oxford and New York: Oxford University Press, 1997). The Friends of Mount Athos issue instructive and delightful annual reports.

Ammons, A. R. *Garbage*. New York: W. W. Norton, 1993.

Anonymous. *The Way of a Pilgrim* and *The Pilgrim Continues His Way*. Translated by R. M. French. New York: Harper, 1954.

Ashton, Dore. *About Rothko*. New York: Oxford University Press, 1983.

St. Augustine. *Confessions*. Translated by Henry Chadwick. Oxford and New York: Oxford University Press, 1991.

St. Basil. *Letters*, 2 vols. Translated by Sister Agnes Clare Way. Washington, D.C.: Catholic University of America Press, 1951, 1955.

———. *The Ascetic Works of St. Basil*. Translated by W.K.I. Clarke. New York and Toronto: Macmillan, 1925.

Benedikt, Michael, ed. *The Poetry of Surrealism: An Anthology*. Boston and Toronto: Little, Brown and Company, 1974.

Bishop, Elizabeth. *The Complete Poems, 1927–1979*. New York: Farrar, Straus & Giroux, 1983.

Brodsky, Joseph. *Less Than One: Selected Essays*. New York: Farrar, Straus & Giroux, 1986.

Bulgakov, Sergius. *The Orthodox Church*. Translation revised by Lydia Kesich. Crestwood, N.Y.: St. Vladimir's Seminary Press, 1988.

Burton-Christie, Douglas. *The Word in the Desert: Scripture and the Quest for Holiness in Early Christian Monasticism*. New York and Oxford: Oxford University Press, 1993.

Buzzati, Dino. *Restless Nights*. Translated by Lawrence Venuti. San Francisco: North Point Press, 1983.

Byron, Robert. *The Station, Athos: Treasures and Men*. New York: Alfred A. Knopf, 1949.

Cabasilas, Nicolas. *Life in Christ*. Translated by Margaret Lisney. West Sussex, UK: Churchman Publishing, 1989.

Carroll, James. *Constantine's Sword: The Church and the Jews*. Boston: Houghton Mifflin, 2001.

Cavarnos, Constantine. *The Holy Mountain*. Belmont, Mass.: Institute for Byzantine and Modern Greek Studies, 1973.

———. *Anchored in God: Life, Art, and Thought on the Holy Mountain of Athos*. Belmont, Mass.: Institute for Byzantine and Modern Greek Studies, 1991.

Celan, Paul. *Glottal Stop: 101 Poems*. Translated by Nikolai Popov and Heather McHugh. Hanover, N.H., and London: Wesleyan University Press/University Press of New England, 2000.

Igumen Chariton of Valamo. *The Art of Prayer*. Translated by E. Kadloubovsky and E. M. Palmer. Edited by Timothy Ware. London: Faber and Faber, 1966.

Chave, Anna C. *Mark Rothko: Subjects in Abstraction*. New Haven, Conn., and London: Yale University Press, 1989.

Archbishop Chrysostomos. *Orthodox and Roman Catholic Relations from the Fourth Century to the Hesychastic Controversy*. Etna, Calif.: Center for Traditionalist Orthodox Studies, 2001.

The Cloud of Unknowing and *The Book of Privy Counseling*. Edited by William Johnston. New York: Doubleday, 1973.

Curzon, Robert. *Visits to Monasteries in the Levant*. London: John Murray, 1849.

Dalrymple, William. *From the Holy Mountain: A Journey Among the Christians of the Middle East*. New York: Henry Holt and Company, 1997.

Dostoevsky, Fyodor. *Demons*. Translated by Richard Pevear and Larissa Volokhonsky. New York: Alfred A. Knopf, 1994.

———. *The Brothers Karamazov*. Translated by Richard Pevear and Larissa Volokhonsky. San Francisco: North Point Press, 1990.

Elder Joseph the Hesychast. *Monastic Wisdom: The Letters of Elder Joseph the Hesychast*. Florence, Ariz.: St. Anthony's Greek Orthodox Monastery, 1998.

Elytis, Odysseas. *Open Papers: Selected Essays.* Translated by Olga Broumas and T. Begley. Port Townsend, Wash.: Copper Canyon Press, 1995.

———. *The Axion Esti.* Translated by Edmund Keeley and George Savidis. Pittsburgh: University of Pittsburgh Press, 1979.

———. *The Collected Poems of Odysseas Elytis.* Translated by Jeffrey Carson and Nikos Sarris. Baltimore and London: Johns Hopkins Press, 1997.

Eusebius. *The History of the Church.* Translated by G. A. Williamson. Revised and edited by Andrew Louth. London: Penguin Books, 1989.

Felstiner, John. *Paul Celan: Poet, Survivor, Jew.* New Haven, Conn., and London: Yale University Press, 1995.

Fennel, Nicholas. *The Russians on Athos.* Bern: Peter Lang, 2001.

Frederiksen, Paula. *From Jesus to Christ: The Origins of the New Testament Images of Jesus.* New Haven, Conn., and London: Yale University Press, 1988.

———. *Jesus of Nazareth, King of the Jews: A Jewish Life and the Emergence of Christianity.* New York: Alfred A. Knopf, 1999.

Frost, Robert. *Collected Poems, Prose, & Plays.* New York: The Library of America, 1995.

Gibbon, Edward. *The History of the Decline and Fall of the Roman Empire.* London, 1813.

Gillet, Lev. *The Jesus Prayer.* Crestwood, N.Y.: St. Vladimir's Seminary Press, 1995.

Greenfield, Liah. *Nationalism: Five Roads to Modernity.* Cambridge, Mass.: Harvard University Press, 1992.

Gregory of Nyssa. *The Life of Moses.* Translated by Abraham J. Malherbe and Everett Ferguson. Mahwah, N.J.: Paulist Press, 1978.

St. Gregory Palamas. *Treatise on the Spiritual Life.* Translated by Daniel M. Rogich. Minneapolis: Light and Life Publishing Company, 1995.

Herbert, George. *The Essential Herbert.* Edited by Anthony Hecht. New York: Ecco Press, 1987.

Herodotus. *The Histories.* Translated by Aubrey de Sélincourt. Revised by John Marincola. London: Penguin Books, 1972.

Horsley, Richard A., and Neil Asher Silberman. *The Message and the Kingdom: How Jesus and Paul Ignited a Revolution and Transformed the Ancient World.* New York: Penguin Putnam, 1997.

Hughes, Rosemary. *Haydn.* New York: Farrar, Straus & Cudahy, 1950.

Archimandrite Ioannikios. *An Athonite Gerontikon: Sayings of the Holy Fathers of Mount Athos.* Kouphalia-Thessaloníki, Greece: St. Gregory Palamas Monastery, 1997.

John Climacus. *The Ladder of Divine Ascent.* Translated by Colm Luibheid and Norman Russell. Mahwah, N.J.: Paulist Press, 1982.

Kadas, Sotiris. *Mount Athos: An Illustrated Guide to the Monasteries and Their History.* Athens: Ekdotike Athenon S. A., 1997.

Kierkegaard, Søren. *Fear and Trembling* and *Sickness unto Death*. Translated by Walter Lowrie. Princeton, N.J.: Princeton University Press, 1954.

Larkin, Philip. *Collected Poems*. Edited by Anthony Thwaite. New York: Farrar, Straus & Giroux, 1989.

Lewis, C. S. *Reflections on the Psalms*. New York: Harcourt Brace & Company, 1958.

Lossky, Vladimir. *The Mystical Theology of the Eastern Church*. Crestwood, N.Y.: St. Vladimir's Seminary Press, 1998.

Matthews, William. *A Happy Childhood*. Boston: Atlantic Little Brown, 1984.

Mayer, Wendy, and Pauline Allen. *John Chrysostom*. London and New York: Routledge, 2000.

Merton, Thomas, tr. *The Wisdom of the Desert: Sayings from the Desert Fathers of the Fourth Century*. New York: New Directions, 1970.

———. *The Monastic Journey*. Edited by Brother Patrick Hart. New York: Doubleday, 1978.

———. *Life and Holiness*. New York: Doubleday, 1990.

———. *Mystics and Zen Masters*. New York: Farrar, Straus & Giroux, 1999.

Merwin, W. S. "Aspects of a Mountain." In *Regions of Memory: Uncollected Prose, 1949–1982*. Edited by Ed Folsom. Champaign: University of Illinois Press, 1987.

Meyendorf, John. *The Orthodox Church: Its Past and Its Role in the World Today*. Revised and expanded by Nicholas Lossky. Crestwood, N.Y.: St. Vladimir's Seminary Press, 1996.

———. *St. Gregory Palamas and Orthodox Spirituality*. Crestwood, N.Y.: St. Vladimir's Seminary Press, 1998.

Milosz, Czeslaw. *The Land of Ulro*. Translated by Louis Iribarne. New York: Farrar, Straus and Giroux, 1984.

———. *New and Collected Poems, 1931–2001*. New York: HarperCollins, 2001.

———. *To Begin Where I Am: Selected Essays*. Edited by Bogdana Carpenter and Madeline G. Levine. New York: Farrar, Straus and Giroux, 2001.

St. Nicodemus of the Holy Mountain. *A Handbook of Spiritual Counsel*. Translated by Peter A. Chamberas. Mahwah, N.J.: Paulist Press, 1989.

———. *Unseen Warfare: The Spiritual Combat & Path to Paradise of Lorenzo Scupolo edited by Nicodemus of the Holy Mountain & revised by Theophan the Recluse*. Translated by E. Kadloubovsky and G.E.H. Palmer. Crestwood, N.Y.: St. Vladimir's Seminary Press, 2000.

St. Nicodemus of the Holy Mountain and St. Makarios of Corinth. *The Philokalia: The Complete Text*, 4 vols. Translated by G.E.H. Palmer, Philip Sherrard, and Kallistos Ware. London: Faber and Faber, 1979–1995.

———. *Writings from The Philokalia on Prayer of the Heart*. Translated by E. Kadloubovsky and G.E.H. Palmer. London: Faber and Faber, 1951.

Norris, Kathleen. *The Cloister Walk*. New York: Riverhead Books, 1996.

———. *Amazing Grace: A Vocabulary of Faith*. New York: Riverhead Books, 1998.

Norwich, John Julius, and Reresby Sitwell, with photographs by A. Costa. *Mount Athos*. New York: Harper & Row Publishers, 1966.

Paz, Octavio. *Alternating Current*. Translated by Helen R. Lane. New York: Seaver Books, 1983.

———. *The Other Voice: Essays on Modern Poetry*. Translated by Helen R. Lane. New York: Harcourt Brace Jovanovich, Publishers, 1990.

Pelikan, Jaroslav. *The Christian Tradition: A History of the Development of Doctrine*, 5 vols. Chicago: University of Chicago Press, 1971–1989.

———. *Jesus Through the Centuries*. New Haven, Conn., and London: Yale University Press, 1985.

———. *Imago Dei: The Byzantine Apologia for Icons*. Princeton, N.J.: Princeton University Press, 1990.

———. *Mary Through the Centuries*. New Haven, Conn., and London: Yale University Press, 1996.

Popa, Vasko. *Collected Poems*. Translated by Anne Pennington. Revised and expanded by Francis R. Jones. London: Anvil Press, 1997.

———. *Homage to the Lame Wolf: Selected Poems*. Translated by Charles Simic. Oberlin, Ohio: Oberlin College Press, 1987.

Pope, Alexander. *The Poetry and Prose of Alexander Pope*. Edited by Aubrey Williams. Boston: Houghton Mifflin Company, 1969.

Pseudo-Dionysius. *The Complete Works*. Translated by Colm Luibheid. Mahwah, N.J.: Paulist Press, 1987.

Riley, Athelstan. *Athos or The Mountain of the Monks*. London: Longmans, Green, and Co., 1887.

Rilke, Rainer Maria. *The Selected Poetry of Rainer Maria Rilke*. Edited and translated by Stephen Mitchell. New York: Random House, 1982.

Runciman, Steven. *The Great Church in Captivity: A Study of the Patriarchate of Constantinople from the Eve of the Turkish Conquest to the Greek War of Independence*. Cambridge: Cambridge University Press, 1968.

Schmemann, Alexander. *Great Lent: Journey to Pascha*. Crestwood, N.Y.: St. Vladimir's Seminary Press, 1969.

———. *For the Life of the World*. Crestwood, N.Y.: St. Vladimir's Seminary Press, 1998.

Sherrard, Philip. *Athos, The Mountain of Silence*. London: Oxford University Press, 1960.

———. *The Sacred in Life and Art*. Ipswich, UK: Golgonooza Press, 1990.

———. *The Greek East and the Latin West: A Study in the Christian Tradition*. Limni, Evia, Greece: Denise Harvey (Publisher), 1995.

————. *Christianity: Lineaments of a Sacred Tradition.* Brookline, Mass.: Holy Cross Orthodox Press, 1998.

Speake, Graham. *Mount Athos: Renewal in Paradise.* New Haven, Conn., and London: Yale University Press, 2002.

Stevens, Wallace. *Collected Poetry and Prose.* New York: The Library of America, 1997.

St. Symeon of Thessalonike. *Treatise on Prayer.* Translated by H.L.N. Simmons. Brookline, Mass.: Hellenic College Press, 1984.

Traherne, Thomas. *Centuries.* Wilton, Conn.: Morehouse Publishing, 1985.

Trumler, Gerhard. *Athos: The Holy Mountain.* Athens: Adam Editions, 1993.

Tucci, Niccolò. *Before My Time.* New York and London: Moyer Bell, 1991.

Archimandrite Vasileios of Stavronikita. *Hymn of Entry: Liturgy and Life in the Orthodox Church.* Translated by Elizabeth Brière. Crestwood, N.Y.: St. Vladimir's Seminary Press, 1998.

Volkov, Solomon. *Conversations with Joseph Brodsky: A Poet's Journey Through the Twentieth Century.* Translated by Marian Schwartz. New York: Free Press, 1998.

Waddell, Helen, ed. *The Desert Fathers.* Translated by Helen Waddell. New York: Vintage Books, 1998.

Ware, Bishop Kallistos. *The Orthodox Way.* Crestwood, N.Y.: St. Vladimir's Seminary Press, 1999.

————. *The Inner Kingdom.* Crestwood, N.Y.: St. Vladimir's Seminary Press, 2000.

————. *The Orthodox Church.* London: Penguin Books, 1997.

Weil, Simone. *Gravity and Grace.* Translated by Emma Crauford. London and New York: Routledge & Kegan Paul Ltd., 1987.

————. *Waiting for God.* Translated by Emma Crauford. New York: Harper & Row, Publishers, 1973.

Wheatcroft, Andrew. *The Ottomans.* London: Viking, 1993.

Wilken, Robert L. *John Chrysostom and the Jews: Rhetoric and Reality in the Late 4th Century.* Berkeley and Los Angeles: University of California Press, 1983.

Wilson, A. N. *Paul: The Life of the Apostle.* New York: W. W. Norton, 1997.

Wolff, Larry. *The Enlightenment and the Orthodox World: Western Perspectives on the Orthodox Church in Eastern Europe.* Athens: Institute for Neohellenic Research, 2001.

CHRISTOPHER MERRILL is the author of four books of poetry, including *Watch Fire*, for which he received the Peter I. B. Lavan Younger Poets Award from the Academy of American Poets; three works of nonfiction, *The Grass of Another Country: A Journey Through the World of Soccer*, *The Old Bridge: The Third Balkan War and the Age of the Refugee*, and *Only the Nails Remain: Scenes from the Balkan Wars*; several edited volumes, among them *The Forgotten Language: Contemporary Poets and Nature* and *From the Faraway Nearby: Georgia O'Keeffe as Icon*; and the translations of Aleš Debeljak's *Anxious Moments* and *The City and the Child*. He is the book critic for the daily radio news program *The World*; his journalism appears in many publications; his writings have been translated into sixteen languages. He has held the William H. Jenks Chair in Contemporary Letters at the College of the Holy Cross, and now directs the International Writing Program at the University of Iowa. He and his wife, violinist Lisa Gowdy-Merrill, are the parents of two daughters, Hannah and Abigail.

ABOUT THE TYPE

This book was set in Electra, a typeface designed for Linotype by W. A. Dwiggins, the renowned type designer (1880–1956). Electra is a fluid typeface, avoiding the contrasts of thick and thin strokes that are prevalent in most modern typefaces.